For Jhon

with warm regards
Rajyashree Kumari Bikaner
Delhi 2007

The Regal Patriot

OTHER LOTUS TITLES:

The Regal Patriot

Maharaja Ganga Singh
Of
Bikaner

PROF. L.S. RATHORE

LOTUS COLLECTION
ROLI BOOKS

First published in 2007
The Lotus Collection
An imprint of
Roli Books Pvt. Ltd.
M-75, G.K. II Market, New Delhi 110 048
Phones: ++91 (011) 2921 2271, 2921 2782
2921 0886, Fax: ++91 (011) 2921 7185
E-mail: roli@vsnl.com
Website: rolibooks.com
Also at
Varanasi, Bangalore, Kolkata, Jaipur & Mumbai

Cover design: Suchita Agarwal
Layout design: Narendra Shahi
Photographs courtesy: Maharaja Ganga Singhji Trust

ISBN: 978-81-7436-505-7
Rs. 595

Typeset in Photina MT by Roli Books Pvt. Ltd. and
printed at Rakmo Press Pvt. Ltd., New Delhi

Contents

Acknowledgements

$\mathscr{I}$ express my sincere gratitude to Princess Rajyashree Kumari Bikaner, Chairperson of Maharaja Ganga Singhji Trust, Lallgarh Palace, Bikaner, for her valuable help and patronage. Despite being actively involved in many social welfare services, Princess Rajyashree Kumari has, commendably, kept her interest alive in literary pursuits.

I am thankful to Thakur Dalip Singh Khiwansar for making available to me archival and photographic material for the book. His efficiency and promptness in the supply of material for the book has been remarkable.

Shri B.D. Joshi, has shown utmost diligence and precision in typing out the manuscript painstakingly. For this I am indeed grateful.

Professor A.B. Mathur, Jaipur; and Professor C.A. Perumal, Chennai have inspired and enthused me, for which I express my gratitude. I am grateful to Nivedita Mishra for editing this manuscript.

Last but not least, my elder brother Shri Ram Singh, I.P.S. (Retd); my wife and daughter, Snehalata and Yogeshwari have cheered me on with hope and confidence, which I greatly cherish.

Jodhpur   *Professor L.S. Rathore*

Genealogical Tree of the House of Bikaner

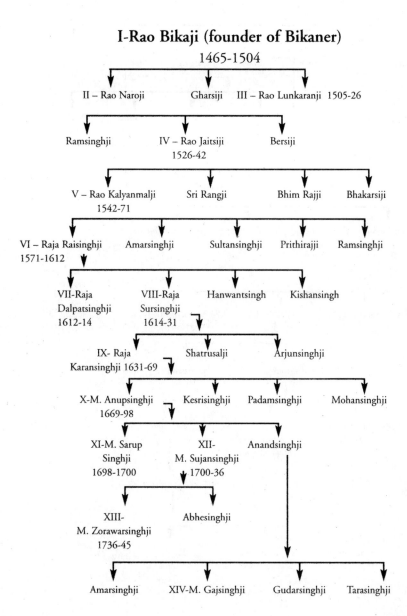

I-Rao Bikaji (founder of Bikaner)
1465-1504

II – Rao Naroji   Gharsiji   III – Rao Lunkaranji 1505-26

Ramsinghji   IV – Rao Jaitsiji   Bersiji
1526-42

V – Rao Kalyanmalji   Sri Rangji   Bhim Rajji   Bhakarsiji
1542-71

VI – Raja Raisinghji   Amarsinghji   Sultansinghji   Prithirajji   Ramsinghji
1571-1612

VII-Raja   VIII-Raja   Hanwantsingh   Kishansingh
Dalpatsinghji   Sursinghji
1612-14   1614-31

IX- Raja   Shatrusalji   Arjunsinghji
Karansinghji 1631-69

X-M. Anupsinghji   Kesrisinghji   Padamsinghji   Mohansinghji
1669-98

XI-M. Sarup   XII-   Anandsinghji
Singhji   M. Sujansinghji
1698-1700   1700-36

XIII-   Abhesinghji
M. Zorawarsinghji
1736-45

Amarsinghji   XIV-M. Gajsinghji   Gudarsinghji   Tarasinghji

1745-87
XIV-M. Gaj Singh

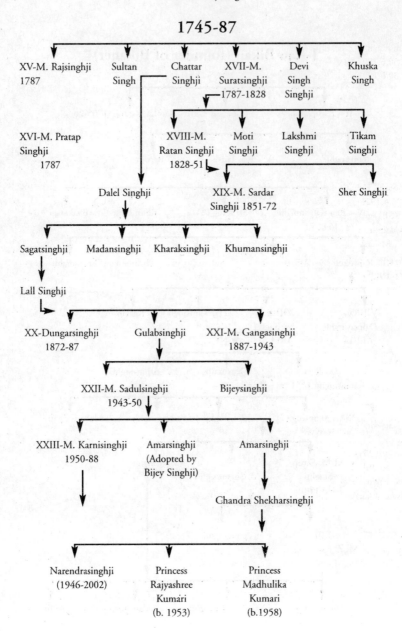

1745-87

XV-M. Rajsinghji 1787   Sultan Singh   Chattar Singhji   XVII-M. Suratsinghji 1787-1828   Devi Singh Singhji   Khuska Singh

XVI-M. Pratap Singhji 1787

XVIII-M. Ratan Singhji 1828-51   Moti Singhji   Lakshmi Singhji   Tikam Singhji

Dalel Singhji   XIX-M. Sardar Singhji 1851-72   Sher Singhji

Sagatsinghji   Madansinghji   Kharaksinghji   Khumansinghji

Lall Singhji

XX-Dungarsinghji 1872-87   Gulabsinghji   XXI-M. Gangasinghji 1887-1943

XXII-M. Sadulsinghji 1943-50   Bijeysinghji

XXIII-M. Karnisinghji 1950-88   Amarsinghji (Adopted by Bijey Singhji)   Amarsinghji

Chandra Shekharsinghji

Narendrasinghji (1946-2002)   Princess Rajyashree Kumari (b. 1953)   Princess Madhulika Kumari (b.1958)

Family Tree of Maharaja Ganga Singh

(1880-1943)

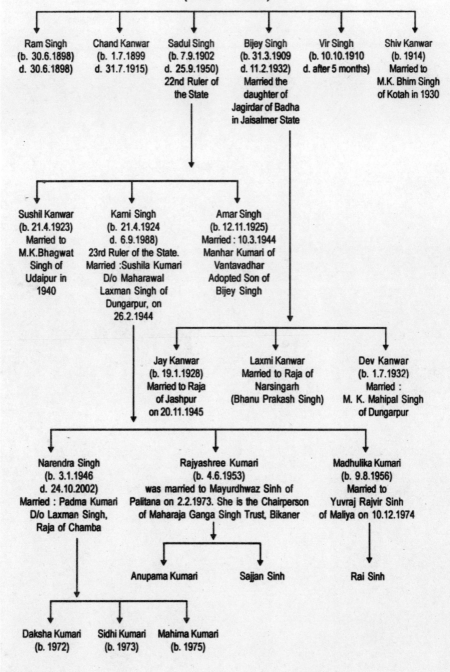

Ram Singh
(b. 30.6.1898)
d. 30.6.1898)

Chand Kanwar
(b. 1.7.1899
d. 31.7.1915)

Sadul Singh
(b. 7.9.1902
d. 25.9.1950)
22nd Ruler of
the State

Bijey Singh
(b. 31.3.1909
d. 11.2.1932)
Married the
daughter of
Jagirdar of Badha
in Jaisalmer State

Vir Singh
(b. 10.10.1910
d. after 5 months)

Shiv Kanwar
(b. 1914)
Married to
M.K. Bhim Singh
of Kotah in 1930

Sushil Kanwar
(b. 21.4.1923)
Married to
M.K.Bhagwat
Singh of
Udaipur in
1940

Karni Singh
(b. 21.4.1924
d. 6.9.1988)
23rd Ruler of the State.
Married :Sushila Kumari
D/o Maharawal
Laxman Singh of
Dungarpur, on
26.2.1944

Amar Singh
(b. 12.11.1925)
Married : 10.3.1944
Manhar Kumari of
Vantavadhar
Adopted Son of
Bijey Singh

Jay Kanwar
(b. 19.1.1928)
Married to Raja
of Jashpur
on 20.11.1945

Laxmi Kanwar
Married to Raja of
Narsingarh
(Bhanu Prakash Singh)

Dev Kanwar
(b. 1.7.1932)
Married :
M. K. Mahipal Singh
of Dungarpur

Narendra Singh
(b. 3.1.1946
d. 24.10.2002)
Married : Padma Kumari
D/o Laxman Singh,
Raja of Chamba

Rajyashree Kumari
(b. 4.6.1953)
was married to Mayurdhwaz Sinh of
Palitana on 2.2.1973. She is the Chairperson
of Maharaja Ganga Singh Trust, Bikaner

Madhulika Kumari
(b. 9.8.1956)
Married to
Yuvraj Rajvir Sinh
of Maliya on 10.12.1974

Anupama Kumari

Sajjan Sinh

Rai Sinh

Daksha Kumari
(b. 1972)

Sidhi Kumari
(b. 1973)

Mahima Kumari
(b. 1975)

Horoscope of Maharaja Ganga Singh

**(Born: 13 October 1880;
Time: 10.31 a.m.; Place: Bikaner)**

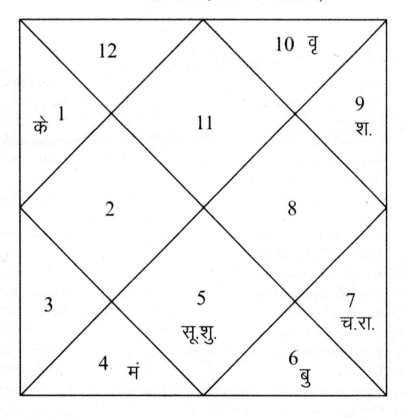

Curriculum Vitae

1. Born   13 October 1880
2. Succeeded as Maharaja   31 August 1887
3. Marriage   8 July 1897
4. Assumed Ruling Powers   16 December 1898
5. Second Marriage of the Maharaja   May 1899
6. Gazetted Honorary Major –
   youngest Major at the time in the British Army   June 1900
7. Proceeded on active service to China in command of
   the Ganga Risala to take part in the Boxer War   August 1900
8. *Kaiser-i-Hind* Gold Medal   1900
9. K.C.I.E for China War services   July 1901
10. Officially attended Coronation of King Edward VII   August 1902
11. Appointed as Honorary A.D.C. to the Prince of Wales   August 1902
12. Awarded the China Medal   1902
13. Birth of son and heir, Prince Sadul Singh   7 September 1902
14. K.C.S.I.   June 1904
15. Prince of Wales' (later King George V) first visit   1905
16. Demise of the first Maharani   1906

17. G.C.I.E.   January 1907
18. Third Marriage of the Maharaja   May 1908
19. Promoted Honorary Lt.-Colonel   1909
20. Demise of the Maharaja's Mother   1909
21. Promoted Honorary Colonel   1910
22. G.C.S.I.   1910
23. Appointed Honorary A.D.C. to His Majesty King George V   June 1910
24. Officially attended Coronation of King George V   June 1911
25. LL.D. (Cambridge)   June 1911
26. Silver Jubilee of Reign   1912
27. Proceeded to Europe to fight in the First Great War   September 1914
28. Demise of Princess Chand Kanwar   1915
29. Elected Honorary General Secretary to the Princes' Conference 1916
30. Promoted Honorary Major-General   July 1917
31. LL.D. (Edinburgh)   1917
32. Represented Ruling Princes of India at Imperial
     War Cabinet and Conference   March 1917
33. Received Freedom of the Cities of London, Edinburgh,
     Manchester, and Bristol   1917
34. The Maharaja's Rome Note   May 1917
35. K.C.B. (Military Division) for services in the First Great War January 1918
36. Received 1914 Star   1918
37. Received Grand Cordon of the Order of the Nile   1918
38. Member of Imperial War Cabinet and the Peace Conference   1918-1919
39. D.C.L. (Oxford)   1919
40. Awarded G.C.V.O.   1919
41. Awarded G.B.E. (Military Division) for Services in the
     First Great War   January 1921
42. Prince of Wales' (King George V) second visit   1921
43. Chancellor of the Chamber of Princes   1921-1926
44. Demise of the Second Maharani   1922
45. M. Clemenceau's Visit   1922

Bikaner State Anthem

May our Sovereign be granted long life,
May the almighty God ever protect him.

May he always have the Divine Guidance
of Shri Lakshmi Narayanji,
May Sri Karniji ever preserve
the Chhatra of Bikaner,
May his Victorious Drums resound all over the World.

May his State be blessed with the highest dignity,
May he be Honoured with the highest respect and esteem,
The 'Ran Banka Rathore',

May he have perpetual happiness and prosperity
to ever enjoy these with his family.

May his reign be benevolent like Indra's
So that auspicious songs may echo all round
wishing 'Jai' to the wise Ruler of 'Jangal Dhar'.

May he rule with justice and ever give us cause
to sing his glories in words full of
everlasting gratitude.

The Bikaner State

(Coat of Arms)

$\mathcal{T}$he components of the State Coat-of-Arms were: Ber tree, the Trident, Kites, Tigers, Red and Yellow colours, and the Motto. Each part had a history behind it.

'**Ber Tree**': Rao Bikaji, the founder of the state, had the blessings of goddess Sri Karniji. When Sri Karniji came to Deshnoke in Vikram Samwat 1475 Sud 9th, there were 'Jal' trees in the area around the village. Sri Karniji turned 'Jal' trees into 'Ber' trees by her miraculous power. The 'Ber' tree is favoured by the 'Devi' (Karniji). As the goddess had been the protector of the state the 'Ber' tree was adopted as a badge and figured on the top of Coat-of-Arms.

'**The Trident**': The Trident is a weapon borne by goddess Sri Karniji, with which she helped the Bikaner Army by killing the foes. This being a symbol of Sri Karniji, it was shown in Coat-of-Arms of her votaries, the Princes of Bikaner.

'**Kites**': The kite is the image of Sri Karniji. When she helped her devotees, she appeared in the form of a white kite. As such in the Coat-of-Arms, the three birds shown were white kites, which represented the image of Sri Karniji.

'**Tigers**': The tiger is the 'Vahan' of Sri Karniji and therefore the supporters of the shield are tigers. In 1877 when Queen Victoria had sent the Bikaner Flag, it showed black leopards as supporters, but the Maharaja wrote back that black leopards had no relevance in the context of the desert, and in their place there should be tigers as supporters. This was accepted and, therefore, in the Coat-of-Arms two tigers were shown as supporters of the shield.

'Red and Yellow'

'Colours': Red is the colour of the 'Dhwaja' of Sri Karniji. 'Peetamber' is worn by Lord Vishnu (Sri Lakshmi Narayanji) as such yellow colour represents Sri Lakshmi Narayanji. Both Sri Karniji and Sri Lakshmi Narayanji, are the supreme deities worshipped by the Royal House of Bikaner, and as their colours are red and yellow respectively; they were shown in the Coat-of-Arms.

'Motto': The Motto 'Jai Jangal Dhar Badshah' inscribed on the Coat-of-Arms had its origin during the time of Raja Karan Singh, when he successfully foiled Aurangzeb's attempts to convert the Hindu Rajas to Islam. This incident had occurred in the seventeenth century at Attock, where the assembled Hindu Rajas saluted Raja Karan Singh of Bikaner in the words, 'Jai Jangal Dhar Badshah', or 'Victory to the King of the Desert', which had ever since been the Motto of the House of Bikaner and was emblazoned on their Coat-of-Arms.

1

Historical Review

$\mathcal{T}$he area which now comprises the four districts of Bikaner, Churu, Ganganagar and Hanumangarh, was known as the Rathore principality of Bikaner, prior to the integration of Bikaner State into Rajasthan Union in April, 1949. It was bound on the north and west by the Bahawalpur State; on the south-west by the Jaisalmer State; on the south by the Jodhpur State; on the south-east by the Jaipur State; on the east by the Loharu State and the Hissar District and on the north-east by Ferozepore District. With an area of 23,317 square miles it had the sixth largest area among all the Indian states and second largest in Rajputana.

The history of the erstwhile State of Bikaner was a record of heroic exploits, epic victories and magnificent gallantry. Founded in A.D. 1465 by Rao Bika, second son of Rao Jodha, the ruler of Marwar State; the rulers of the House of Bikaner belonged to the warrior clan of Rathores. Though the state was founded in the fifteenth century, the lineage of its rulers went back to much earlier times.

Among the many clans of Rajputs, whose patriotism, valour and chivalry decorated Indian history, none stood higher in fame or in the stature of historic tradition than the Rathores. Claiming descent from Lord Rama, the deified King of Ayodhya, the Rathores or the *Rastrakutas* came to be known in Indian history as the first great imperial dynasty in the Deccan. In the first decade of the eighth century the *Rastrakutas* wrested from the Western Chalukyas a sizeable territory, and established their capital at Malkhed, now in Andhra Pradesh. Arab and Persian travellers who visited Malkhed at the time spoke of the monarchs of *Rastrakutas* Dynasty as 'the Emperors of Hindustan' – among the most powerful rulers of the period. By the tenth century the *Rastrakutas* established themselves as the leading power in northern India with their capital at Kanauj. When the Muslims invaded India, they found the great Rajput kingdoms in existence, one of which was that of the Rathores at Kanauj, whose ruler, Jai Chand was at the pinnacle of his fame. The calamitous outcome of the rivalry between Jai Chand, ruler of Aryavarta, and the impetuous Prithviraj Chouhan, constituted a turning-point in Indian history. The invasion of Mahommed of Ghor in the last decade of twelfth century and the disasters that overtook the Rajput arms in the Punjab and the Gangetic Valley completed the ruin of the Empire of Kanauj.

Ancestry of Maharaja Ganga Singh

The Rathores were to emerge again. In 1212, eighteen years subsequent to the overthrow of Kanauj, Rao Sheo, grandson of its last monarch, abandoned the land of his birth, and with 200 retainers, journeyed westward to the desert. According to some chronicles, he intended to make a pilgrimage to the shrine of Dwarka, but, according to others, he wanted to carve his fortunes in fresh pastures in order to further the glorious legacy of Kanauj. Rao Sheo, with the image of the family deity and the emblems of Imperial power, wandered for some time in the wilds of Marwar – 'the Land of Death' – known as Jodhpur. In the fifteenth century Jodhpur was ruled by Rao Jodha, who had founded the city of Jodhpur. Jodha had fourteen sons and many brothers. Valuable estates had then become scarce and the enterprising amongst them looked for new lands to occupy. One of these was Bika, the second son of Rao Jodha. He went north-west to conquer a kingdom for himself and with him began the history of Bikaner.

Rao Bika – Founder of Bikaner (1465-1504)

One day in 1465 Bika came late to the *durbar* held by his father, Rao Jodha, and took his seat beside his uncle Kandhal, with whom he carried on a conversation in whispers. Rao Jodha jestingly remarked that they must be scheming a conquest of new territory. Kandhal at once treated the remark as a challenge, and standing up announced that he now felt compelled to win new lands. One of the courtiers present, who had just returned from a journey, pointed out that the country to the north had been abandoned by the Sankhlas, who had been weakened by losses in war. Bika was discontented with his prospects, as he had then a living elder brother, and spurred by his ambitions, decided at once to set forth to undertake a campaign. With two younger brothers, several uncles, one hundred horses and five hundred on foot, he set out to win himself a new kingdom. His followers comprised not only well-tried knights, sturdy men of arms, but also experienced officials; he possessed a civil and military staff, sufficient for the administration and the conquest of the state he intended to establish.

The area close to Jodhpur, where the little army first marched, was a barren desert abandoned by its previous occupants. Here Bika established his base and gradually penetrated further north. Arriving at Mandore he dedicated himself at the shrine of the local deity to the great work he had undertaken.

The chronicles of Bikaner state that on the following morning:

Bika miraculously found Lord Shiva's amulet among his wardrobe. With the happy feeling of assured success through divine help he reached Deshnoke, a village 16 miles to the south of the present city of Bikaner. There lived a famous lady, Sri Karniji, who was considered to have supernatural powers. When Bika paid his respects to the holy woman, she announced to him that, 'Your destiny is higher than your father's; and many servants will touch your feet.' She gave Bika encouragement and advice for his campaign. For many years he continued to rely on her counsel.

Sri Karniji was born in A.D. 1387 in a Charan family at Suwap in the Jodhpur State. She was the daughter of Meha and was married to Depa, son of Bithu Kaha of village Santhi in the Bikaner State. People recognised her as the incarnation of goddess 'Devi'. She had miraculous powers predicting the future. It was with her blessings that Rao Bika founded Bikaner State. She is still worshipped by the royal family of Bikaner as also by the many people far and wide. Sri Karniji passed away in A.D. 1538. Her temple is at Deshnoke, about 16 miles from Bikaner.

Gradually, Bika conquered areas which were built up into a state. The deserted country was re-populated; the small army with which Bika had set grew in size and strength. Through wars, alliances and matrimonial ties, Bika gradually extended his territory. A fort was erected by Bika at Kodamdesar in

1478, but on account of the continued hostilities of the Bhattis, he considered the area unsafe. Bika decided to find another site for the fort and deputed his maternal uncle, Napo, to select a place. Napo came to a spot called the 'Rati Ghati', where he found an ewe with two lambs defying a pack of wolves, whom Napo drove away and declared the site auspicious. The search for a still more propitious site continued. Not very far, Napo found a man asleep with his head resting on a tuft of *bhurut* grass around which a snake had coiled itself. Napo sat down to watch the movements of the snake who, after some time, uncoiled itself and slithered away. It was here that Rao Bika laid the foundation of a fort in 1485, known as Bika's Fort, and started building of the city of 'Bikaner' in 1488.

For some time the Sultan at Delhi attempted to crush the new state that was growing up on the borders of his territory, but with the help of his father, Rao Jodha, the Imperial Army was put to flight. Bikaner had thus became a factor to be reckoned with in Indian affairs.

Rao Jodha, who was growing old, was anxious to settle the affairs of his family before his death. Bika had already won a kingdom for himself. The Rao, therefore, asked him to remain content with what he had won and not to claim the succession to his father's state. Bika agreed, but stipulated one condition. If after the death of Rao Jodha, his elder brother, the heir-apparent, should die, he desired to claim, not his rightful patrimony which he would leave to his younger brothers, but the heirlooms and the insignia of royalty brought from Kanauj on the downfall of the old Rathore Empire. Kingdoms he might conquer but these cherished emblems of imperial sway, which should go to the eldest line, he could not legitimately give up. Rao Jodha agreed to Bika's demand and ordered that should Bika become the eldest surviving son, these would be sent to Bikaner. In 1491 Rao Jodha died. His eldest son, Rao Satal, followed him shortly afterwards to the pyre. Bika now laid claim to the heirlooms, but Rao Sujo, who had succeeded Jodha, would not give them up. Bika thereupon collected a large army, invaded Jodhpur, defeated the Jodhpur forces and occupied the city. He was besieging the fort, where his brother had taken refuge, when Sujo's mother intervened. She came to see Bika and at her request he agreed to raise the siege and return to his state provided the heirlooms were given over to him. Soon afterwards the heirlooms were delivered to Bika who brought them in triumph to his capital, where they still remain. These Rathore heirlooms are: the Sandalwood *Singhasan* (throne) of the emperors of Kanauj brought by the Rathores from Kanauj; the *Hiranyagarbha* idol of Lakshminarayanji; *Karand* (a small box held to be sacred); large silver idol of the goddess, *Nagnechi*; the royal umbrella; a diamond studded shield of Rao Jodhaji; a sword; a dagger; the steed *dal singar* (the ornament of the Army); *bhunjai degs* (the ancient cauldrons); *bairisal Nagara* (the foe-frightening kettle drum); *Bhanwar Dhol* (Big Drum) of Rao Choondaji; and some other royal emblems. They are now vested in Raja Rai Singh Trust, and are on display in the Fort Museum under the 'Will' of Maharaja Karni Singh. Most of these heirlooms are regularly worshipped on special occasions by the Royal family. The Family Goddess is housed in a large temple outside the city.

Rao Lunkaran (1505-26)

Rao Bika had passed away in 1504, leaving room on the screen for his brave son, Lunkaran, 'the sun of the race'. Rao Lunkaran was not slow in loosening the strings of his purse to captivate the affections of his subjects: he fed the poor in a year of famine, and ingratiated to himself the bards by gifts of horses and elephants. The newly founded capital of the desert was greatly dressed in all the pomp and circumstance of a great court: gems glittered in the *durbar* hall which was filled with robleman and caparisoned elephants were tied at the posts outside the gate. Flags fluttered on the top of the palace, while bards and dancers from Gujarat recited panegyrics and performed in the presence of the Rao.

The sword of Rao Bika did not rust in the hands of his son. The indomitable Lunkaran defeated the chief of Nagore, subdued the Bhattis of Jaisalmer, and marched towards Narnaul in the east, where he was attacked by 'a large body of Pathans'. Two of his sons fell in battle. Lunkaran was asked to surrender his elephants, but he did not oblige his enemy. Almost single-handed, against overwhelming odds, Lunkaran, threw himself into the middle of the enemy army and was felled by a hundred spears.

Rao Jaitsi (1526-42)

Rao Jaitsi, who succeeded the *gaddi* (throne) of Bikaner in 1526, marked the beginning of a new epoch, not only in the history of Bikaner, but also that of northern India. At the time the hostile armies of Babur and Ibrahim Lodi clashed on the plain of Panipat (April 21, 1526) and Lodi was defeated. On March 16, 1527, Babur secured another historic victory over Rana Sanga of Mewar at the battlefield of Khanua and laid the foundation of the Mughal Empire in India.

After the death of Babur, his son Kamran attacked Bhatner, in 1538, and captured it. Emboldened by this victory, he marched on to Bikaner; but the Mughal army was routed by Rao Jaitsi, near the village of Chotariya. Kamran, accompanied by his troops in the panic flight, dropped his umbrella, which is still preserved in that village in memory of a proud feat.

Raja Rai Singh (1574-1612)

Bikaner eventually made peace with the rising Mughal Empire, and, during the reign of Akbar, became one of the premier states of the empire. After the chief of Amber, Raja Rai Singh of Bikaner was, according to the historian P.W. Powlett, 'the Hindu of the highest rank at the court of Akbar.' Rai Singh was in fact Akbar's most trusted general and fought with distinction in all the emperor's campaigns. He enjoyed a *mansab* of 5,000, which was the highest dignity conferred upon those who were not members of the imperial family. In the expedition against Ahmedabad, Rai Singh held high command under Akbar, distinguished himself in the assault on the city and slew in single combat the governor, Mirza Mohammad Hussain. He maintained his honour and authority both in the time of Akbar and his son Jehangir; in the troubles preceding the succession of the latter, Jehangir himself acknowledged that he depended greatly on Raja Rai Singh, 'one of the most considerable of Rajput Amirs.'

It was Raja Rai Singh who built the present Fort of Bikaner (1594) and laid the foundations of the palaces, which are among the most beautiful gems of Indian architecture. Raja Rai Singh's brother, Prithwi Raj, known as *Peethal*, was one of the most renowned poets and scholars of his time. He was equally at home on the battlefield of battle and at the council table. His great epic poem, *Veli-Krishna Rukmani* is undoubtedly a masterpiece of Rajasthani literature.

Among the successors of Raja Rai Singh, the most prominent were Raja Sur Singh (1614-31), Raja Karan Singh (1631-69), and Maharaja Anup Singh (1669-98). There were nearly fifty-one *farmans* issued by Jehangir and Shah Jahan to Raja Sur Singh, a testimony to his rise in royal favour as a trusted counsellor and defender of the empire.

Raja Karan Singh (1631-69)

Raja Karan Singh, as heir-apparent, held the governorship of Daulatabad. He served in the Deccan and, later, in the principal battles between Aurangzeb and his brothers for the Imperial Throne. Two of his formidable sons – 'warriors as brave as any who have sprung from the Rathore stock', Rajkumar Kesri Singh and Rajkumar Padam Singh – specially distinguished themselves in the battle of Khajwa 'in appreciation of which the Emperor Aurangzeb with his own handkerchief brushed off the dust from their persons as they stood before him hot from the battle.' Aurangzeb presented Kesri Singh a sword with a hilt encased in gold, still preserved in Bikaner as a family heirloom.

Though loyal, the Bikaner rulers were not servile towards the Mughal Emperors. The most celebrated incident of their readiness to resist Imperial authority, when their honour was at stake, was the occasion from which the Bikaner rulers derived their proud motto, *Jai Jangal dhar Badshah* or Victory to the King of the Jungle. Emperor Aurangzeb intended to convert by force all the great Hindu Rajput Princes to Islam. He summoned the armies of the various princes to join the Imperial Army, ostensibly for a campaign beyond the River Indus. His idea was to get the Rajputs across the far bank, where they were helpless and there give them the choice between the sword and Islam. The plot was discovered and the rajas before crossing the river held a secret meeting to decide on their course of action. It was agreed that the Muslim force should be induced to cross the river first, and when the boats returned to fetch the Hindu contingents, they should be destroyed. Accordingly, the rulers sent their messengers to take possession of the boats, pretending that the Hindus wished to cross the river first. The Muslims resented this move as impertinence and declared that they would use the boats first. Just as the fleet containing the Muslim troops had crossed the river, news arrived that the mother of the Ruler of Amber (Jaipur) had died; on this pretext all the Rajas delayed the crossing for 12 days. They had now the river between themselves and the Imperial Army, but they still had to destroy the means by which the Imperial forces could return to set upon them. Accordingly they asked for the boats to be sent back, saying that they intended to cross.

The Rajas then came to Raja Karan Singh of Bikaner. They pointed out that since his territories were the least susceptible to invasion, he could, without risking his ruin, save their religion and bear the brunt the imperial displeasure by destroying the boats. Raja Karan Singh assented, but not without a condition, that he should be seated on an improvised *gaddi* in the forest, and receive homage of the assembled rulers as 'Emperor of

Hindustan'. To this condition the Rajput chiefs agreed. A throne was speedily constructed and emblazoned with the Coat-of-Arms, which Queen Victoria had granted to the Maharaja of Bikaner in 1877, soon after she had assumed the title of 'Empress of India'.

The Bikaneris and other rajas destroyed the boats in the presence of the Imperial messenger, and the Rajput forces set off securely for home.

All the princes saluted the ruler of Bikaner with the cry: '*Jai Jangal dhar Badshah.*'

The jubilant cry with which all Rajputana paid homage to Raja Karan Singh on that day remained the proud motto of the rulers of Bikaner till the integration of the state in 1949.

The breach of good understanding caused by this incident, however, did not last long. Raja Karan Singh rendered outstanding services to the Mughal Empire, for which he received a grant of land near Aurangabad. This estate, with three villages of Karanpur, Padampur and Kesrisinghpur, named after the House of Bikaner, were in the possession of Bikaner till 1904, when the Maharaja ceded them to the British Government for cantonment purposes, together with the fourth village named Kokanwari. He was given, in exchange, a certain cash compensation and two villages adjoining the Bikaner border.

Maharaja Anup Singh (1669-98)

Raja Karan Singh's successor was his eldest son, Anup Singh, who was the first to be invested with the title of the *Maharaja*. He was a remarkable ruler, described by Powlett as having revived the 'golden time of Bikaner valour and fame.' A great patron of art, music and learning, the Maharaja was himself a versatile genius, a distinguished scholar in Sanskrit, a mathematician and an astronomer. His manuscript collection, now housed in the Lallgarh Palace, has some rare and valuable books and is considered one of the best Indian libraries now in existence. Maharaja Anup Singh's achievements unique on the battlefield were unique. He captured for Aurangzeb the Fort of Bijapur (1673), and was in command of Mughal armies in the attack on Golcunda (1687). He stormed the Fort of Golcunda, the principal stronghold of the Deccan. In fact he was one of the great leaders in the Deccan campaign of Aurangzeb, and one of the emperor's most trusted generals.

It was during the time of Maharaja Anup Singh that his brother, Rajkumar Padam Singh, distinguished himself by feats of magnificent valour, the stories of which are still told to the boys of Bikaner by their parents. Padam Singh, says Powlett, 'is the hero of Bikaner and occupies in the minds of the people the same place which Richard the lion-hearted holds or held in the minds of the people of England. To the present day his huge sword is reverently preserved and at certain seasons *puja* is performed before it. Reckless courage, great personal strength and extreme generosity were the characteristics on which Padam Singh's popularity rested.' An often told story is one about how an Imperial Officer had treacherously killed Mohan Singh, a Prince of Bikaner, by stabbing him in the back. Enraged, Padam Singh rushed with drawn sword into the emperor's *durbar* and severed the murderer's head from his body, the blow leaving an indelible mark on a pillar near by. Padam Singh then carried off his dying brother. So revered was Padam Singh, that no one including the Emperor questioned this act; in fact, the emperor himself treated him with singular affection.

Padam Singh died fighting against the Marathas on the bank of the River Tapti on March 24 1683. During the battle he wielded his spear and the two swords, which he invariably carried, so effectively, that he slew nearly sixty people from the enemy camp before he was surrounded, and fell 'like a wounded lion'.

Rajkumar Kesri Singh (1638-73)

Padam Singh's brother, Rajkumar Kesri Singh, was also a distinguished Imperial Officer and a valiant fighter. There are many stories about the daring and prowess of Kesri Singh. Colonel James Tod in his *Annals and Antiquities of Rajasthan* narrates that this young prince once fought and killed a tiger with his bare hands. For this, the emperor rewarded him with the grant of a *jagir* of twenty-five villages. While fighting an encounter during the Deccan Wars, he struck off with one blow the head of his opponent, who was commanding the army of the Bahmani King. Kesri Singh was slain in the storm of Bijapur (1673).

Maharaja Gaj Singh (1745-88)

Maharaja Gaj Singh was well known among his contemporaries as a powerful ruler, who received in 1752 the hereditary title of *Sri Raj Rajeshwar Maharajadhiraj Maharaja Shiromani* together with the *pargana* of Hissar from the Mughal Emperor Mohammad Shah in recognition of his valiant services.

Bikaner-Mughal Relations

Over 164 years, covering the total period of the effective Mughal dominion in India, the rulers of Bikaner rendered distinguished services to the emperors, generation after generation, either at the head of their own troops or in command of the Imperial Army, as well as in responsible posts of viceroys and governors, Imperial representatives and ambassadors. The numerous *farmans* they received from the emperors attest the exceptional dignity which the rulers of Bikaner enjoyed at the Mughal court. There was no honour which the emperors did not bestow upon them. And they were not only the recipients of the hereditary titles of *Maharaja*, *Maharajadhiraj* and *Raj Rajeshwar*, but of the great dignity of *Mohi Maratib* – the Order of the Fish – given only to the most important territorial sovereigns. This order was bestowed upon the maharajas of Bikaner on three different occasions.

There were some important factors which caused the Mughals to establish close collaboration with the rulers of Bikaner. The first was the people of the area possessed war-like traits, so Bikaner offered a good recruiting ground for the Mughal army. The second was its close proximity to the kingdom of Delhi which made it obligatory on the part of the mughal emperors not to under-rate the strategic importance of a principality situated so close to their vicinity. The third was the importance of two impregnable forts – Bhatinda and Bhatner – situated on the northern boundary of Bikaner. Lastly, the Bikaner region had a commercial importance as well. The town of Rajgarh, located in Bikaner, was a great commercial mart and a point of rendezvous for caravans, from all parts of northern India.

At the same time, there was equally the need for the rulers of Bikaner to develop cordial relations with the Mughals. Bikaner, though not open to external danger, had, however, been a victim of internal anarchy arising mostly out of the lawless activities of the clans and other indigenous elements of the indigenous population. Bikaner's rulers had to seek outside assistance to curb the disorderly activities within its territories. This made them establish a relationship with the emperors of Delhi which was further facilitated and strengthened by Akbar's policy of tolerance towards the Hindus. From an overall perspective, the Bikaner-Mughal collaboration was mutually beneficial to both parties.

Treaty with British

During the reign of Maharaja Surat Singh (1788-1828), the historic fort of

Bhatner or Hanumangarh, which during the past four centuries had frequently changed hands, was finally conquered by Bikaner.

By the middle of eighteenth century the Mughal Empire, which the Bikaner House had supported so long, was crumbling to pieces. In the shadow of Imperial Power the Bikaner dynasty had grown to greatness and eclipsed the other Rajput states. The anarchy that followed the decay of the Mughal Empire brought about a slow decline in the prosperity and power of Bikaner. Its geographical position, and the valour and wisdom of its Rulers, however, saved Bikaner from the indignities to which the other great states of Rajputana were subjected as a result of the Maratha aggression. Though Udaipur, Jaipur and Jodhpur had all to bend before Scindia, Bikaner was never conquered and paid neither *chauth* nor tribute to him. In its sandy isolation it maintained its majestic independence.

Internal troubles gradually beset the desert kingdom. The nobles of Bikaner, encouraged by the support of the marauding Pindari forces, defied the authority of the Maharaja and rose in rebellion.

At that critical juncture in the history of Bikaner, a new factor entered the Indian scene. The rising British power gradually extended its control over large parts of the crumbling Mughal Empire. Lord Hastings offered British protection to the rulers of Rajputana – an offer, which was gladly accepted and led to the liberation of Rajput states from the yoke of the Marathas. Bikaner welcomed the new power that was taking the place of the Mughals and concluded on March 9, 1818, a treaty of 'perpetual friendship, alliance and unity of interests.'

British troops under General Alner entered Bikaner to aid the Maharaja in his campaigns against his rebellious Thakurs. The insurrection was quelled and the British Force withdrew soon afterwards. From that time onwards the rulers of Bikaner had lived up to the mutual pledge contained in the Treaty of Alliance that 'the friends and enemies of one party shall be the friends and enemies of both'. The protection of the British power secured internal and external peace to Bikaner, and gradually the state was transformed from a military camp into a civil administration. The transition was fraught with many difficulties and internal conflicts, and was finally achieved by Maharaja Ganga Singh in the first decade of the twentieth century. K.M. Panikkar in the *Biography of Maharaja Ganga Singh* writes: 'In the early days of the transition, during the time of Maharaja Ratan Singh (1828-51) even the Raja of Mahajan, the premier noble, was in open revolt. The Thakurs were in a constant state of disaffection and open defiance, and over large areas state authority practically broke down. In fact the military state had ceased to function and the civil state was yet in its infancy. The reign of Ratan Singh is a weary tale of insurrections and punitive expeditions, in which by slow degrees the government obtained the upper hand.'

In spite of the troubles at home, however, Bikaner gave strong support to the British Government in the latter's period of crisis. In the Afghan War of 1841, the Maharaja supplied 200 camels for the Kabul expedition. During the Second Sikh War in 1848, a body of horse and artillery was provided by the state and it co-operated actively with the British forces, especially near Ferozepur; a number of camels were also supplied for the use of the British Army. For this help Maharaja Ratan Singh (1828-51) was thanked by the Governor-General, Lord Ellenborough, in person at Delhi.

During the time of Maharaja Sardar Singh (1851-1872), Bikaner's internal situation worsened because of the defiant behaviour of some Thakurs. Despite this, when the Great Mutiny broke out in 1857, the Maharaja, harassed as he was, never forgot his obligations under the Treaty of Alliance. True to the pledged word, he treated the enemies of the British Government as his own enemies. The authority of British in the north of India was practically extinguished, as a result of the rising; and it became clear that the future of British rule in India would be decided by the attitude of the Punjab. The northern boundary of the State of Bikaner marched along the southern boundary of the Punjab. The British districts, which touched the state, had risen in revolt. Sirsa, Hissar and Hansi were in the hands of rebel forces.

Maharaja Sardar Singh recognised the necessity of immediate and decisive action, and at the head of his own troops, marched without any delay to the disaffected area. His forces consisted of regular, well-disciplined infantry and cavalry and a large auxiliary camel force. This force took the field in British India and engaged the rebels in the bordering districts. Under the personal leadership of the Maharaja, the Bikaner forces won a lot of glory. They besieged and occupied Hissar, a strategic stronghold commanding the old routes to Delhi. They stormed Hansi and occupied the town till the arrival of the British troops. They attacked Jamalpur, a rebel stronghold, where the Bikaner cavalry by their ferocious charge pulled sharply apart the rebel resistance. Apart from these and other notable actions, (in the battles of Tosham, Mangali, Sirsa, and Fatehabad) the very presence of the Maharaja

Maharaja Ganga Singh at the age of five with his elder brother, Maharaja Dungar Singh, ruler of the Bikaner State from 1872 to 1887.

A view of the Old Fort, Bikaner.

Maharaja Ganga Singh in his ninth year.

Maharaja Ganga Singh between Sir Charles and Lady Bayley. Sir Charles was President of the Regency Council of Bikaner for three years during Ganga Singh's minority.

Maharaja Ganga Singh (seated) with the members of Regency Council of Bikaner State during his minority.

Maharaja Ganga Singh (seated fourth from left) at Mayo College, Ajmer with his English tutors and their wives.

Maharaja Ganga Singh (sitting extreme right) with his English tutors.

Maharaja Ganga Singh (seated fourth from right) with Lord Curzon at Bikaner - 1902.

Maharaja Ganga Singh holding Prince Sadul Singh, the heir-apparent.

Maharaja Ganga Singh with his staff, L to R (sitting): Lt. Col. Th. Deep Singh Gharsisar, Maharaja Ganga Singh, Maj. Th. Gop Singh Malasar. L to R (standing): Maj. Th. Bhaktawar Singh Syani of Samandser, Th. Prithviraj Singh of Daudsar.

Maharaja Ganga Singh with his daughter, Princess Chand Kanwar; son, Prince Sadul Singh;
Duke and Duchess of Hesse at Munich Hospital (Germany).

Maharaja Ganga Singh (right) with King George the V and Queen Mary in India in 1911, with (L to R) Maharaja Jai Singh of Alwar, King George the V, Maharaja Sir Pratap Singh Idar, Queen Mary (sitting) and Maharaja Sumer Singh of Jodhpur.

The coronation of King George the V was held at Delhi (1911). Maharaja Ganga Singh of Bikaner is standing by the side of King George the V.

Maharaja Ganga Singh with his children. L to R - Princess Chand Kanwar, Prince Sadul Singh, and Prince Bijey Singh.

The Viceroy, Lord Minto, his daughter Lady Eileen Elliot and Lady Minto with Maharaja Ganga Singh seated, at the end of a day spent shooting black bucks in Bikaner State in1908.

with his troops in the field had a great impact on the morale of the forces. The support and the personal example of the Maharaja, and the zeal with which he threw himself on the side of the British Government was largely responsible for preventing discontent spreading to the Punjab. British authorities gratefully recognised the importance of the support which they received from the Bikaner State in the hour of their trial. Brigadier-General G.St.P. Lawrence, in his official dispatch to the Government of India, while praising the loyal friendship, spirit and energy of the Maharaja, wrote:

'I consider the Maharaja is deserving of the highest scale of reward which the government may be pleased to sanction to the most meritorious of Rajput States. His Highness, by his courage and the example of his loyalty, checked disaffection and gave confidence to the wavering. No Prince in Rajputana save Bikaner took the field in person in our favour without hesitation. No Prince gave such aid in searching out and rescuing fugitives, though all gave their hospitable shelter and support. And no other Prince exhibited such purely disinterested motives in giving us his active assistance. And none but the Bikaner Raja suffered so heavy a loss of Rajput kindred and chiefs whilst fighting purely in our cause. It was for these reasons that I considered, and still consider, the loyalty and good services of the Bikaner Raja superior to those of any other Chief in Rajputana, including Jaipur.'

The services of the Maharaja were fully appreciated by Queen Victoria, who through the Secretary of State for India sent an illuminated *kharita* in 1859 which was presented in *durbar* with due formality to Maharaja Sardar Singh. Narrating the loyalty and devotion of the Maharaja, the *kharita*, said: 'It is in such times that the true quality of friendship is best tested; and it will ever be among the most cherished recollections of Her Majesty that Your Highness and other princely representatives of the ancient Houses of Rajputana were, during the eventful years which have just passed, among the most steadfast of her friends.' The Maharaja's services were rewarded. The British Government granted the *pargana* of Tibi along with 41 villages to Bikaner.

Maharaja Sardar Singh died in 1872 without settling the issue of succession. There were three claimants. The matter was settled in favour of Dungar Singh for strong reasons. The first, was that he was the son of Maharaj Lall Singh, who held the larger grants of Chutterpore, as such Dungar Singh owing to his consanguinity was treated with marked consideration compared to the other claimants. The second was that the eldest Maharani of the deceased ruler favoured Dungar Singh, and she exercised her right of adoption in his favour. The third was that the case of Dungar Singh was supported by the Royal House of Udaipur, because he was related to the Maharana of Udaipur. These arguments appeared convincing to the Political Resident, who, after hearing the claims of both the parties, recommended Dungar Singh for adoption, which was consented to by Lord Northbrook, the Viceroy.

Maharaja Dungar Singh (1872-87)

From the taxing exertions made during the Mutiny and the depletions caused by a long succession of internal revolts, Bikaner did not fully recover till after the accession of Maharaja Dungar Singh in 1872, at the age of 18. At that time the revenue of the state had fallen to a mere five lakhs of rupees, while the treasury was in debt to the extent of eight and half lakhs of rupees. Neither roads, nor schools, nor hospitals existed. A large and untrained army kept up for the sake of earlier traditions, swallowed up the revenues of the state. There was no regular administration in the modern sense of the word, and the entire energy of the ruler and his ministers was devoted to the maintenance of a precarious authority over the chiefs and nobles.

From this deplorable position the state was rescued by the wisdom, courage and statesmanship of Maharaja Dungar Singh. From the early age of 18, when he assumed ruling powers, he started to modernise the state administration. He divided the state into regular districts and *tehsils*, each in the charge of a trained officer. The pernicious system of farming out land revenue was abolished in favour of a fixed assessment and direct payment to the state. The Maharaja organised a regular police force and put down dacoity with a heavy hand, giving security of life and property to his people. Regular courts of law were established and laws based on British Indian models were adopted. The finances of the state were conserved and many revenue-yielding schemes were taken in hand. Hospitals and dispensaries were established and education was made free throughout the land, the first state school was opened by the Maharaja himself. It was characteristic of his far-sighted vision, that as early as 1886, as the first ruler of an Indian state, he installed electric power in his capital. He took up in earnest, considerable schemes of canal irrigation and railway communications – schemes which were carried out after his death by

Maharaja Ganga Singh. During the fifteen years of Maharaja Dungar Singh's reign, the revenues of the state more than trebled; the treasury's debt was wiped out; and many important reforms were carried out. Maharaja Dungar Singh had been justly called the founder of modern Bikaner and his achievement was recognised without exaggeration in the inscription, which the people of Bikaner had placed upon his monument: 'Benevolent and sagacious ruler, beloved by all his people and subjects, who by his prudence and foresight opened the gates for the advancement of Bikaner along the paths of modern progress, who constantly strove for the happiness and prosperity of those whom he governed, and who was renowned for his piety and charity of disposition.'

Maharaja Dungar Singh had four *Ranies* – the first was Mahatab Kanwar, the daughter of Thakur Mool Singh of Sattasar; the second was Naval Kanwar Shekhawat, the daughter of Raghunath Singh of Shahpura; the third was Chand Kanwar Kachhawa, the daughter of Thakur of Bhaleri; and the last was Bai Rajba, the daughter of Maharao Prayag Das Jareja of Kutch. Naveen Patnaik in *A Desert Kingdom: The Rajputs of Bikaner*, writes: 'When Maharaja Dungar Singh married a princess of Kutch, the journey to her state on the coast of the Arabian sea and the subsequent wedding celebrations took six months. A hundred restless young men who had accompanied their ruler to his wedding party suddenly decided to wed one hundred young maidens of Kutch on the same evening as their sovereign. When Maharaja Ganga Singh narrated this tale to a visiting Viceroy, the Englishman exclaimed, "Phew! What a night"!'

Maharaja Dungar Singh had no heir. In the latter years of his reign the question of succession was a matter of deep concern to him. When, therefore, it was announced that his father, Maharaj Lall Singh, was soon to be father again, the matter was considered to be one of the highest political importance affecting the succession of the state and the future of the dynasty. When Dungar Singh fell ill, he sent a *kharita* on August 7, 1887, to A.P. Thornton, Political Resident, which ran as follows: 'As I have no son and heir and had long intended to adopt my younger brother, Ganga Singh. Now as my health had not been good for some time past, I have according to my intention, adopted my brother, Ganga Singh, who will succeed me, to this there will be no objection, nor has any one else any claim to succession. I, therefore, request you will be good enough to inform the AGG for Rajputana of this matter, so that the Government of India may confirm the succession to my brother, Ganga Singh, after my demise and may show the same kindness to him as they have shown to me.' The *kharita* was confirmed and consented to by Lord Dufferin, the Viceroy. Maharaja Dungar Singh expired on August 19, and on August 21, a proclamation was issued about Ganga Singh's succession to the throne. His immediate lineage is given in the following table.

Genealogical Table

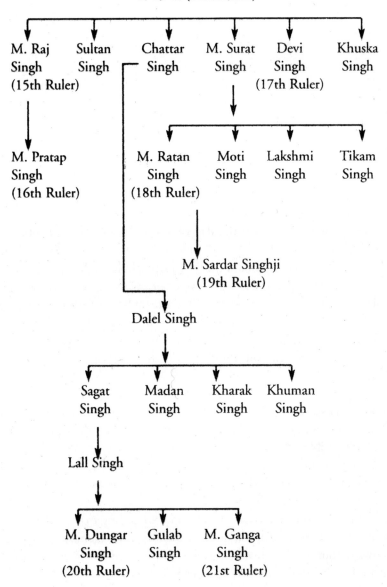

Maharaja Gaj Singh
1745-87(14th Ruler)

M. Raj Singh (15th Ruler) — Sultan Singh — Chattar Singh — M. Surat Singh — Devi Singh (17th Ruler) — Khuska Singh

M. Pratap Singh (16th Ruler)

M. Ratan Singh (18th Ruler) — Moti Singh — Lakshmi Singh — Tikam Singh

M. Sardar Singhji (19th Ruler)

Dalel Singh

Sagat Singh — Madan Singh — Kharak Singh — Khuman Singh

Lall Singh

M. Dungar Singh (20th Ruler) — Gulab Singh — M. Ganga Singh (21st Ruler)

2

The Maharaja's Rule: Early Phase

*I*t was at half-past ten on the day of Vijay Dashmi, as a October 13, 1880, (sacred to all Hindus as a celebration of the victory of Lord Rama over Ravana, the King of Lanka), that the birth of Ganga Singh took place. As the half-brother of Maharaja Dungar Singh, who had no son, the child from the moment he was born was marked out to be the future successor of the *gaddi* of Bikaner. The day and the hour of his birth were considered auspicious by the Hindus, and specially for Kshatriyas, and the court astrologers predicted a glorious future for the little Prince.

His father, Maharaj Lall Singh, was a prince of outstanding ability, highly esteemed by all for his piety and kindness of heart. During the minority of his eldest son, Maharaja Dungar Singh, and even during the earlier period of his rule, Maharaj Lall Singh was closely associated with the administration. He held the responsible office of the president of the State Council for four years after Maharaja Dungar Singh assumed full powers, and had, in that capacity, a share in all the important measures and reforms carried out during the period. After withdrawing from active service in the administration, he was always ready to advise and assist his son, never forgetting that though he was the father, he was also the subject of the Ruler. Maharaja Dungar Singh on his part, always showed the greatest possible respect and consideration to his father, so that their relations were most cordial.

The mother of Ganga Singh was a lady with remarkable personality and charm. She was the second wife of Maharaj Lall Singh, the first having died shortly after the birth of Dungar Singh. The future Maharaja loved and venerated for his mother, always maintaining that one of the most important influences in his life was her character and pious disposition. As heir-presumptive, the young prince was brought up in the royal apartments in the old fort under the supervision of Dungar Singh himself. When the young prince was hardly seven years old, Maharaja Dungar Singh passed away, in the prime of his youth. 'It was a warm August evening and the boy', writes K.M. Panikkar, 'without a care in the world, was playing with his companions in one of the shaded courtyards of the old palace in the fort. His game was interrupted by the sudden appearance of two venerable court dignitaries whose gravity of demeanour announced that something serious had happened. The important thing was to get the boy changed into suitable clothes, since he was, as usual, clad in brightly coloured clothes with golden braid. With practiced tact, the Prince – now Maharaja – was wheedled to his suite of apartments, persuaded to change into more sobre clothes and led away to accept the homage of his people.' After thirteen days of mourning were over, the young Maharaja, on August 31, 1887, ascended the throne of his ancestors in the presence of the chiefs and nobles and high officials of the state. A fortnight later Maharaj Lall Singh, who had thus seen his second son, ascending the throne of Bikaner, also passed away. The young Maharaja felt deeply the loss of paternal guidance at the very beginning of his reign.

The Council of Regency

During Maharaja Ganga Singh's minority, the Council of Regency was set up by the Government of India. Sir Charles Bayley, the Political Resident, was its president. The council carried out some administrative reforms initiated earlier by Maharaja Dungar Singh. The construction of railway to Bikaner and its extension to Dalmera; the raising of the Bikaner Camel Corps; the establishment of the State Public Works Department; the conversion of the local currency; the introduction of the land revenue system; the construction of the Ghuggar canals; the discovery of the coal mine at Palana; and the re-organisation of judicial machinery, were some of their conspicuous achievements. The council administration, however, was not free from flaws. Neither was there de-centralisation of work nor were the powers of the members of council defined. Everything important or petty was referred to the president, who, busy with his own normal work as Political Agent, was unable to devote due attention to the affairs of the state. Naturally intrigues flourished and corruption went on unchecked; district officers relieved from the watchful eye of the Maharaja reverted to bad old ways, and the people of Bikaner felt the truth of the old adage that 'it is ill for a kingdom when its ruler is a minor'. The council had no proper appreciation of the local traditions, the bureaucracy had become indifferent, and little was done to improve the finances of the state. The council was a slow-moving machine; its tardiness hamstrung the progress of the state; and left for Maharaja Ganga Singh a legacy which took many years of patient toil and constant vigilance to combat, after he assumed full powers.

The Maharaja's Early Education

The Maharaja's education was one of the major concerns of the Regency Council. His early teaching was entrusted to Pandit Ram Chandra Dube, whose conscientious care of the Maharaja's interests and of his studies was deserving of the highest praise. From the beginning the Maharaja gave evidence of more than ordinary intellectual power. The quite surprising facility with which the minor Maharaja spoke English at this early age was no doubt greatly due to his having associated freely with the children of Sir Charles Bayley, who was the Resident at Bikaner. His study was well regulated, and besides a regular literary course, it included a system of military training. True to Rajput traditions, from boyhood the Maharaja was a keen soldier and took equal pleasure in his studies as on his saddle. The Regency Council thereafter sent the Maharaja to the Mayo College at Ajmer, when he was just nine years old. He was a resident pupil there for five years (1889-94). The Maharaja's record at the school was evidence both of his natural ability and of his application. He always won the first prize for English, and came a close second in all other subjects. He won a number of coveted academic prizes and medals. Early in his school days he demonstrated an extraordinary prowess for extempore speech and elocution, which in later years was to mark him out as one of the leading orators in the empire. Gifted with a resonant voice, he spoke English with a purity rarely attained by foreigners, without a trace of accent; the Maharaja established a reputation even at school as a speaker and debater of distinction. He excelled in poetry recitation competitions which took place annually at the school.

Sir Brian Egerton: The Tutor

The Maharaja left Mayo College in September 1894 when he was only 14. The Government of India thought it necessary that the ruler of a premier Rajput state should be provided essential administrative and military training, before entrusting him with full powers. Sir Brian Egerton was the person on whom the choice fell, for he combined sympathy and tact with firmness and a wholesome belief in discipline. Scion of an old English family of high standing in Cheshire, an accomplished and well-read gentleman, a keen sportsman of distinguished manners and fine bearing, Brian Egerton won the affection of his young charge from the very beginning. Sir Brian possessed many exemplary qualities. There was one great trait in his character – the absolute identification of his interests with those of the young Maharaja, that touched the sensitive heart of the Prince. On his arrival, the Political Agent advised Sir Brian not to stay in the fort as it was impossible for a European to stay there. Sir Brian's response, however, was that his place was with his ward and he insisted on residing in the fort.

With so conscientious and sympathetic a tutor, the young Ganga Singh made steady progress, not only in his studies but in all accomplishments. 'He taught me to ride and to shoot', said the Maharaja a year and a half after the arrival of Sir Brian, 'I did not care for either but now I am awfully fond of both. He has taught me many more things and his kindness is more than I can express.' While Ganga Singh was assiduous in his studies, his activity was amazing. Riding and shooting before breakfast, study morning and afternoon, polo in the evening, and at a later date roller skating to finish up was an ordinary day's routine it varied on holidays by a ride out eighteen miles to Gajner, shooting and pig-sticking there, and riding back in time for evening polo. Study at this time was more or less on the lines of traditional education, but frequent visits to various places in the districts, close touch with the affairs of his state, and with his troops, interviews granted to nobles and land-owners, together with the punctual performance of all religious and state ceremonies, were part of the Maharaja's regimen.

His military training also progressed side by side. Deeply interested in family traditions, Ganga Singh took more than ordinary interest in this aspect of his education. He was sent in 1898 for training to Deoli with the Deoli Regiment under the command of Lt. Col. J.A. Bell.

Sir Brian Egerton had demonstrated that Indian princes should be trained in India and should not be subjected to the visits and disappointments which too often attend an education in England. The young Maharaja was fortunate in his tutor, but Sir Brian Egerton was equally fortunate in his pupil. Quick, industrious, and observant, he soon assimilated all that the West had to offer, but was learning at the same time all that was best in Indian wisdom and Bikaner traditions. 'During the few years of my tutorship', wrote Sir Brian Egerton, 'I had seen His Highness develop into a tall young man, of striking appearance, a brilliant polo player, a marvellous shot, a keen pig-sticker, and a perfect host. He had been most assiduous in his studies – passionately devoted to his state and its interests, he had been all along determined to master every detail of its administration, and the introduction of a canal into his territory was already a fixed object of his ideals.' The Maharaja was greatly indebted to Sir Brian, and in later years while acknowledging it, he said: 'I owe an immense debt of gratitude, which I can never repay so long as I live, to my tutor and guardian, Sir Brian Egerton, than whom I have no greater friend in the world.'

The happy years spent with Sir Brian Egerton had a further result. The Maharaja gained a thorough insight into English character and learnt to appreciate the great qualities of the British race. He came to be perfectly at home in their company, with a full knowledge of the courtesies, manners, and conduct appropriate to the best European society. At no time, however, even in those early days, was he anything other than a Rajput prince. The false pretences of many of the younger princes, who in their desire to imitate European modes and manners, forgot their own social and cultural inheritance, never affected him. Sir Brian Egerton's 'influence was always on the side of tradition modified by circumstances.' Sir Brian held that as an Indian prince and as a Rajput, Ganga Singh, in the conduct of the affairs of the state and in his own personal life, should be the embodiment of Indian culture and tradition; at the same time he should have the advantages of modern education, and of the accomplishments necessary for success in the changed conditions of India. Therefore, while Sir Brian Egerton helped the Maharaja 'to extract from the West a special knowledge of the West, he impressed on his young charge that true greatness for him lay in remaining an Indian and a Rajput with a genuine pride in his own race and country.' Sir Brian Egerton's influence on Ganga Singh was deep and all-pervading. The Maharaja imbibed what was good both in the East and the West; and developed traits of gentlemanliness and honour. For thoroughness of administrative training Ganga Singh was greatly indebted to Egerton, who, in his opinion, was the embodiment of all the qualities 'of courage, sympathy and unselfish devotion to duty'.

Lord Elgin's Visit

One important event that occurred in the early days of the Maharaja was the visit of the Viceroy, Lord Elgin, to Bikaner, in November 1896. This was an occasion for the first official exposure of Ganga Singh before the Viceroy. He took part in all the functions and made an extraordinary impression by the manliness of his bearing, and the untutored dignity with which he went through all the ceremonies.

At the banquet given in honour of the Viceroy, the Maharaja in his maiden speech, said: 'I stand before you, but a boy with all my work and all my toils before me and it is my most earnest wish that I should prove myself worthy of the position in which I am placed. I want not only to be the ruler of my people but their best friend too. What I look to is this that a successor of Your Excellency's may at some future date honour me with a visit and if he should express approval of what I have been doing – I shall indeed be happy.'

Ganga Singh's words were strongly impressed on Lord Elgin's memory; and the effect produced on his mind was deep. While replying to the above speech Lord Elgin declared: 'I am confident that the appearances which His Highness made in the *durbar*, on the parade ground, and here at this table have given every promise that when his time comes he will fully discharge the duties of the ruler of this state... I shall look with pleasure on the success which I have no doubt he will achieve when he assumes the administration of this state.' So favourable was the impression that the Maharaja had created upon Lord and Lady Elgin that both of them 'always retained the most pleasant recollections' of their visit to Bikaner. In October, 1897, Lord Elgin wrote to Ganga Singh: 'I trust you will count us among the friends who will always look out with interest for goodness of you and of your state.'

Marriages

Ganga Singh was approaching marriageable age, and it was part of the duty of the Regency Council to arrange for a suitable match. The bride selected was Princess Vallabh Kanwar Ranawat, daughter of Maharawat Raghunath Singh of Pratapgarh. Horoscopes were matched, deputations proceeded hither and thither, and minute details were settled according to long-established customs. The Regency Council had in all these matters the guidance of Ganga Singh's mother. The wedding was celebrated with great pomp on July 7, 1897. By this marriage Ganga Singh had three children, of whom the eldest, Prince Ram Singh, died after a few hours of life. The second was Princess Chand Kanwar born in 1900, whose health was also a source of concern to the Maharaja, since she was the apple of his eye. The Princess, in fact, fell victim to tuberculosis, as will be revealed later. The third child was Prince Sadul Singh who was born on September 7, 1902.

Maharaja Ganga Singh was married a second time on May 26, 1899, to the daughter of Thakur Sultan Singh, brother of Thakur Jeoraj Singh, of Reri in Bikaner, but unfortunately, did not have any children from this marriage.

In accordance with the injunctions of the Hindu religion, the Maharaja was therefore married again on May 3, 1908, to the daughter of Thakur Bahadur Singh of Bikamkore. This marriage also bore him three children: Prince Bijey Singh, born March 29, 1909; Prince Vir Singh born 1910; and a daughter – Princess Shiv Kanwar – born in 1916.

The Prince Assumes Charge

The Maharaja reigned for 11 years as a minor, while the administration was carried on by the Regency Council on his behalf. He assumed full powers of government on December 16, 1898. That day was, as history was to show, the end of one epoch and the beginning of another in Bikaner.

In the presence of the chiefs and nobles of the state and the members of the Regency Council, the Agent to the Governor-General, Sir Arthur Martindale, at a grand *durbar* held in the old fort, read out the *kharita* of the Viceroy confirming the Maharaja in his ruling powers. On the very same day Maharaja Ganga Singh showed that he intended to be the effective ruler of the state without delay. To the chiefs and nobles he spoke out his mind regarding the administration of the state and the factions and intrigues which were rampant in the state.

'The first thing that I want to say today is something about the past. You will know that a minority of 11½ years is a very long time and unfortunately, if the people have no strong hand over them, they are apt to go wrong and quarrel with each other and form intriguing parties. I am sorry to find that this has also been the case at Bikaner… These parties I am sorry to say have been the ruin of Bikaner. What I want very much now is that this party feeling should stop at once.

I want you to understand that whatever I shall do in the future I shall do because I think that, that is the right and just thing to do, not by favour … I wish it to be known that I strongly disapprove of bribery and mean to put a stop to it. God help the men who give and take bribes because I certainly will not help them.

Sardars, let it be known to the "ryot" through you that there is no bribe taking or bribe giving in future. If the "ryots" think they are ill-treated tell them to come to me but tell them not to waste their hard-earned income by giving it as bribe to any "Raj" servant be he great or small.'

This was a strong utterance from a young ruler who was but 18 years old. It was the voice of one born to rule, to take his responsibilities seriously, of one who was going to spare neither himself nor his officers in the work of administering the state. This determination, which he articulated on that first day of his effective rule, pervaded the entire administration of the state like a strong fresh breeze.

Great Famine of 1899-1900

Hardly one year had elapsed since Ganga Singh's attainment of majority when the great famine of 1899-1900 – devastating and calamitous in its effects, decimated the land. The whole of northern India fell into the grip of a great famine. Bikaner, where the rainfall is precarious in the best of years, had already suffered from serious scarcity in the preceding years. As the famine of 1899-1900 occurred in immediate succession to several bad years in which scarcity or famine prevailed more or less it was the most severe and widespread within memory than any that had preceded it.

The famine of 1899-1900 was unparalleled in intensity. It had affected the entire population of the state which, according to census of 1891, was 8,32,000. The parched desert yielded no crops. Cattle and other livestock began to die in large numbers through extraordinary heat, lack of fodder, and scarcity of water. The misery of the villagers was so great that emigration began to take place on a large scale towards the Punjab, Malwa, and other areas. To add to the misery, diseases also began to play havoc. Dysentery and cholera began to take a heavy toll, and smallpox and measles began to spread.

The Maharaja who had to face this calamity of unparalleled magnitude was only a stripling of 18, but he rose magnificently to the occasion. The training he had received from Sir Brian Egerton was now put to the test. The famine gave an opportunity to the young ruler to show his mettle. He bore the brunt of the unpleasant work entailed, and earned the gratitude of his people by promptly sanctioning liberal expenditure, and laying down well-devised measures of relief. Relief works and famine camps were started in August 1899 and maintained till October 1900. The work was devised in such a way as not only to provide effective relief, but also to bring in some profit to the state eventually. All but one were managed on the same system; the labourers were gauged and given fixed tasks and all payments were made daily in grain; poor houses were maintained; the land revenue was suspended and advances made to agriculturists. The Maharaja's share of the work was not limited to what he did or directed to be done in Bikaner; he visited the suffering villages, and formed an independent opinion on the sufficiency of the methods employed. His presence was welcomed by the villagers as an assurance that government was doing that was possible to save them. Ganga Singh took the bold step of substituting the army for the ordinary revenue machinery in this work. The Bikaner Camel Corps was converted, for the time being, into a kind of famine agency and the novel experiment justified itself. Through the help of the Camel Crops the work of transporting grain was carried out with success. The experiment of utilising an efficient and well disciplined military force for famine duties was carried out for the first time on the Maharaja's own initiative, and proved a complete success.

Ganga Singh personally superintended the operations. As distress became general, a famine relief department was constituted directly under his supervision. He also appointed a famine committee which met weekly and discussed the management of the various branches of relief and the provision of labour for the number estimated to require it. He made adequate medical arrangements in the camps. Qualified doctors were placed in charge of the camps and compounders were sent round to the villages twice a day to attend to the needs of the people. Strict supervision was enforced over the water supply of the city and wells were effectively protected. Untiring and in continuation, the Maharaja toured the villages on horse and camel with only three small tents for the accommodation of himself and his staff. Such tremendous energy and interest in the work of administration in the case especially of a young ruler of 18 was indeed uncommon and unparalleled.

A detailed programme of works and relief measures was drawn up with care. The preparations for relief were made on a scale of unexampled magnitude. The work decided upon was both useful and remunerative and permanent benefit to the state. The railway line was extended towards Bhatinda, giving relief to 38,876 persons. Relief centres and poor houses in different parts of the state were opened. Taccavi or interest-free loans amounting to Rs. 85,300 were advanced to the agriculturists; and land revenue amounting to Rs. 4.7 lakhs was remitted. Nine irrigation projects, two railway lines, three roads, extension of the city wall enclosing 740,000 square yards, and nine miscellaneous works were executed during the course of the famine. No cases of fraud or embezzlement occurred at any of the camps. In total 91,87,085 units with 16,78,670 units of dependents were relieved. The state spent Rs. 8.5 lakhs on famine relief works, of which half of the amount was subscribed by the leading *seths* of Bikaner.

The peasants found in the Maharaja their best friend. The Maharaja, frank and outspoken, took them into open confidence about the policies and intentions of the government, stood with them in their hour of distress, and did not ignore or deceive them. He always held that a ruler was the first servant of the people, and in their adversity he should have broad shoulders and share their burden. The Maharaja scrutinised not merely the current requirements of the hour, but the abiding needs of the state; and built not only for the present but for the future too.

'Never again, if human enterprise and skill can prevent it' was the unspoken decision that Ganga Singh took in his own mind. After the frightful experience of the famine, he resolved to make Bikaner a modern and progressive state. His instinct told him that the future of Bikaner lay in a twofold policy – railway development and irrigation. The Maharaja began to devote attention to this end. To leave Bikaner stronger and more prosperous, to add to the elements of stability in its existence, to develop communications and irrigation, and, thereby enable the government to confront the dangers or vicissitudes in the future, became the Maharaja's ambition, which he attained, admirably.

Ganga Singh's famine work and the success which attended it attracted a great deal of attention. Colonel Dunlop Smith, the Famine Commissioner of Rajputana, greatly appreciated the 'personal interest' and 'initiative' taken by the Maharaja and characterised him as 'the guiding spirit of the relief operations'. 'The energy and shrewd capacity he brought to bear on the conduct of affairs made his famine administration in some respects a pattern not only to other states but to British districts also.'

Sir Denzil Ibbeston, Revenue Member of the Viceroy's Council, in the course of a speech in the Imperial Legislative Council, declared that the personal interest taken by the Maharaja of Bikaner was not only 'highly creditable' to himself as a ruler, but had also contributed largely to the success which had attended the famine organisation.

Sir Arthur Martindale, Agent to the Governor-General in Rajputana, during his visit to Bikaner in 1900, spoke about the famine administration of the Maharaja 'as the best in the whole of Rajputana'. The Maharaja, he said, faced his foe squarely across the countryside and mitigated the distress of the people. He had no idea of sitting down with folded hands. His watchword was 'action' and the entire resources of the state in men and money, unaided from without, had been devoted to the struggle.

The Queen-Empress in recognition of Maharaja Ganga Singh's personal activity conferred upon him the '*Kaiser-i-Hind*' Gold Medal, a coveted decoration, for humanitarian work. Lord Curzon, while awarding the *Kaiser-i-Hind* to the Maharaja paid a glowing tribute to him for 'such splendid an opening'. 'His Highness of Bikaner was his own famine officer, throughout the fearful time and he conducted his campaign with indefatigable energy and skill.'

Countering External Interference

Between 1899 to 1907, the Maharaja had to face the petty interference in his administration by the Political Resident, who behaved like a virtual ruler invested with the right of supervision, direction and asserted the authority to interfere in any matter he liked. H.A. Vincent, the Resident, in his letter dated November 19, 1898, wrote to the Maharaja that no measures or acts of the Council of Regency during the minority be altered or revised without the concurrence of the Political Officer. The Maharaja, however, was not content to be a nominal ruler. He had experienced many drawbacks in the administration carried out by the council for eleven years during his minority, and wanted to introduce significant reforms and innovations in administration in order to push ahead the state from medievalism to modernism. The pettifogging interference by the Political Resident, however, irked the Maharaja's pride and independent spirit. Petty employees dismissed in the ordinary course of events for corruption or inefficiency, professional malcontents, disloyal nobles and others, knew that however unreasonable their case, they could get a hearing with the Political Resident. Many troublemakers exploited this shared authority and played up to the Political

Resident, whose interference on trifling matters, at times hurt, even humiliated Ganga Singh.

Exasperated by this increasing interference the Maharaja wrote to the Political Resident, Captain S.F. Bayley: 'Hardly a day goes past villainy or other, if you ask on each case, the people who petition do get to know of it through your clerks or mine and it puts their back up and even if you don't interfere it, in a way, upsets my authority. I mean they know I can't do anything very much myself without your asking an explanation. This is the gist of my whole letter.' But Bayley, refused to budge an inch. At the same time the Maharaja was equally determined that nothing could prevent him from gaining his objective.

The relations of the Maharaja with S.F. Bayley were hardly harmonious. In January 1900, when Captain Bayley embarked on a tour of the Hanumangarh district, the Maharaja, as a matter of courtesy, sent him a shooting licence on January 24, which was taken by Bayley as an offensive, who wrote back: 'I am very much amused at your sending me a shooting licence. I will have it framed, I think, and show it to my cousin and others as a specimen of the advanced Government of Bikaner where not even the Political Agent may shoot without a licence.'

The Maharaja in his reply to Captain Bayley on February 2, 1900, emphatically wrote: 'I think it is very unkind of you to make such sarcastic remarks about my sending you the shooting licence. To begin with you say you will have it framed and show it to people as a specimen of the advanced Government of Bikaner where not even the Political Agent may shoot without a licence. And then you say you hoped to give one to the A.G.G. and his staff. I am afraid you have made a mistake when you state that not even the Political Agent may shoot without a licence, for this is not the case ... I only sent you the licence the other day as the duplicate was being sent out to the "Shikar" Department as I told you before, we are very strict in the district ... I thought you would be pleased at my sending you a formal licence ...' Bayley, arrogant that he was, remained dissatisfied with the Maharaja's reply, but Ganga Singh, with the resolution which characterised him from childhood, refused to be brow-beaten, and made his protests to the government.

Bayley adopted a policy of obstruction and put several bottlenecks to the Maharaja's reform plans. There was a great deal of correspondence on the details. Each point raised by Bayley was answered in detail with his hand-written notes. He was polite and persuasive, but he answered note for note. In this warfare of words, Bayley, unaccustomed to a ruler who wrote his own 'aide memoire' and who was prepared to debate, not merely to sulk in an attitude of injured dignity, found himself the loser. Bayley's interference finally ended in 1907, but long before that date, Ganga Singh's sagacity and administrative skill had earned the confidence of the Government of India sufficiently to allow him to introduce important reforms without hindrance.

Troublesome Lieutenants

Though the chiefs and nobles of Bikaner had on the whole been generally loyal to their Ruler, but some of the discontented group of nobles, mainly the Thakurs of Ajitpura, Bidasar and Gopalpura had tried to create an unrest in the state in 1904. They began spreading disaffection by the usual methods of exaggeration and misrepresentation. A well-organised seditious movement was orchestrated. When Ganga Singh came to know about the movement, he warned them against disloyal activities and promised consideration of any genuine grievances which they had. He soon came to know that the conspiracy was much more serious than what he had apprehended. He appointed a special tribunal which after careful inquiry unanimously found that the Thakurs of Ajitpura, Bidasar, and Gopalpura were dissatisfied with the state and 'took it into their heads to create a serious disturbance by making other chiefs and subjects hostile to the state by whatever means possible; and concluded that the charge of sedition against them was clearly proved.'

Ganga Singh kept Major Stratton, the Political Agent, fully informed; who to the surprise of the rebels supported the action of the Maharaja. In consultation with the members of his Council, Ganga Singh decided on administrative punishment, and confiscated only one-half of the estate of the Thakur of Ajitpura and a village each from the estates of Bidasar and Gopalpura. Though the policy of the Maharaja was a mild one, he was not moved by any spirit of vengeance; but the offended nobles made a representation to the Government of India. The Foreign Department was sympathetic to the Thakurs and said that their action against the reforming activities of the ruler was nothing but a formal protest. The Maharaja took the matter to Lord Curzon and had no difficulty in proving that the tentative advice of the Foreign Department was based on wrong premises. The Maharaja's arguments carried the day and Lord Curzon overruled his Foreign

Secretary and upheld the Maharaja's decision, which was communicated to the later on December 7, 1905. This was a great diplomatic victory for Ganga Singh. He had worked strenuously and finished the hardest of battles, breaking the back of the rebellious Thakurs. That was the last uprising of the nobles in the state, and Ganga Singh had put them in their place. His period of trial and trouble was nearly over; he had *skillfully* eliminated the unwanted elements in his state. He had demonstrated that the Maharaja intended not only to reign but also to rule.

The manner in which Ganga Singh had handled the unrest of the nobles was acclaimed by A.J. Bruce, who was the Political Resident from May 1905 to September 1906. In his confidential note, he wrote that the misunderstanding which arose between the Maharaja and some of his principal Thakurs was much to be regretted; the situation was faced by the Maharaja with energy and promptitude which happily prevented any prolonged or serious unrest in his state. The Maharaja, he thought, was 'to be congratulated upon the firm and yet judicious manner in which he dealt with this troublesome affair.'

The Coronation of Edward VII

The year 1902 was full of activity. The Maharaja attended the coronation of King Edward VII held on June 26 in London. It was a great, a rare occasion for the Maharaja. He was received with unusual distinction everywhere he went. His fine appearance and amiable disposition attracted the attention of all those who came into contact with him. His conduct and magnetism along with his indepth knowledge impressed everyone. Their Majesties King Edward VII and Queen Alexandra showed him many marks of favour; in all functions he was invited to stand behind His Majesty along with members of the royal family. A personal honour which the Maharaja valued greatly came to him from this visit to England was his appointment as honorary Aide-de-Camp to the Prince of Wales, later King George V. After some time of his return to India, he attended the Coronation *Durbar* in Delhi on January 1, 1903.

In a short time Ganga Singh had established a very good rapport with the King-Emperor and the royal family. His Majesty was greatly impressed by him, and had a strong regard for his 'opinion and counsel'. Ganga Singh cultivated a close relationship with the King-Emperor and was in regular correspondence with His Majesty. His remarkable felicity with the English language helped him to maintain this relationship. Colonel Arthur Bigge, Assistant Private Secretary to the King-Emperor, in his letter dated January 4, 1911, to the Maharaja, wrote: 'His Majesty is much struck by your command of the English language, and your letter, written without a mistake in spelling or phraseology, reaches a high standard of English scholarship.'

Lord Curzon's Visit

The year 1902 was also marked by the visit of Lord Curzon of Kedleston, the Viceroy, to Bikaner, from November 24 to 26 . The Viceroy arrived by official train on the morning of November 24. During his stay at Bikaner, the Viceroy performed the opening ceremonies of the Victoria Club and Curzon Garden. On November 26, Lady Curzon laid the foundation of the *Zenana* (Women's) Hospital which bore her name. Their Excellencies then drove to Devi Kund Sagar and saw the cenotaphs of the deceased members of the Royal House of Bikaner. At the state banquet held on November 25, the Viceroy said that the personality and career of no ruling chief in India had warmed him more than that of the Maharaja of Bikaner, who he had been observing from his days as Viceroy. He was glad to say that the Maharaja had started on the right lines, and the four years that had passed since he received full powers, had been 'packed full of industry and experience of many kinds and in many different lands'. He said that the achievements of the Maharaja were known to all and that he was 'revealing no secret'.

The state, said Lord Curzon, was 'in the hands of a young Maharaja, in the fresh morning of manhood with all life before him, and great opportunities await him. He could combine the merits of the East and the West in a single blend and could be, at the same time, a liberal and a conservative, each in the best sense of the term.' He expressed the hope that the Maharaja would live for his people, he would know them, mingle with them, typify all that was best in their national character and traditions. He was sure that his host would remember that 'he was not merely the Maharaja in rank but Maharaja of Bikaner in particular, that would not only add to his personal reputation but would bring happiness and credit to his people.' What Lord Curzon ventured to sketch in his observations, Maharaja Ganga Singh of Bikaner fulfilled them during his reign!

Lord Curzon's fondness for Ganga Singh is disclosed in his letter in September 1905: 'I have then (at Bikaner) formed a regard for you, and the visit has led me to follow with the warmest interest every incident of your career. This interest will not cease when I leave India. From time to time I shall hope to see Your Highness when you come to England.'

Arrival of the Prince of Wales

An important visit to the state was that of the Prince and Princess of Wales, for three days in November 1905. His visit was a matter of 'great pride' to the Maharaja and his family. The Prince of Wales (later on King George V) arrived in Bikaner by the royal train from Jaipur on November 24.

The visit of the Prince of Wales to Bikaner was mainly for a little relaxation after the long round of ceremonies so carefully and exactly observed. His main object was a few days' shooting. He was one of the finest small game shots in England and a whole-hearted enthusiast in the pursuit of game.

The area surrounding Bikaner has the best sand-grouse shooting in India, perhaps in the world. The species chiefly visiting those parts is the imperial grouse, about 13 inches in length and 17 to 18 ounces in weight, and amazingly strong and rapid on the wing. A great resort for the birds is the Gajner Lake, about 20 miles from the city. On the fringe of water stands the Gajner Palace, 'a charming shooting box in a delightful old-world garden'. Gajner is an oasis with its garden paved with paths and flowers, shaded by tall trees and at the end of a long visit of palaces, a succession of buildings with the arches and terraces rising straight from the banks of a large lake. Here the Prince of Wales had demonstrated his shooting skill on the Gajner lake, where in two days, his eleven guns accounted for 2,841 birds. Gajner is almost as famous for its pig as it is for grouse. 'Four boars were speared by the Prince and his staff one of which showed stubborn fight and gave the English visitors an excellent idea of what a Rajputana pig could be.'

The visit of the Prince to Bikaner was brought to a close with a state banquet. The Prince at the banquet speech touched upon his old friendship for Ganga Singh. He said: 'In any case the Maharaja's face is very familiar to us and our children, for, besides having had the pleasure of seeing him in England two years ago, there hangs at Marlborough House an excellent portrait of His Highness – his gift to me – in the uniform of the Bikaner Camel Corps.' This full-length portrait of the Maharaja in uniform of Commandant of the Imperial Service Camel Corps was painted by M. Collier. 'I have been much struck', the Prince of Wales continued, 'by the fine soldierly appearance of the Bikaner Camel Corps. We know what they have done on active service. It will give me much pleasure to tell the King-Emperor of the smart appearance of the men, most of whom wear medals for China and Somaliland, and of the excellent condition of the camels. I shall assure His Majesty that he has every reason to be proud of Your Highness' contribution to the Imperial Service Troops, and also inform him of your further generous offer to augment it by the addition of half a regiment of your infantry.'

The Prince of Wales was very pleased with his visit to Bikaner. The Maharaja's friendly welcome and generous hospitality made him feel as if he was at home. He had heartily approved the Maharaja's suggestion to commemorate his visit by erecting a library building, which would also contain the beautiful and historic armoury of Bikaner. 'The Maharaja has also permitted me', said the Prince of Wales, 'to see and enjoy what may fairly be described as one of the wonders of Bikaner – its sport. My experience of two delightful mornings' shooting at Gajner will never be forgotten.'

Lord Minto's Visits

Lord Minto visited Bikaner twice. The first visit of Lord and Lady Minto and their daughters was in 1906; and the second in 1908. The first was the official visit, and the second unofficial. During the first visit the Maharaja had received Lord Minto on the railway station platform, 'resplendent in brocaded silk and looking magnificent in rainbow hued breeches with jewelled aigrette. The escorts, in gold and white uniform, were mounted on camels with crimson trappings decorated with necklaces of shells. Troops lined the road up to the palace, some dressed in chain armour with visors over their faces, silver bullock-carts drawn up in formation, with the horns of the bullocks were encased in embossed silver; behind the troops the crowd made a riot of colour.' As Lord Minto and the Maharaja drove by, the people shouted *Khoma, Khoma* – meaning, 'Pardon mighty Lord.'

Apart from seeing the historical places, Lord Minto also undertook the review of troops. Ganga Singh took him to Gajner as well where the Viceroy stayed two days for sand-grouse shooting. 'We have much enjoyed our shooting expeditions', wrote the Viceroy, 'some times stalking black-buck and *chinkara* from a bullock-cart and some times galloping over the desert in a barouche and six, while *shikaries* or camels indicated the position of the herds. Bikaner himself is a very fine shot. He never shoots unless the animal is moving, considering it as an unsportsman-like, as they should a sitting pheasant.'

At the banquet speech during Lord Minto's first visit, on November 24, Ganga Singh spoke of his endeavours, the success which his administration had so far achieved, the sympathy and help he had received from the agents to the Governor-General, and of his hopes and ambitions for the future. For the economic salvation of the state and relief of people from their bond of misery, the Maharaja opened out his heart before Lord Minto, and earnestly pleaded for the feasibility of bringing a canal from some big river in the Punjab. 'I venture to say, that would constitute one of the greatest achievements and transformations under British rule in India.'

Lord Minto listened with the deep interest to all that the Maharaja eloquently spoke. He appreciated Ganga Singh's hopes and anxieties for the future welfare of his people, the difficulties that stood before him and his firm confidence that he would overcome them. He admired the all-round progress in the state in the fields of revenue, railways, mineral development, education, industries, electricity, buildings and administrative reorganisation. All this was encouraging, said the Viceroy, but, behind so much that was encouraging 'there lurks that awful ghost of possible famine, ever ready to haunt the broad lands over which you rule.' The Viceroy extended his support in the possibilities of irrigation which he had already worked, and hoped that his miracles would ultimately triumph in Bikaner, aided by the energy of its Ruler and the hardiness of its people. Lord Minto promised sympathetic consideration of the request made by the Maharaja for sharing the water of the Sutlej. The ice had been broken. The great scheme towards the realisation of which the Maharaja was to devote a quarter of a century was clearly charted out.

'The Maharaja of Bikaner is a wonderful host', stated Lord Minto, 'who has shown us princely hospitality and, I think I may say, too, unrivalled sport'; ... ' we left Bikaner with great regret in the Viceroy's magnificent white train, a quarter of mile long which standing in the desert siding seemed to belong to a different era from the local transport of camel teams and bullock wagons.'

Lord Minto's appreciation of the Maharaja's kindness was disclosed to the Maharaja by Field Marshal Lord Birdwood, Commander-in-chief of Indian Army, who, in December, 1906, wrote: 'We were dining with the Viceroy last night (13th December) and after dinner he remembered you and was telling me how much he had enjoyed his time with the great Maharaja of Bikaner.'

Lord Minto came to Bikaner again in 1908. He stayed for two weeks, and visited Gajner, Hanumangarh and Suratgarh. The visit was informal, but it was clear to all that it established a new relationship between the ruler of Bikaner and the representative of the Crown. Everyone knew that Bikaner was an important state; that its young ruler had achieved much and had been marked out for special courtesies. The official visit was a matter of formality. The informal visit was purely in the spirit of friendship.

On one occasion when Ganga Singh's wrote to him about a shooting done at Gajner, Lord Minto replied, 'I wish I had been with you.' The Maharaja's loyalty to old friends was perhaps one of the most attractive elements in his character.

Sir Harcourt Butler

A word should be said about Sir Harcourt Butler, who was the foreign secretary during Lord Minto's Viceroyalty, and, who, in November 1910, became member of the Viceroy's Council; he was another good friend of Ganga Singh.

Sir Harcourt Butler infused a new spirit in the Foreign Department. He believed that India was entering on a new era, and there still remained much to be done to face new challenges. He felt that the native states were in such different stages of development, chiefs varied so much in tastes, ability and character, that any general policy was not practicable. He was pleased to see that Bikaner was moving steadily forward.

On November 15, 1910, when Sir Harcourt Butler left the Foreign Department and joined his new assignment as member of the Viceroy's Council; he wrote, the same day, to Ganga Singh: 'I shall carry with me among my warmest recollections the remembrance of your kind hospitality and the free frank discussion which we have brought to bear on public affairs.' In appreciation of the Maharaja's co-operation and assistance during his tenure as foreign secretary, he stated: 'What I value most is the confidence that you had ever reposed in me and the confidence that I had ever reposed in you.'

The next foreign secretary to the Government of India was Sir John B. Wood, who also held Ganga Singh in high esteem. In his letter dated August

5, 1910, to the Maharaja, John Wood, wrote: 'I have read your Administration Report with the greatest interest. Bikaner seems to be rapidly developing into a modern state.'

In Laughter and in Sorrow

Though the first phase of the Maharaja's effective reign had been of trial and trouble, nothing dampened his spirits. Despite obstacles in the way, his energies were ceaselessly directed towards the interests of the state. No hindrance prevented him, or checkmated his plans and reforms. He remained unmoved by both failure and success. He was realistic yet optimistic in his vision and had clear action plans for every objective. He judged things on their merit. His ideas were realistic and accurate. He showed zeal for a cause, worked with great ardour and enthusiasm for the well-being of the people, and never allowed pleasure to interfere with duty. He had diagnosed the ailments of the state, and moved forward, with grim determination, to remove illness and poverty. Working hard through good times and bad, the Maharaja, demonstrated the truth of what William Blake in *Gnomic Verses*, wrote:

> 'Great things are done when men and mountains meet;
> This is not done by jostling in the street.'

3

The Silver Jubilee

*M*aharaja Ganga Singh completed twenty-five years of his reign in 1912 and the celebration of his Silver Jubilee saw much rejoicing in the state. Since December 1898 he had put in place a remarkable administrative system. The new reforms initiated by him from 1902 onwards greatly accelerated the pace of growth. In almost every field of state activity a marked change was visible. The Prince of Wales (later on King George V) was happy to witness the progress achieved by the Maharaja and, on June 1, 1909, he wrote: 'I am always delighted to hear from you, as I take a great interest in you and in your state.'

As a reformer he showed great strategic vision. He was a good judge of people and things, and seldom went wrong in his assessment. He could see things from the other person's point of view. 'Think how that word or letter will read at the other end,' he often used to say in correcting the abruptness of official suggestions regarding reforms. He sought to improve the efficiency and responsiveness of the government machine by introducing reforms. He accelerated the pace of development and put a new face on the state; the visitors who came during the Silver Jubilee of the Maharaja in 1912 were astonished to see the great strides, clear and tangible, that had taken place in Bikaner.

Ganga Singh reorganised the finance and revenue departments of the state. In 1898 the revenue of the state was Rs. 20 lakhs and by 1910 it had jumped up to Rs. 44.50 lakhs. Buildings for public institutions and purposes were constructed. Water supply projects were undertaken. A large modernised electrification system was installed. Telephones connecting all important courts, offices and residences were installed. New railway projects were completed. In 1897-98 the total mileage of railway line was 85.5 miles, while by 1911 the total mileage of railway line became 384.13 miles. Tarred roads were constructed in the city and its adjoining areas. The cause of education received the Maharaja's zealous attention. Hospitals and medical aid were greatly developed. An X-ray unit was installed at the main hospital and a new women's hospital was constructed. Questions of sanitation and public health received the utmost attention. The police department was reorganised. The judiciary was made independent of the executive. A Chief Court was established in 1910. The creation of the Chief Court was a momentous step and with it the state embarked on a novel experiment, which was found nowhere in any other part of Rajputana. Administrative conferences were held periodically, where developmental schemes were formulated. These conferences provided the best example of the Maharaja's method of administration through deliberation and discussion. Weekly diaries were regularly scrutinised to keep a watch over the administration. He expected the Regency Council to exert themselves to their utmost and, on occasions reminded them: 'Put your souls and body into the work, take interest in it, and do your utmost.' The Maharaja abhorred self-propagation and paper reforms; he believed in examining facts himself to reveal the true nature of things.

There is hardly any measure of administrative reform that escaped the attention of Ganga Singh. The state was given a stable foundation by 1912, the year of the Maharaja's Silver Jubilee. Fine buildings, parks and public institutions indicated the spirit of progress in Bikaner. All that was worth keeping for posterity was carefully preserved and fitted into the new order of things; the future of the state seemed prosperous and rosy.

Bereavement

The Maharaja's first wife, Maharani Sri Ranawat passed away in 1906, after nine years of married life. The Maharaja greatly mourned the loss of his wife, and poured out his sorrow to Sir Arthur Bigge, Assistant Private Secretary to the King-Emperor, in his letter dated August 22, 1906: 'My dear wife passed away on the 19th August. It is a cruel blow and made all the harder to bear on account of the little children left motherless on my hands.' Maharani Sri Ranawat's age at the time of her death was merely twenty-four.

Another tragedy occurred on December 13, 1909, when the mother of the Maharaja, Maji Sri Chandravatiji, expired. The Maharaja, who was greatly devoted to her, was constantly at her side during her illness. She was ailing for some time, but her death came quite suddenly, and the whole state was plunged into grief. Her piety, charity, and high sense of duty had endeared her greatly to the people of Bikaner. Her role in the education and upbringing of the Maharaja and her keen interest in all matters affecting his welfare were fully recognised by Sir Charles Bayley and Sir Brian Egerton who had charge of the Maharaja during his boyhood. She never stood in the way of any arrangements made for the better education and training of her son; and co-operated in every way with the guardians and tutors under whose charge the Maharaja was brought up, thereby earning the gratitude of both the Maharaja and the people of Bikaner. 'Her piety and charity', writes K.M. Panikkar, 'were proverbial in the state. Her efforts to alleviate the sufferings of the poor and the sick and her solicitude for the welfare of the people of Bikaner made her a venerated personality throughout the state.' Her death was a public loss for the entire state.

Though by nature the Maharaja was a proud man who kept his sorrows and joys to himself, on this occasion he was unable to contain his feeling of desolation, and he greatly mourned his mother's death. He poured out his grief into the sympathetic ear of the Prince of Wales, who knew what the Maharaja's mother had meant to him.

The Maharaja was still in deep mourning for his mother when Prince Vir Singh, who was then only five months old, fell ill and died. Pouring out his tale of misfortunes the Maharaja wrote to the Private Secretary of the King-Emperor: 'In addition to losing my wife, … as you know, from the same disease I have had the misfortune to lose two out of my four sons.'

The demise of his mother and his son were sorrowful events in the life of Maharaja Ganga Singh, and for a considerable length of time he lamented their death.

The Imperial *Durbar*

The Maharaja was nominated a member of the *Durbar* Committee by Lord Hardinge, which at the time was regarded as a great honour. He had participated at the Imperial *Durbar* in December 1911, in his dual capacity, as one of the premier ruling princes of Rajputana, and as A.D.C. to His Majesty. 'Standing by the side of the King-Emperor, his soldierly figure attracted much attention. So far, the public of India knew him only by report as one of the progressive princes of Rajputana. The Coronation *Durbar* brought him prominently to the public eye and made his personality familiar to the leaders of British India. Constant attendance on His Majesty also brought him into closer contact with the royal family, though his association with the King-Emperor dating from the coronation of his father had already ripened into friendship.'

At the Imperial *Durbar* Maharaja Ganga Singh was personally invested with the 'Order of the Knight Grand Commander of the Star of India' by His Majesty the King-Emperor, at the Investiture held in December, 1911. From none of his Indian lieges did the King-Emperor receive a more cordial welcome on his arrival in India than from the Maharaja of Bikaner; and his services in organising the Coronation *Durbar* were warmly acknowledged by Lord Hardinge.

At the Coronation *Durbar*, Gopal Krishna Gokhale, an important moderate leader of Indian National Congress, and the most outstanding personality in British India, came into contact with the Maharaja of Bikaner. Both men decided to send a message of goodwill and friendship from the princes and people of India to the English nation through the Prime Minister of Britain, expressing the high appreciation of the influence exercised by the visit of their Majesties in drawing closer the bonds that united England and India. The Maharaja's contact with G.K. Gokhale, which started from Imperial *Durbar* gradually developed into friendship. At Gokhale's suggestion, the Maharaja came in touch with other princes, and, as a result, a long and affectionate message was sent from India. Apart from expressing the cordial goodwill and fellowship of the princes and people of India, the message said: 'Their Imperial Majesties, by their gracious demeanour, their unfailing sympathy and their deep solicitude for the welfare of all classes have drawn closer the bonds that unite England and India.'

The Jubilee Celebrations

The Silver Jubilee was celebrated with great pomp and show; the occasion was applauded by everyone. Ganga Singh received a direct cable from King George V, who, said: 'I heartily congratulate you upon your having completed twenty-five years' rule over your state and I wish you and your people many years of happiness and prosperity.'

The jubilee celebrations in the state took place in September 1912. The Maharaja went through different religious ceremonies; visited the temples of his family deities – Sri Lakshmi Narayanji and Sri Karniji – and the temples of Bhairunji at Kodamdesar, and the Nagneechiji and Sheobari; he made gifts to charity according to tradition; received addresses from various public bodies; and finally announced various grants according to old Hindu custom. In the innumerable congratulatory messages and addresses presented by his subjects on this occasion there was a feeling of joy and loyalty on the part of the people and affectionate pride in the achievements of their Maharaja.

The Durbar at Ganga Niwas Hall

On September 24, 1912, the Maharaja held a public *durbar* at the Ganga Niwas Hall, where the Resident, the nobles, and the officials of the state were present in their full dress uniform. Colonel Windham, the Resident, in a congratulatory speech, applauded the Maharaja's successes, praising his earnestness and conspicuous ability in governing the 'splendid heritage of an ancient kingdom'. He said that both the friends and foes of the Maharaja, acknowledged the unqualified success of nearly all of the Maharaja's ventures. He acknowledged that the revenue had doubled and the internal rebellion and other troubles had ceased to exist. He spoke about one of the most distinctive results of the Maharaja's rule which had always struck him. 'There is probably no state in India where the immemorial culture and genius of the East and the traditions of the ruler and his race are more happily blended with the science, energy, and practical activity of the West than they are in Bikaner. Evidences of it are to be seen in every direction; in fact of Bikaner it can I think quite truly be said that good healthy tradition and reform are, so to speak, the warp and the woof of the administration.'

The Maharaja's speech at the *durbar* was characteristic; it was marked by a review of the past and challenges that lay ahead. He narrated how he and his administration had laboured earnestly to promote the prosperity of the state and the welfare of the people. Though the Maharaja was conscious that much yet remained to be done, looking back with satisfaction, he said: 'The introduction of far-reaching and important reforms in the various branches of the state administration – executive and judicial, the strengthening of the finance department of the state and the placing of it on a sound footing by the appointment at its head of an expert and able officer, the removal of defects that existed before, the employment of better paid and more competent officers, the liberal expenditure of public money on much-needed public works, on education, on sanitation, and on medical relief, on the extension of railways, on the increased means of water-supply in the shape of constructing and repairing wells, tanks, and bunds, the suppression of dacoities and the marked decrease of serious crime, the security of life, liberty and property, which is now enjoyed by everyone throughout the length and breadth of the state, and the perfect peace and tranquility which reign within my borders – these are all indications of the fact that the efforts which have been made to promote the well-being of the state and the people, have not been without success; whilst the vast improvements and the many buildings, which have tended to beautify the capital, have altogether changed Bikaner from what it was even 14 years ago.' The Maharaja expressed confidence that the efforts which were in process to secure the priceless blessings of canal irrigation from River Sutlej in the Punjab would be a success within a measurable period, and an era of unknown prosperity would be opened to the people of Bikaner.

Peoples' Representative Assembly

Maharaja Ganga Singh was not a man 'to rest on his laurels.' He was a far-sighted ruler, who recognised that conditions were fast changing, and new ideas and ideologies were evolving in British India, which required suitable adjustments in the traditional system of government. He was familiar with the movement of the Indian National Congress which had started in 1885. Ganga Singh had correctly anticipated the developments in India and realised that the strength of a ruler in the future would lie only in a close association of his people with the government. He took a notable decision, on his own, during the Silver Jubilee, and established the Peoples' Representative Assembly for Bikaner in 1913. It was a great landmark in the history of Bikaner, by which the Maharaja had blended prudent conservatism with modern ideas.

The Assembly consisted of 35 members, of whom 10 were elected, 19 nominated, and 6 were ex-officio. It had the same powers as the Imperial Legislative Council, established under the *Act of 1909*. It ushered in an era of associating the people with the active governance of the state. It broke through the icy portals of personal autocracy to let in the ingress of democracy.

The Maharaja inaugurated the Assembly on November 10. In the galleries of the hall, the British Resident, Maharao of Kotah and the Nawab of Palanpur were present as honoured guests.

In his inaugural speech, Ganga Singh made it clear that the new experiment was intended to make the lives of people more interesting and comfortable, and 'at least a portion of the desert should blossom, if not as the rose, at any rate as the cornfield.' He said: 'My people who were children have now grown up, and I can deal with them as men', and added, 'Those who have to steer the ship of state must not look behind to the mere memories of an illustrious past, but must peep out into the distance to descry what lies ahead and in doing so I am satisfied that this milestone placed today lies on the line of happiness and progress.'

In 1917, four years after its inauguration, Ganga Singh felt that the experiment had justified itself. He took a further step and increased the number of elected members from 10 to 15, and the strength of the body was raised to 45. The word 'Representative' was replaced by the word 'Legislative'; as such the body came to be known as Legislative Assembly. In subsequent years, the number of elected representatives were increased and powers of the Assembly were enhanced in 1921, 1925 and 1937.

The Assembly, indeed, was a remarkable political experiment; it was deserving as an example of political foresight; as a blending of the old with the new in a way which gave the advantages of both without the defects of either. This was a novel constitutional innovation, in which the Maharaja had anticipated what was to follow in the years ahead. It was the first of its kind in northern India. While in the southern states of Travancore, Mysore and Baroda, representative institutions had already been in existence for over two decades, the conditions were different as compared to Bikaner, where the creation of an Assembly in Bikaner was a bold step. *The Bombay Chronicle* (November 7, 1913) wrote that the Maharaja had given 'wide powers for initiative and control' to the Assembly. *The Tribune* (November 14,1913) called it 'a very important event not only for the Bikaner State, but gradually for India'.

Felicitation by British Residents

Maharaja Ganga Singh's Silver Jubilee celebrations had a lot of functions

A portrait of Maharaja Ganga Singh unvieled on the occasion of his Silver Jubilee celebrations in 1912.

Maharaja Ganga Singh (second from left) with the Commander-in-Chief of the British Indian Army, (on his left) and a group of British officers in 1913.

Maharaja Ganga Singh, (seated second from left), with the Meerut Division in France in 1914.

King George the V riding with his honorary Aide-de-camp, Maharaja Ganga Singh, in London shortly after the Great War.

Maharaja Ganga Singh (sitting left) and the famous Bikaner polo team with Rajputana Polo Challenge Championships Trophy.

Maharaja Ganga Singh of Bikaner (right) with Prince Sadul Singh, who shot his first panther at Mt. Abu.

Maharaja Ganga Singh (sitting fifth from left), Chancellor of the Chamber of Princes, with senior rulers for a meeting of the Chamber in Delhi.

Maharaja Ganga Singh (standing in second row, second from left) at the Imperial War Conference in 1917.

Maharaja Ganga Singh and Maharaja Scindia of Gwalior with Hon. Mr. Clemenceau, Prime Minister of France at Gwalior in 1920.

Maharaja Ganga Singh with Prince of Wales (later on, King-Emperor Edward VII) at the ramparts of Bikaner Fort during his visit.

Three Generations: Maharaja Ganga Singh with his son, Maharaj Kumar Sadul Singh, heir-apparent of Bikaner and grandson Prince Karni Singh.

Maharaja Ganga Singh in military uniform during the First World War.

A portrait of Maharaja Ganga Singh taken at Geneva in 1930 at the Assembly of the League of Nations.

and attracted the atten‑ion of subjects as well as British officers. The British residents of Bikaner gave a banquet to the Maharaja at the Victoria Memorial Club. The Maharaja had from the beginning availed himself of the services of selected European officers for his more important technical departments; and they had served the state with utmost loyalty and devotion. Colonel A. Wake who presided over the function held on September 28, 1912, alluded to the Maharaja's administration. While he did not propose to recount the history of the past 25 years – 'the most momentous epoch in the history of Bikaner', Colonel A. Wake reminded his audience to bear in mind that for 15 years out of 25, the whole burden of the state had rested on the shoulders of the Maharaja. If the toil was his, the results and the credit were also his own. In all his plans and enterprises the Maharaja had claimed the services of British officers, and they, with rare exception, had repaid him with loyal service and hearty appreciation. The hospitality the Maharaja had shown and the friendship with which he had honoured many were unique. British officers had seen many reforms carried out and many more planned. 'We have watched the Maharaja', said Colonel A. Wake, 'in his daily wrestle with the growing accumulation of work, personally direct and inspire every department in his state. We have seen palaces and pleasure gardens spring from the desert, and mud hovels transformed into avenues of carved stone. We have stood by while he broke records in sport, led his troops in the field, and took his place among the premier Princes of India round the King-Emperor.'

Visits by Lord Hardinge of Penshurst

The social celebrations of the jubilee were postponed to December in order to enable the Viceroy to attend in person. Lord Hardinge (1910-16), who had a personal relationship with the Maharaja, arrived in Bikaner on November 25 and stayed up to December 2, 1912. It was his first visit to the state and the occasion was eventful.

On November 26, Lord Hardinge declared the Public Park open and expressed the hope that in the dim and distant future, when young men, would walk on its green turf, enjoy its cool shade and 'look upon the various memorials with which they are surrounded, they will tell one another how this beautiful park was made during the rule of Maharaja Ganga Singh, remind one another that its very existence is a memorial of one of the best of

Bikaner's rulers, and each in his own way try to emulate his example of devotion to duty and to his country's interests.'

On November 30, there was the state banquet in honour of Their Excellencies. The Maharaja in his speech said that 'as the Sutlej Canal Project has in the last six years advanced a step further, in that the surveys have been completed, we shall eagerly await the issue in due course of the final orders of the Government of India on this question of such vital importance to us.' Lord Hardinge assured the Maharaja that the Canal Project would receive his sympathetic consideration. He praised the liberal and true statesmanship of the Maharaja and his tact and friendliness with which he had maintained excellent relations with the political officers. He congratulated the Maharaja for his bold announcement to create a peoples' representative assembly which was in fact a liberal and progressive measure. The Silver Jubilee, he said, was truly a memorable occasion and it was as much a privilege as a pleasure for him to join in the celebration, and 'in the years to come these days will ever remain days of pleasant memories and happy recollections.'

Appreciating the Maharaja's record of performance during the past fourteen years Lord Hardinge said: 'While violating no reasonable custom or tradition of the people, you have with true statesmanship introduced improvements and reforms without destroying the old-time characteristics of your state.' 'If Bika, the founder of the state, returned to the earth he would marvel at and approve the great changes which were directed for the good of the state.'

Lord Hardinge testified that Maharaja had achieved extraordinary progress in Bikaner, 'a desert state with many natural disadvantages, but which, nevertheless, has made more material progress and achieved greater prosperity than many other states in India blessed with greater advantages by climate and nature.' It was quite impossible for him, stated Lord Hardinge, to enumerate all the measures of reform adopted by the Maharaja, but the endeavours that had been made by free money-grants to improve the water supply and the efforts devoted to encourage the growth of trees, had caught his attention, as particularly appropriate in so thirsty a land as Bikaner; and no one could fail to appreciate the amenities which the Maharaja had added to his capital with beautiful buildings, fine roads and parks. These were some of the results to which the Maharaja could contentedly point, but below them all lay the mainspring of finance to which the Maharaja had given so much attention. The Viceroy added: 'Finance is the backbone of all administration, and Your Highness's firm grasp of that fact and the financial reorganisation which you have effected will, I think, prove to be one of the most substantial reform of all.' The Viceroy devotedly hoped that it was possible for Ganga Singh to look forward to a long future of useful and distinguished rule.

The Viceroy's visit which was an important part of the celebration had been both a pleasant and an instructive one, for while he had enjoyed the lavish hospitality for which the Maharaja was famous, he had at the same time seen how smoothly events moved in a state where administration was completely organised and everything was well ordered.

Lord Hardinge visited Bikaner again, privately, from October 17 to 25, 1913. He enjoyed shooting at Talwara *Jheel*, Suratgarh, Chhaper, Kodamdesar and Gajner. At a banquet given by Ganga Singh in his honour, Lord Hardinge disclosed his happiness when he received the cordial invitation to come back to Bikaner. 'I need hardly tell you how readily I jumped at the chance of breathing once more the glorious air of Bikaner and meeting its distinguished Ruler in friendly intimacy untrammelled by the exigencies of ceremonial.' Expressing his deepest sentiments, Lord Hardinge, said : 'When I stepped once more upon the friendly soil of Bikaner, I felt like a school boy out for a holiday, and that is a sensation, let me assure you, that a Viceroy does not often have, at any rate in these latter days; but its very rarity gives an edge to one's appetite, and I really think it would be difficult to find a more delightful combination of circumstances than the present, with a goodly company of friendly faces around me, with the best of sport placed lavishly at one's disposal, and by my side a chief who has filled to the brim the bright promise of his early days as a conscientious and high-minded ruler, whose word carries weight in the counsels of his brother chiefs, whose support is as one of the pillars of the Indian Empire, and who has given me the privilege of his true and genuine friendship.'

Hardinge's third visit for ten days was between November 18 to 28, 1915. On November 24, he unveiled the statue of Maharaj Lall Singh, Ganga Singh's father.

To show his admiration, Ganga Singh built a large municipal hall in 1922, and had named it Hardinge Municipal Hall. Lord Hardinge did not try to conceal his friendship, wrote: 'My own personal relations with the Maharaja were those of great mutual friendship and esteem … I cherish the friendship of His Highness the Maharaja of Bikaner …' Again, in 1916, when departing from India, Lord Hardinge poured out his feelings to the Maharaja on April 7: 'From the day of my arrival in India you have always been nice and helpful to me in every way ... Your kindness I shall always keep alive in my heart ... I feel this parting from you more deeply than I can say, and I only hope that you will always think of me as a true friend.' He added: 'Amongst many things that have tended to cloud my recollections of India, my relations with you will always stand out as bright spot and will always be a joy to me to work back upon.'

A Galaxy of Visitors

Many good friends and well-wishers visited Bikaner on the occasion of his silver jubilee. E.S. Montagu, (later, Secretary of State for India) Sir Louis Dene Leuth, Governor of the Punjab; and a number of rulers of native states. The Maharaja of Jaipur, Sawai Madho Singh, on December 19, 1912, wrote: 'The success which the Maharaja of Bikaner has achieved in the administration of his state is splendid.' The Maharaja of Mysore, Krishnaraja Wadiyar, on December 23, wrote: 'During the past 25 years there had been continued prosperity under the Maharaja of Bikaner's enlightened and liberal rule.' The tone of the numerous congratulatory messages that the Maharaja had received from other princes, friends and admirers was similar.

End of Isolation

The festivities went on at intervals during the years 1912 and 1913. Among the many important dignitaries and potentates who came to rejoice in the achievements of the young Maharaja in 1912-13, had not guessed what the future held in store for their host. The Maharaja was soon to acquire a national presence. 'The jubilee was in that sense more than the end of an administrative period. It marked also the end of the period of the Maharaja's isolation, the confinement of his interest to his own state; it saw the beginning of a new period when the Maharaja stood forth as a representative of his own Order and as a champion of his motherland.'

Beating all obstacles, Ganga Singh had broken the path of medievalism. The state had changed enormously: the feudal visage had been stripped and Bikaner had emerged as an advanced modern state. Full of pioneering zeal, firm in resolution and unmindful of pitfalls along the way, Ganga Singh was ready to embark upon a new voyage – one that was bound to open new vistas for the state and its ruler.

4

On the Battlefield

The Rathore clan of Rajputs had always been a race of warriors. The warlike spirit of the race had remained intact and on more than one occasion Maharaja Ganga Singh had proved himself a worthy scion of the distinguished race of warriors to which he belonged. The martial traditions of the historic race were not only upheld by him, but his daring deeds in three continents had added to the rich heritage of his forbears and brought him glory. He fought for the Crown in China, France and Egypt.

From his early boyhood Ganga Singh had taken a keen interest in military training. Inclined towards family traditions, he took more than ordinary interest to cultivate his physical capabilities. The Bikaner Army at that time was not a modern and efficient force, and the opportunities for superior training were not available with his own troops. He was therefore sent in 1898 for training to Deoli with the Deoli Regiment under the command of Lt. Col. J.A. Bell. That regiment had the reputation of being one of the smartest in India. On his return from training, the Maharaja was given command of the Sadul Light Infantry, named after Prince Sadul Singh, who was born in 1902. With natural keenness he attended to his duties and it was to his training that the regiment owed its smart marching which was so greatly admired.

Boxer Rising in China

The Maharaja from the very beginning was greatly inspired to demonstrate his worth on the battlefield. In 1895 when war was declared between the British and Chitral, and again in 1896 when war broke out in Sudan, the Maharaja offered his personal services but they were gratefully declined in view of the Maharaja's tender age, who was only 15 at the time and the fact that the wars in question were of no serious magnitude. In 1899 again the Maharaja offered his services for the Boer War but the government did not consider it desirable for him to participate in person. In June, 1900, the Maharaja was gazetted as an honorary major in the Indian Army and attached to the Second Bengal Lancers. He was at the time probably the youngest major on record outside members of the European Royal families.

The first opportunity for personal service in the field came to the Maharaja in 1900, when the Boxer rising in China necessitated the dispatch of an Indian expeditionary force to Peking. The Maharaja at once offered services of himself and his army, an offer Lord Curzon accepted with enthusiasm. The first Indian Prince to go overseas to fight under the British flag, the Maharaja sailed from Calcutta on September 1, arrived at Hong Kong on September 14, and disembarked on September 17. The Maharaja was in command of his Camel Corps, which he took as a dismounted unit. He and his regiment took active part in various battles including the siege of Potingfu and the victory of Pitang. He served with distinction at the front and was mentioned in dispatches. The young Prince, though hardly 20, and invested with full powers merely a year and a half before, had his first experience of active warfare. On the signing of Peace Treaty, the Maharaja returned to India in December 1900. On landing in Calcutta he received a grand ovation from his subjects whose shouts of *Jai Jangal Dhar Badshah*, resounded far and wide. The Maharaja was given a public welcome at Calcutta on behalf of the Government of India. The reception at the quay was with full ceremonial, and the Foreign Secretary, the representative of the Viceroy, and the high military and civil officers in uniform were there to honour him.

Ganga Singh, the only Indian prince to visit this theatre of war, was awarded the 'China Medal' and the dignity of a K.C.I.E. by the King personally in June 1902 when he went to England to attend the coronation of King Edward VII.

The Maharaja's soldierly appearance in the China War had created an everlasting impression, which later on was disclosed by Sir Arthur Lothian, Resident for Rajputana, in 1942, who, at a banquet in Bikaner, said: 'I remember as a boy seeing a picture of His Highness the Maharaja of Bikaner in the picturesque uniform of the Bikaner Camel Corps when he was proceeding to China during the Boxer rebellion. I certainly will never forget him, though I met him personally at the original Conference of Ruling Princes in 1916.'

Somaliland Campaign

The next was the Somaliland Campaign of 1902-04, where the Maharaja was not permitted to take the field in person, but the Ganga Risala, the Bikaner Camel Corps, was dispatched to the theatre of war on November 4, 1902, and returned on July 14,1904.

Being the only unit from India which was mounted on camels, the Camel Corps' services were much in demand; in addition, to taking part in the fighting their 'volley firing' at the enemy in several points was appreciated. The regiment particularly distinguished itself in the battles of Jidbali and Dharatol.

In the battle of Dharatol, Captain (afterwards Major-General) W.G. Walker, Special Service Officer, won the Victoria Cross; and as the Victoria Cross in those days was not awarded to Indian Officers and men, including those belonging to the Indian States Armies, the 'Indian Order of Merit' was conferred on Major Kishan Singh of Ganga Risala who was with Captain Walker and who was wounded in that fight.

Field-Marshal Sir Charles Egerton, General Officer Commanding the Somaliland field force, had recorded his appreciation of the services of the Ganga Risala. On the return of the Ganga Risala, Lord Curzon, in his telegram dated July 9, 1904, congratulated the Maharaja for 'the great courage and bravery under most trying circumstances', shown by Bikaner Camel Corps, and emphatically said that 'they have not only done excellent service to the empire, but also great honour to the Maharaja and the state both.'

On June 25, 1909, the Maharaja was promoted to the rank of Lieutenant-Colonel in His Majesty's Army and on June 3, 1910, on the accession to the throne of His Majesty King George V, the Maharaja was promoted to the rank of a full Colonel, and made an A.D.C. to His Majesty.

The First Great War

A sterner task awaited the Maharaja in the trying ordeals of the Great War in 1914. On August 4, the British Empire declared war on Germany. The Maharaja at once offered not only the entire resources of his state, but also his own personal services at the disposal of His Majesty. He realised that in this great period of crisis for the Empire, lay his opportunity for emulating the glorious record of his ancestors on the field. To one so filled with the traditions of the Bika Rathores, 17 of whom out of 21 had actually led their own troops in warfare in distant parts, a great European war in which the forces of the Empire were engaged in a life and death struggle with a mighty enemy, was too unique an opportunity to be lost. Placing his own sword and services at His Majesty's command, the Maharaja implored that as the opportunity was one of a life-time he should not be left here inactive, and 'if the forces of the Empire are engaged, for the duty of a Rathore Chief calls me to fighting service, which was his highest ambition.' The Maharaja's warm-hearted offer met with immediate response. The Bikaner Camel Corps (Ganga Risala) proceeded to the Front and the Maharaja was himself attached to the Head-Quarters Staff of the 7 Division of the Indian Army under orders for France.

Those were indeed days of great activity in Bikaner. *Rana Banka Rathore* – Rathores gallant in war – was the old and true description of the Maharaja's clan and the opportunity for serving in such a war was every Rathore's desire. At the parade of the (Bikaner troops on the eve of the departure of the Camel Corps on active service) August 25, 1914, the Maharaja addressed them in words that stirred the heart of every true soldier. 'These indeed are great days,' he said, 'for us Rajputs and for the matter of that for all other soldiers too! Such an opportunity presents itself but rarely. It gratifies our life dream and ambition as Rajputs.' He further added: 'Remember, my brave men, what our traditions are! We came to Bikaner as fighting men. Soldiers we were and soldiers we have ever since remained. We fought for the British in the time of the great Mutiny. We have fought for them in China and Somaliland. Now we go to fight again ...' The Bikaner Camel Corps proceeded to Egypt, where for 18 months it was the only Camel Corps available and was accordingly relied upon for all patrol and reconnaissance duties East of the Suez Canal. In the defence of the Canal the Corps took a prominent part, fighting in many actions against the Turks, who were pressing upon this vital artery of trade and defence.

Shortly after Great Britain took up arms, the Maharaja sailed for France, leaving behind a broken-hearted Prince of twelve, his heir, who had pleaded, as only a boy could, that he too be allowed to go and fight for the King-Emperor. The Maharaja was first appointed on the Head-Quarters Staff of the Meerut Division. It was with that force that he had sailed. Till the beginning of December he was mostly at Locon, near Bethune. When His Majesty King George V visited that front he was pleased to command that the Maharaja be appointed to the staff of the Commander-in-Chief, Sir John French, afterwards the Earl of Ypres. There he remained till the end of January. Though the Maharaja appreciated the honour of these appointments, but his war-like spirit was in no way happy to remain at head-quarters when fighting was in progress. 'To so proud a spirit, anxious to rival the records of his great ancestors who had fought at the head of Imperial troops and won victories for their sovereigns, service on the staff was a source of intense disappointment.' The British Government, however, fully aware of the changed conditions of modern warfare and its responsibility in exposing an Indian sovereign prince to the dangers of a modern war, was on no condition willing to post him to front-line duty.

On one occasion the Maharaja was, however, insistent and unyielding. He insisted on being treated exactly as others similarly placed and on sharing their hardships and difficulties. He did not allow things to be made easy for him. This characteristic of the Maharaja elicited spontaneous tributes from all the officers with whom he served, especially from General Sir Charles Anderson in command of the Meerut division, who wrote that in sending the Maharaja of Bikaner to his staff they had sent a 'kindly, simple, self-effacing English gentleman.'

Ganga Singh took everything seriously. What there was to do he did with characteristic thoroughness, and General Sir James Willcocks who commanded the Indian forces, wrote: 'Both you and I can fairly say that we saw the Great War in its most trying days. No boarded trenches then: we had to fight in the mud and slush... I always recall your good work in those terrible days: never afraid of mud or discomfort or anything else, you showed a fine spirit, Maharaja, worthy of your great name and race.' In another communication to the Maharaja, dated January 27, 1915, the gallant General bore the following characteristic testimony: 'You really are not only a chief, but a hard-working soldier.'

The Maharaja's work and example were greatly appreciated and he was mentioned in dispatches. He looked forward in time to greater activity at the front, but news reached him from home which made his return to India imperative. His daughter, Princess Chand Kanwar, was reported by doctors to be suffering from consumption. Early in January, 1915, the Maharaja received alarming reports about the Princess's health. The doctor who was in charge of her, declared her condition very serious. He was therefore obliged to return; but not before he was enabled to take part in the campaign in Egypt during the fortnight he stayed there on his way back.

Before leaving the Maharaja asked Lord Kitchener to let him spend some time in command of his own Camel Corps, which was then in service in Egypt. Lord Kitchener appointed the Maharaja to the staff of General John Maxwell, General Officer Commanding in Egypt. The Maharaja arrived at Port Said on January 29, 1915, where information reached him that his daughter was better. At Port Said, the Maharaja heard that the Turkish army was actually approaching the Canal, and instead of reporting himself in person at head-quarters in Cairo he received permission from General Maxwell to serve at the head of his own troops which were then stationed at the Ferry Post at Ismailia. General John Maxwell, in reply to the Maharaja's request, wrote: 'You have decided to do exactly what I would have wished you to do. I regret very much to hear of the cause that brought you to Egypt but what is loss to the army in Flanders is a gain to the army in Egypt.'

During the advance of the Turkish force under Djemal Pasha in January and February, 1915, the Bikaner patrols were in continuous touch with the enemy; and during the final attack on the Canal early in February were in the trenches at Ferry Post under the actual command of the Maharaja of Bikaner. One day when out at the head of a small detachment of troops the Maharaja came upon a large concentration of the enemy in the neighbourhood of Katib el Khel. In the encounter which resulted the Maharaja himself took part, fired 17 rounds from his own rifle. On February 21, the Turkish army had to retreat, and the Maharaja at the head of the Ganga Risala took part day by day in the pursuit of the enemy.

The role of the Ganga Risala was highly appreciated. General John Maxwell wrote: 'They are a most useful Corps, I do not know what we would have done without them.' Similarly, General Archibald Murray, General Officer Commanding-in-Chief, Egyptian Expeditionary Force, mentioned: 'The Bikaner Camel Corps have shown soldierly qualities in action, discipline and endurance.' Likewise, General H.V. Cox, wrote: 'The Camel

Corps continues to do splendid work in this country, and everyone speaks with the highest praise of this. They understand the desert naturally, and never make a mistake.'

After the defeat and retreat of the Turks from the Canal area the Maharaja returned to India. He was extremely unhappy because of the illness of his daughter – Princess Chand Kanwar, of whom he was extremely fond. Her mother – Maharani Ranawatji Sahiba – had expired in 1906 because of tuberculosis. Princess Chand Kanwar too had developed a tubercular infection at the age of fifteen. She was brought to King Edward Memorial Sanatorium in United Provinces for consumptives, where a specialist, Major Cochrane, was looking after her. Her condition was declared very serious. Her deteriorating condition created a great anxiety in the Maharaja's mind, which he expressed to Lord Stamfordham, Private Secretary to His Majesty, in his communication dated June 28, 1915: 'I recently wrote and said to Sir Walter Lawrence, to see what was a fine healthy young girl of sixteen laid low and confined to bed and gradually wasting away from this awful disease. Our anxiety is, as you can imagine, very great.' Despite the Maharaja's best efforts, the disease could not be cured, and Princess Chand Kanwar passed away on July 31. Her demise was most heart-breaking to the Maharaja. To perpetuate the memory of his beloved daughter, he built a cenotaph at Bhowali. Once, when Sir James Meston, Lieutenant Governor of United Provinces, rode over to Bhimtal, he, on his way took the liberty of going in to see the mausoleum which the Maharaja was building in memory of his 'dear little girl'. On August 10, 1917, Sir Meston wrote to Ganga Singh: 'It (the mausoleum) stands in a beautiful position and is a most graceful piece of work, or the gem of architecture. The workmen were very nearly finishing it, and the ground has been enclosed in the most picturesque manner.'

After the demise of his daughter, the Maharaja's own health was none too good. He had high fever, his health declined and he had lost 26 lbs. during the illness. The Maharaja was hoping that this was only a temporary indisposition, and when he spoke to the Viceroy about his return to the War in the late spring as he intended doing – Lord Hardinge told him that he could not dream of letting him go back in the present state of health. The Viceroy wrote: 'Much as I admire and appreciate your desire to return to the scene of conflict, I have come to the conclusion that in the interests of India and of your state, it is Your Highness' duty to remain in this country.'

When the Maharaja was in Delhi, he asked Sir James Roberts, the

Viceroy's surgeon, who told him that he could not pass him fit even if the Viceroy allowed him to return to the war. Though there were no bad symptoms visible but due to the uncertainty about the real nature of the fever the Maharaja had in June, and the fact that both his father and brother died of consumption, the doctors, as a precautionary measure, were inclined to take a somewhat serious view of his weight loss and ill health. The Maharaja was kept under observations and given tuberculine injections.

The Maharaja had an earnest desire to go back to the Front, but the Viceroy did not agree to his proposal. Later on, in March 1916, the Maharaja disclosed his inner feelings to his old friend, Vivian Gabriel. 'Though I should like to have been "in at the death" of the Germans and would have dearly loved to have been in a big battle – it looks as if it is crying for the moon to hope in this War for a good old-fashioned hand to hand fight on horseback – still I cannot say that for other reasons I am disappointed.' His enforced retirement from the War, however, proved to be of the highest political importance, both to the states, and to India as a whole.

The Maharaja, during the Great War, had received mention in dispatches for 'gallant and distinguished conduct in the field', and in recognition of his personal services at the Front, the King-Emperor promoted him, on August 1, 1917, to the rank of honorary Major-General in the British Army.

Among the various honours and distinction Ganga Singh received were the K.C.B – Knight Commander of our most Honourable Order of Bath, (Military Division), '1914 Star', the Grand Cordon of the Order of the Nile by the Sultan of Egypt, General Service and Victory Medals as well as mentions in the Emperors' Honours Gazettes.

The Maharaja wore his medals and decorations with great humility and respect. The medals were hard won, and exemplified his courage and commitment as a soldier. A man of deep integrity and courage in all aspects of life, he always led by example.

The valuable services rendered in the field by the Maharaja and his Camel Corps received very special praise in official communications from the King-Emperor, the Viceroys, and others. A number of decorations and distinctions were won by the Ganga Risala on the field of battle during the War.

The King-Emperor in his cablegrams to the Maharaja, dated March 14, 1918, appreciated the war services of Bikaner, and observed: 'Your illustrious

House has long been distinguished for its loyal devotion to the British Crown and I am well aware how worthily these traditions are maintained in Your Highness' own person.' Earlier also, in the beginning months of the war, the King-Emperor was gratified to know about the splendid conduct and behaviour of the Camel Corps, and on November 5, 1914, wrote to the Maharaja: 'We all quite realise that no troops could have been more tried, and to be pitchforked into one of the greatest, if not the greatest battle in the history of the world.' He added: 'It is a splendid performance that four of the Rathore ruling chiefs (Bikaner, Jodhpur, Ratlam and Kishengarh) are at the front pulling their weight in the boat.'

Lord Hardinge in his farewell *kharita* to the Maharaja, wrote: 'Your Imperial Service Troops in Egypt have fought most gallantly for the King-Emperor, and added to the reputation they had already won on other fields for courage and efficiency.'

Like him, Lord Irwin, the Viceroy, in a speech at Lallgarh Palace, Bikaner, in January, 1927, alluded to the Maharaja's qualities of statesmanship and wisdom: 'He was also a great soldier whose sword was unsheathed in three continents in the service of the King-Emperor.' His views were reiterated by the Prince of Wales (King George V) in December, 1921: 'The Maharaja had worthily maintained the Rajput tradition of staunchness and fidelity.'

The Second World War

In 1938, when the Germans presented their demands to Czechoslovakia, and the situation in Europe became surcharged with tension, the Maharaja was quick enough to recognise the dark clouds looming large over the horizon. He cabled the King-Emperor, placed unreservedly at his disposal his own sword, the services of his army and the entire resources of the state. He repeated this offer in August and September, but the King-Emperor graciously declined. 'I thank you warmly for your message which has given me the greatest satisfaction. I can assure you that I appreciate very deeply the sentiments of loyalty and devotion which have prompted your valuable offer of assistance at this critical time.'

Ganga Singh saw the Viceroy in Delhi in December 1939, who told him that the war was different from the last one, and it had been decided, at least for the time being and especially in regard to France that no Prince would be allowed to proceed on active service. On December 21, the Maharaja expressed his feelings to the Maharana of Udaipur that, 'when the Viceroy first told me he only spoke about myself, and I cleared up the point by asking whether this decision applied only to myself or was because of my age; and it was satisfactory to find that this was a general rule about all Princes and their sons. So here I am very disappointed, but one must the make best of it.'

The Offer Accepted

The Maharaja renewed his offer of active service in August, 1941, at the age of sixty-one, and wrote to Lord Linlithgow: 'Your Excellency will realise how profound has been the disappointment to one like me who has all his life been a keen soldier, how I have chafed at having to stay behind and sit at home in luxury when the empire was in the grip of a life and death struggle and when my own troops have taken the field in the service of the King-Emperor, and how I have longed, and am still longing, to have the privilege of taking some personal part in this war also.' The Government of India at this stage gladly accepted the offer made by the Maharaja.

The Maharaja had tried for two years since the outbreak of the war to get off on active service, and at last in October 1941, the Viceroy accepted his offer. The Maharaja was tremendously looking forward to it, and when he got the acceptance, he wrote on October 16 to General Claude Auchinleck, Commander-in-Chief, Middle East British Army Headquarters: 'My elder grandson, a young lad of 17½, is, if that is possible, even more keen than I am – in fact, the boy is really mad with joy – and the same applies to my two young A.D.C's who will be accompanying me and who are sons of old and faithful friends of mine'. The Maharaja further stated that although, of course, he would be glad to meet the Indian and other troops, but his one and only desire was to go to the Front and 'to see, and if possible be in, some fighting'. He had requested General Auchinleck that he should be taken at least to the Front at or near sollum for a few days; and if by any chance 'our advance in Libya should be on then, I would most earnestly beg you to let us be there also for it. That would be wonderful. I and my grandson', continued the Maharaja, 'and the young fellows accompanying me do not want, as you will appreciate, to come home without our even hearing a shot fired on this occasion; and I am afraid due to over-keenness you may find us rather a nuisance, but I feel sure you will understand and forgive my troubling you.' The Maharaja, along with his grandson, Prince Karni Singh, proceeded to Middle East War Front on

October 30, 1941, where two units of state Army – Ganga Risala and Sadul Light Infantry – were already stationed.

On the War Front

The Maharaja was on the War Fronts in Egypt, Iran and Iraq for one and a half months. He saw several Indian units including regiments of his own state, and also visited some Indian general hospitals. He found the brave Indian troops well prepared and in the best of health and spirits. He was greatly impressed by their gallantry, heroism and discipline. The exploits of Indian troops was a general topic of talk in Libya and they had gained laurels in the hard fighting there. The Maharaja quoted one well-known American journalist who described Indian gallant soldiers not as men but 'lions'; another American journalist, whom he met and who had seen one of the Rajputana rifle regiments in action, told him that 'he wished he was a Rajput and could enlist in that unit'.

From all accounts, said the Maharaja, the Indian troops and the Bikaner State forces seemed to get on very well with their British comrades. They had put the fear of God in the Italians who never waited to face their bayonet charges; while like the British troops, the Indian soldiers had proved themselves the better than Germans. General Sir Claude Auchinleck told the Maharaja that 'no praise could be too high for our Indian troops'.

The Maharaja was in Egypt at the time when the third Battle of Libya started. He and his grandson, Prince Karni Singh, during those momentous days had been to the Western desert as far as advance battle head-quarters which then were near Fort Maddalena. A highly mechanised war, full of rapid movement and great surprises was going on. Many German and Italian tanks, planes, vehicles and other equipment were destroyed. The War was fast, furious, fluid and fluctuating; the Indian troops and the Germans moved great distances. Ganga Singh was more convinced than ever that the Arms of the King-Emperor would triumph over the enemy and that by God's grace ultimate victory was assured. The Maharaja left Egypt, and returned to Bikaner on December 21,1941.

Rank of a Full General

His Majesty's government was fully aware of Ganga Singh's meritorious services rendered to the empire, on different continents and on different battlefields, and never hesitated in recognising his worth. With one distinction after another, he was promoted finally to a full General in 1937 – a rank which no other Indian ruler had attained.

The conferment of the highest military rank upon the Maharaja was a signal distinction, and he, descending from a long line of soldiers, particularly valued it. Not only did the Maharaja take great pride in his achievements, but the people of Bikaner, equally, felt deeply gratified and honoured. It aroused justifiable pride among the people of the state.

Ganga Singh's character was that of a true soldier unconquerable will, and dauntless courage, 'never to submit or yield'. His prowess on the battlefield, and adherence to his commitments earned him many laurels.

5

The Imperial War Conference and Rome Note, 1917

After his Silver Jubilee, Maharaja Ganga Singh extended his interests from the internal problems of his own state to the affairs of India as a whole. He was looking into the future and had, as early as January 1914, defined his ideas in a note to the Viceroy, Lord Hardinge. He put forward his views concerning the position of the states with a firmness and clarity to which the Government of India had hardly been accustomed to at that time. The Maharaja had realised that the lack of co-operation not only permitted the gradual reduction of the ruler's powers, but was preventing the states, as a whole, from taking their full share in the social, economic and administrative advancement which was then in progress in British India. His note to Lord Hardinge was only one of the many moves by which, for a number of years, he fought battles for the Princes of India. In defining his ideas regarding the execution of the principle, the Maharaja wrote: 'In this way a federal chamber representing all the states – and if necessary … the provinces of British India as well – would gradually grow up.' He envisaged an ideal of which he would be a staunch exponent 16 years later. Even at this early stage his mind was working towards a federation and he visualised the organisation of princes as a necessary first step. The seed of the idea sown by the Maharaja bore magnificent fruit.

At the outbreak of the Great War, he had already established so great a reputation as an Imperial statesman that he was chosen to represent his brother princes in particular and India in general, at the sessions of the Imperial War Cabinet and Conference, held in London in 1917. Maharaja Ganga Singh thought that it was a unique chance, to serve at one and the same time the emperor, India and the states.

The Maharaja knew that he was going to London not only as the ruler of Bikaner, or even as the representative of the Princes of India, but as spokesman of his mother country. From now onwards a new note came in his speeches. At the banquet given by the princes in his honour at Bombay on February 7, 1917, prior to his departure for London, the Maharaja spoke 'for the first time publicly not only as the ruler of a great state, but as an Indian statesman'. The Maharaja in his patriotic speech, told the assembled princes:

'Whether we come from the territories of British India, or those of the Indian states, we are all Indians, who are entirely united in loyalty and attachment to our King-Emperor; in our affection for our mother country; and in our deep and genuine solicitude for our brethren of all creeds and communities throughout India. I know I am voicing the feelings and sentiments of Your Highnesses when I further state that we of the Indian states ... deeply sympathising with all the legitimate aspirations of our brother Indians in British India, just as much as, we feel sure, our brethren in British India sympathise with the legitimate aspirations of the Princes and people of the Indian states and our desire to see maintained unimpaired our dignity, privileges, and high position.'

The Maharaja voiced the deep sympathy of the princes 'for the legitimate aspirations of our brother Indians in British India', which had a special or suggestive meaning. Not only did he express sympathy but he took the bold and the unprecedented step of effectively pleading in public for greater reforms in British India. Showing no fear the Maharaja frankly said: 'I sincerely believe that the British statesmanship and British sense of justice and fairness will rise equal to the occasion and accord to our country that place to which her position in the empire and her loyal services to the Crown entitle her.'

This was indeed a note that had never been heard in India before – so long it was complacently argued by British authorities in India that the demand for reforms was confined to the *babus*, or the intelligentsia, as they were contemptuously called. The princes were greatly agitated about this demand, and the impression had been created that the rulers of Indian states were alarmed at the prospect of British Indian political freedom. Not only was this grossly unfair to the princes, but, as the Maharaja realised, dangerous to their future position, as it was likely to create hostility between British India and the states.

No prince had so far openly declared himself in favour of reforms for British India. For the first time the Maharaja of Bikaner at a banquet presided over by a governor and attended by many ruling princes had given unequivocal expression to nationalist and patriotic sentiments. He had in no uncertain terms pleaded for 'the just claims and aspirations of India to enable her to work out her destiny under Britain's guiding hand and protection.'

The Maharaja's categorical statement had caused much surprise to a great many. As K. M. Panikkar writes: 'Political India gasped in surprise, but friends and foes alike realised that this open declaration in favour of reforms by a representative of the Ruling Princes selected by His Majesty's Government as the spokesman of princes at the Imperial War Conference and Cabinet, to a gathering of princes, had changed the complexion of the Indian political movement. Old-fashioned friends admonished the Maharaja on the boldness of the step; others hinted at the unwisdom of taking sides with agitators, but in British India itself the enthusiasm created by the speech was great. Nationalist newspapers hailed it as the dawn of a new era when princes and peasants would work together for the greater glory of India. And so in a sense it was.' The Maharaja's speech at Bombay was the beginning of that political collaboration between British India and the Indian states which was to find its consummation in the enactment of the federal constitution of India twenty years later.

The Maharaja stayed with the Ganga Risala in Egypt for a few days, and reached London in March 1917, and took part in the various meetings of the Imperial War Conference up to May. The other two representatives from India were Sir James Scorgie Meston, Lieutenant-Governor of the United Provinces of Agra and Oudh; and Sir Satyendra Prassanna Sinha, lately Law Member of he Governor-General of India's Executive Council and Member of the Executive Council of the Governor of Bengal. Originally Indian representatives were only advisers of the Secretary of State, who, in his dual capacity of a Minister of the Crown and a representative of India, sat as a member of the conference. There was some doubt about the position which India should occupy at the conference, whether she was entitled for full membership or not. But the British Prime Minister, Lloyd George, who was fully aware of the sacrifices of blood and treasure which India had unreservedly made at the call of the Empire, stood staunchly by the intentions of the cabinet, and India was accorded the rights of full membership, in what he himself had called the Executive Cabinet of the empire.

Recognition on Foreign Shores

It was quite natural that on an occasion like the session of the Imperial Conference, the Maharaja who was one of the representatives of India was feted wherever he went. He received the Freedom of the City of Edinburgh and an honorary degree of Doctor of Laws from Edinburgh University, in recognition of his eminent public services and the high position he held in India.

The civic function was held at the Usher Hall, where apart from Lord Provost and the members of the City Council, a number of other dignitaries were also present. The Maharaja in his speech, said:

'As a boy at school, I well remember reading with fascination stories illustrative of the noble and widespread reputation of your country for prodigal hospitality, loyalty, and valour ... I have been greatly impressed with the close resemblance in so many things between the Scotsman and the Rajput – that warrior race of India to which I have the honour to belong. The strong sentiment of clans and kinship which prevails so widely in Scotland as in Rajputana, is a link between us ... We Rajputs, like you, have also had our clan and blood feuds and are rich in the possession of ancient history and tradition with a wealth of folk-lore and bardic literature recounting imperishable deeds of heroism and romance.'

The conciseness and lucidity of his speech earned great cheer from Lord Provost and members of the City Council. The Maharaja assured them that this great event would never pass from his memory, and 'the scroll which is the badge of my freedom of Edinburgh and the beautiful casket in which it is enshrined will be treasured in my House for generations to come.'

The *Senatus Academicus* of the University of Edinburgh gave a cordial and enthusiastic welcome to the Maharaja , whose presence was an event of no ordinary significance; it signalled the admission of India for the first

THE IMPERIAL WAR CONFERENCE AND ROME NOTE, 1917

time into the inner councils of the British Empire. The citation referred to the many benefits the Maharaja had conferred on his country; his beneficent measures to cope with the recurring perils of famine, and, of the representative assembly he had lately set up to associate his subjects with himself in the tasks of government. The citation read: 'As befits a Rajput prince of ancient lineage and martial traditions, the Maharaja is an accomplished soldier and sportsman, noted for his skill with the rifle and in the saddle ... Maharaja Ganga Singh of Bikaner stands pre-eminent as a just and enlightened ruler, whose constant concern is the welfare and happiness of his people.' The *Senatus Academicus* had conferred on the Maharaja their honorary LL.D. as a token of their admiration for the Maharaja's princely qualities, and as a pledge of their friendship and good-will towards the millions of Indians whom he represented.

The Maharaja expressed his gratefulness for all the generous hospitality and kindness which 'the Athens of the North' had extended to him, and said that what a pleasure it was 'to receive the degree from the hands of so distinguished a scientist and educationist as Sir Alfred Ewing, principal of our university.'

Freedom of Manchester

On April 23, 1917, the Maharaja received the Honorary Freedom of the City of Manchester, being the highest honour which it was in its power to bestow. The Mayor of the City of Manchester, Sir James Dunlop Smith, presented the illuminated scroll conferring the 'Honorary Freedom of Manchester City' upon the Maharaja, in a silver casket.

Amid a large gathering Ganga Singh expressed his pride in being associated with the City of Manchester, valued the honour, specially as it had come from the heart of 'time honoured Lancaster'.

At the luncheon given by the Lord Mayor and the Corporation of Manchester, the Maharaja alluded the glorious tradition of the Manchester Regiment and, said: 'I saw them engaged in great action in France just before Christmas in 1914. The Manchester Territorials shortly afterwards went to Egypt and gained imperishable glory during the historic landing of the British Army in Gallipoli.'

The Imperial War Conference

At the Imperial War Conference, the meetings of which were held at the

Mansion House, the Prime Minister and other members of His Majesty's government, had shown consistent sympathy and courtesy to the Indian delegates – the Maharaja of Bikaner, Sir James Meston and Sir Satyendra Sinha. The Maharaja was highly impressed by Austen Chamberlain, the Secretary of State for India, not only by his sense of duty and his frankness and fair-mindedness in the council chamber and in discussing Indian problems with him and others in private, but also by his courtesy in giving the delegates every encouragement to speak for themselves both in the cabinet and the conference meetings.

The Maharaja had established cordial relations with his two colleagues – Sir James Meston and Sir Satyendra Sinha. His relations with them throughout had been of the happiest and frankest description. He observed that 'the calm judgement and broad outlook of Sir Satyendra Sinha, who has long been known as a true son of India, have greatly contributed to the understanding and sympathy with which the Indian cause has been handled in the Imperial sessions.' Similarly, he said: 'Sir James Meston, alike in conference and private consultation, has shown insight and broadmindedness, and the utmost loyalty to the land of his adoption.'

Ganga Singh, in the sessions of the Imperial War Conference and Cabinet, had praised the loyal enthusiasm of India for the war, and of the scorn with which she had rejected the subtle and nefarious overtures of Germany to seize the opportunity to rebel. The absorptions of the early months of the war had given the British Government little leisure to reflect on the wider implications of India's rally to the British flag of freedom. He stated: 'I note with the keenest gratification a greatly quickened interest in Indian problems, accompanied by a growing recognition that they must be solved on lines which will promote the greatest good of the greatest number, and will, as far as is consistent with the high ideals England has taught us, be most in accordance with the sentiments and hopes of educated Indian opinion.'

Certain misgivings prevailed in India at one time as regards the holding of the Imperial Conference, but they were soon dissipated, because of the conclusions unanimously reached by the Imperial Conference, notably the acceptance of the principle of reciprocity of treatment in relation to the position of Indians in the Dominions. A new spirit towards India was shown at the conference. 'Some differences of view may remain,' observed the Maharaja, 'but we shall agree to differ now that India, no longer able to regard herself as a Cinderella of the empire, takes a place at the council board. Trust begets trust, and India has to give as well as receive. I am persuaded that she will cheerfully respond in peace, as in war, to the readjusted demands and sacrifices of Imperial citizenship, as readily as she enters upon its great privileges and noble opportunities.'

Lloyd George himself, in his '*Memoirs*', wrote about the Maharaja's work in the Imperial War Conference and Cabinet, 'Bikaner' as he was familiarly and affectionately called – the Indian Prince – was a magnificent specimen of manhood of his great country. We soon found that he was one of "the wise men that came from the East". More and more did we come to rely on his advice, especially on all questions that affected India.'

Empire Parliamentary Association

The Maharaja's speech at the luncheon given to the Indian representatives by the Empire Parliamentary Association in the House of Commons, Harcourt Room, on April 24, 1917, was of special significance. At the Empire Parliamentary Association, in the presence of ministers of Great Britain and of the Dominions and members of the British Parliament, he made a powerful appeal for a liberal measure of reforms for India. It was, for instance, news to some of his erstwhile colleagues in the cabinet that the Princes of India were not opposed to constitutional reform. The Maharaja declared: 'Our aspiration is to see our country under the guidance of Britain making substantial advance on constitutional lines in regard to matters political and economic, and ultimately attaining, under the standard of our King-Emperor, that freedom and autonomy which you in this country secured long ago for yourselves and which our most fortunate sister Dominions have also enjoyed for some time past ... I decline to believe that British statesmanship will not be equal to the occasion, for it depends on the various complex and important Indian problems being handled with sympathy, with imagination, and with a generous and broad-minded perspicacity and boldness by the responsible Ministers of the Crown, whether or not such unrest dies out or continues. It is further the considered opinion of many who have given thought to the subject, that if the people of India were given a greater voice and power in directions in which they have shown their fitness, we should hear much less of unrest, agitation and irresponsible criticism ... No reasonable-minded person will contend that India is ripe at the present day for self-government in the full sense of the term, but there are many who think that there is room for further political reforms and advance ... To you we look for sympathy, help, and readiness to recognise the changes which are taking place in India and to help Indians to achieve further progress, and in due time to realise her cherished aspirations.'

No Indian ruler at the time ever dared to speak with confidence and effortless ease in the presence of ministers of the Crown and members of the British Parliament; and no Prince had advocated the need for 'further political reforms and advance', more than Ganga Singh of Bikaner. He upheld that the demands for which India was striving were 'perfectly reasonable and legitimate', and that her ideals were not 'unworthy'. Neither were the Indian states alarmed, or did they ever resent the political advances in British India. On the contrary, the Indian states were alarmed nor they ever resented political advance in British India on the contrary the Princes had rejoiced at such progress, for their greatest anxiety was to see India progressing and prospering and her people receiving what was their due. The Maharaja made contrary an emphatic call for further advance. The British, he said, had doubtless heard of the 'Unchanging East' which

'... bowed low beneath the blast,
In patient deep disdain,
She let the legions thunder past,
And plunged in thought again.'

He assured the British that India at least had been, and was, changing very rapidly and beyond conception, and that under the invigorating influence of Great Britain she was making remarkable and gratifying strides. Her political advance, therefore, was a necessity; and it should no longer be prolonged or side-tracked.

Speech at the Guildhall

Similar was the tone of the Maharaja's speech at the Guildhall on May 1, on the occasion of receiving the Freedom of the City of London. He made an intimate appeal to all that was best in the British peoples illustrating examples of the loyalty, generosity, and insight of their Indian subjects. The Maharaja recounted, with just pride, the glorious role of the campaigns in which Indian troops had served side by side with the British – in China, South Africa, and, in the Great War, Gallipoli, East Africa, Egypt, China again, and Mesopotamia, and France above all. Speaking from personal experience, the Maharaja narrated how when the Indian troops had arrived in France they were rushed straight to the firing line. 'The fate of nations and of civilisation then hung in the balance; every additional man counted; we had veritably a thin khaki line, with very little but our loyalty, and patriotism, and sense of duty to carry us through.'

Emphasising the need to raise India by gradual stages from dependence to equality, the Maharaja said: 'We are not of the same kith and kin with you, but India is attached to Great Britain and to the Empire, and they to her, by very real and strong ties. In the last three years these have been cemented and consecrated with the blood of your sons and brothers, and of ours, in this titanic struggle. Out of the crucible of common danger and of mutual sacrifice you and we will emerge with a closer and better comprehension of one another, linking us in stronger bonds of understanding, brotherhood, and affection than were ever dreamt of by our ancestors on either side. Those who still say that India is held by the sword do a grave injustice to both countries. I should be sorry, and I feel sure you would all be sorry, to hold so narrow a view.' The Maharaja in his Guildhall speech made a powerful appeal for a liberal measure of reforms for India.

Interview to *The Times*

The Maharaja's interview in regard to Indian political matters, given to the representative of *The Times*, London, on May 2 and 13 were significant. On May 2, the Maharaja had explained his 'new angle of vision', and observed that British policy looked steadily forward to a gradual increase of the self-governing function for India; but that this policy was too seldom expressed in terms, and that the moment to declare it with authority was now, while the war was still in progress, and not as a reply to agitation when the war was over. The Maharaja on May 13 said: 'I would say that the advances to be made should be conceived with the breadth and generosity of view that has marked British policy in so many other parts of the world, and which, so far as I can recall the history of her colonial expansion, she has never had occasion to repent. Sentiment counts for a very great deal in India, and the changes made should be of a character to strike the imagination. The old saying that he gives twice who gives quickly applies with singular felicity to the constitutional reforms recently stated by the Viceroy to have been submitted by the Government of India to the Secretary of State for consideration. Excessive caution would be an error almost as great as the acceptance of rash and ill-considered proposals.' The Maharaja added that some further steps in the internal political evolution of India were desirable as well as essential. He did not wish to minimise the immense difficulties ahead in the adaptation of Indian internal affairs to the changed conditions, but they were not insoluble, and should not deter British and Indian statesmen from marching along the road of ordered development. 'There can be no more mistaken view', said the Maharaja, 'than that the Indian Princes will look with disfavour or apprehension upon these political developments. On the contrary, they will rejoice to see India politically progressing on constitutional lines under the British flag.'

The Rome Note

The importance of the Maharaja's advocacy of India's constitutional advancement and the fulfilment of her cherished aspirations of freedom could not be easily brushed-off. The British public realised that agitation in India was not to be equated with sedition as they had so long been inclined to think, but was the expression of a new vigour in national life which was justly entitled to their sympathy and support. Sir Austen Chamberlain, the Secretary of State for India, was so greatly impressed by the Maharaja's views that he requested him to send to him his detailed views on Indian reform. The Maharaja welcomed this opportunity and on May 15 forwarded to the Secretary of State for India from Rome just before sailing for India a detailed minute on the whole question. This was his famous Rome Note, which was important in two ways. It was the first official expression by a Ruling Prince to His Majesty's Government on the vital question of British Indian reforms. Secondly, the historic pronouncement of August 20, 1917, which had changed the course of Indian political evolution, was not only anticipated in the Note, but was definitely traceable to it. The Maharaja therefore was certainly, without doubt, the forerunner of Montague's famous announcement of August 20, for which he would be ever remembered.

The Maharaja's suggestions to meet the situation were positive and concrete. In his Rome Note, the Maharaja put forward his four-point suggestions.

1. The extreme importance – indeed, the vital necessity – of a formal and authoritative official declaration being made by the British Government at the earliest possible opportunity to the effect that self-government

within the British Empire is the ultimate object and goal of British rule in India.

2. The advisability of inaugurating, on liberal and sympathetic lines, further political reforms in the constitution and function of the Provincial Legislative Councils as well as the Imperial Legislative Council in British India.

3. The desirability of greater autonomy being granted to the Government of India as well as to Provincial Governments.

4. The vital importance to the Indian states, their rulers and their subjects, of establishing at an early date on constitutional lines a Council or Assembly of Princes to deal with matters which concern the British Government on the one side and the states, their rulers and their people, on the other.

The Maharaja had an emphatic opinion that self-government within the British Empire alone could be the object and goal of British rule in India, for which an unequivocal declaration of British policy was required. 'If the granting, when the right time comes, of self-government within the empire is not the goal of British rule in India, then it is impossible to conceive what the goal is.' The Maharaja asserted that the declaration should be formal and authoritative, simple and clearly worded, without being hedged in with numerous narrow and petty restrictions and qualifications. For reforms both in the Centre and in the Provinces the Maharaja argued with equal force. 'No reforms', he stated, 'leaving intact the Central Government would be acceptable to India.'

This was the Maharaja's Rome Note which he dispatched to Austen Chamberlain on May 15, along with a covering letter, in which he wrote: 'I regret that I could not hand it over to you before leaving England, but the rush, as you know, was very great and I have only just finished it today. I have appended a note to it apologising for its length and the poor paper and ink, but it has not been an easy matter dictating it and having it typed during this trying journey, and I had to get the paper, etc. here.' He further wrote: 'I hope, however, that it has enabled me to put before you the strong view I honestly hold of the very serious situation that is likely to be created in India in certain eventualities ... liberality, sympathy and bold statesmanship have always paid in the past, and if England will rise fully to the occasion in her future handling of Indian affairs I am firmly convinced she will never have any cause for regretting her policy and action.' The Maharaja wanted that the people of India should be equally happy as citizens of other countries. He wished that men and women, without distinction of caste or creed should have opportunities to grow to the full height of their stature, unhampered by cramping and unnatural restrictions. He pleaded for India to take her proper place among the great nations of the world, politically, industrially, in religion, in literature, in science and in arts. He emphasised all this, and asserted that this aspiration could, in its essence and its reality, be realised within the empire. His grand ideal of freedom was akin to Gopal Krishna Gokhale, the illustrious Indian patriot and friend of the Maharaja.

The Rome Note reflected the Maharaja's shrewd political insight in which he revealed his inmost feelings. It laid before the Secretary of State a clear picture of the Indian demands, whose basic propositions were: an unequivocal declaration of British Government's policy, defining the goal of British rule in India; provincial autonomy; increased powers for the Central Legislature; and a Council of Princes. As an Imperial statesman, aware of his responsibilities, the Maharaja claimed these reforms for India as the minimum which would satisfy the legitimate aspirations of her people. The ruler from the East was a man of action, not content just to talk. He had shown the way, and it was now for His Majesty's Government to take action.

When, owing to the Mesopotamian troubles, Sir Austen Chamberlain had to resign almost immediately after the Maharaja had sent his Note, he wrote privately to his successor, him to Edwin Montagu, calling attention to the document and appealing to him to give effect to the recommendations. Montagu made his historic Declaration on August 20, which was found to follow closely the lines which the Maharaja had advocated. Though others had claimed to have influenced, and no doubt did influence, the momentous decision taken by His Majesty's Government, the Maharaja of Bikaner could justifiably claim not only to have originated the idea, but to have worked out the details which were embodied in the declaration that was to change the course of Indian history. The vital passages of the declaration read as follows: 'The policy of His Majesty's Government, with which the Government of India are in complete accord, is that of the increasing association of Indians in every branch of the administration and the gradual development of self-governing institutions with a view to progressive realisation of responsible government in India as an integral part of the British Empire. They have decided that substantial steps in this direction should be taken as soon as possible...' This declaration had drawn its inspiration from the Maharaja's historic Rome Note, but it fell short of his expectations.

Esteem of the Maharaja's Work

At the luncheon given in honour of the Indian delegates by the Empire Parliamentary Association, Austen Chamberlain, spoke of the Maharaja as 'the model of a great Indian ruler ... a soldier in many fields and statesman both in India and in the Conference here at home.'

The Secretary of State, in his letter dated May 15, wrote: 'Let me say how pleasant I have found our association in the representation of India at the Imperial gatherings which we attended together and how glad I have been of the opportunity for getting to know you well and discussing Indian questions with you. You have taken part in a series of historic gatherings of the first importance and will, I feel sure, carry back to India with you a wider interest in Imperial affairs and a prouder conception both of what the British Empire is and what it may be made.'

The Viceroy expressed appreciation of what the Maharaja had done, and on July 1, wrote: 'You have discharged your mission faithfully and well.' On the occasion of opening the Princes' Conference in November 1917, the Viceroy made the following observations in his speech to Their Highnesses: 'You know, too, how the Indian representatives, including Your own able and distinguished representative, His Highness the Maharaja of Bikaner, were admitted to the innermost Councils of the Imperial War Cabinet, and so were in a position to exercise a voice in shaping the policy of the British Empire.'

An important testimony to Ganga Singh's valuable contribution at the Conference was that of Lord Satyendra Sinha, who, after his arrival in India, wrote to the Maharaja from Darjeeling, on June 13, 1917: 'I do not know what you found on enquiry at Bombay but in Bengal people of every shade of opinion are simply enthusiastic about your work in England and in particular about the speeches you made there ... It is not only newspaper men in Bengal who appreciate your work, but there is not a single man whom I have met who has not spoken in terms of fervent praise of all you have done. I am so glad that Bengal at any rate has no fault to find with everything you said.'

The Indian press had shown appreciation of the work done by the Maharaja at the conference in bringing closer the English people and the Indians and in creating an understanding and sympathy for the aspirations of India. 'He falsified', writes Maharaja (Dr.) Karni Singh, 'the gloomy forebodings entertained at the time of his selection as an Indian representative on the Imperial Conference and displayed a wide grasp of his country's best interests. He laid down the lines on which advancement in British India was likely to proceed for years to come.' This was indeed a remarkable accomplishment of the Maharaja, deserving attention in India's constitutional and national history.

The work of the Maharaja at the Imperial War Cabinet and at other forays in England was greatly appreciated and he was lionized when he returned home. The Maharaja had won his spurs; his honour and reputation both in British India and the Indian states moved up quickly. Gifted with wisdom and a broad-minded outlook in Indian affairs, the Maharaja had unmistakably shown the high qualities of statesmanship.

Trust Begets Trust

Ganga Singh's modus operandi was the maxim: 'Trust begets Trust'. At the Imperial War Conference meetings he had won over the trust of his two colleagues – Lord S.P. Sinha and Sir James Meston – to a remarkable degree. On June 13, 1917, Lord Sinha in a letter to the Maharaja, wrote: 'I do not think I never thanked you sincerely for your many kindness to me during the four very pleasant and eventful months we passed together, but I am sure you know how thoroughly I appreciate your kindness and what a pleasure it was to me to have such a long spell of your company.'

Sir James Meston, who was at the time Lieutenant-Governor of United Provinces, wrote to the Maharaja on August 10, from Nainital, that 'I have the liveliest memories of the very happy time that we spent together, or the warmest gratitude for the unceasing kindness and friendliness that you showed me during our work together. That friendliness has been greatly enhanced by the perfectly charming way in which, since your return to India, Your Highness has spoken about the share that I tried to take in our common work.' Sir Meston had also written letters to the Viceroy regarding the work of the representatives in England, which were strictly private, but he believed in the honesty and reliability of the Maharaja, and sent those copies to him, with a remark: 'Do, like a good friend, cast it into the flames after you have read it; for I would not like anybody, except us three, to see this confidential, though very imperfect, production.'

Another Invitation

The role of the Maharaja was so admirable, that Lord Chelmsford, the Viceroy, pressed him again in April, 1918, to accept nomination to the Imperial Conference. The Maharaja had received the Viceroy's letter on April 14, when he was in the remote jungles of Panna. He had appreciated the importance of the offer made by the British Government, but reluctantly declined owing to pressing state affairs demanding his attention.

The most significant outcome of the Imperial War Conference for the Maharaja was that he had grown in stature; he became the mentor of Indian princes and statesmen, for there was no important question of the day concerning India in which he had not played a prominent part. For him a new era of active involvement in the affairs of India, and the globe had commenced. His wisdom and statesmanship, exhuberance and genial personality, charmed luminaries in many meetings and conferences, in which he had an opportunity of participating in the following years.

6

The Peace Conference, 1919

The Allied and Central Powers concluded an armistice on November 11, 1918; with it the First World War (1914-18) came to an end. The problem of settlement after the great upheaval, however, remained. Something like a new world-order had to be attempted: for the peoples had been promised that this should be a war to end war; that the world should be made safe for democracy; that their country should be made a land fit for men to live in. It was perhaps sanguine to expect these consequences from four years of hatred, carnage and wholesale destruction. Nevertheless men felt that humanity was entering upon a new era, and they expected the leaders, on whom fell the task of negotiation, to fix the character of this new era at the Peace Conference.

On November 15, Maharaja Ganga Singh of Bikaner was again offered the honour of representing his Order at the Peace Conference. Lord Chelmsford requested the Maharaja to proceed immediately to England: 'Your Highness will be gratified to learn that Prime Minister himself expressed a wish that you should go to London now.' The fact that Lloyd George had himself asked that the Maharaja should be selected, served to show the impression that he had made on the Imperial War Cabinet in 1917.

The Maharaja sailed for England in *H.M.S. Dufferin*, and reached London on the afternoon of the December 14, 1918, where he first attended the meetings of the Imperial War Cabinet.

The first matter with which the Imperial Cabinet had to deal was a visit to England by President Wilson, who was arriving during the Christmas holidays as that was the only time which he could spare for this visit. The Imperial Cabinet was in two minds. They knew that Their Majesties the King and Queen, who had a most strenuous time during the War, were anxious to spend a quiet family Christmas at Sandringham. They were equally anxious that the President of the United States should be accorded the courtesy of a ceremonial reception in London. The Maharaja spoke out his mind in the Cabinet and strongly urged that President Wilson should be requested to put off his visit to a more convenient time. In this he was supported by W.H. Hughes, the prime minister of Australia, 'who warned his colleagues in his shrill voice and with much thumping of the table of the dangers of hitching the British lion to the chariot-wheel of President Wilson.' His Majesty, however, removed the difficulty by agreeing to forgo his Christmas holidays, and President Wilson paid his visit to London.

This visit, as narrated by K.M. Panikkar, was the occasion of another extraordinary experience for the Maharaja. President Wilson, as the head of the great state which was associated with the Empire in the War, was received with all due pomp and ceremony at Victoria station. Their Majesties and the members of the royal family, together with the Cabinet, were present to receive him. The Maharaja was also there, standing just behind His Majesty. The president, on alighting from the carriage, bowed neither to the King nor even to the queen, but shook hands stiffly with a bare 'How-do-you-do?' The Maharaja was greatly shocked by this discourtesy and quietly fell back, as he did not desire to be introduced to the president. But a member of the royal family saw the Maharaja disappearing behind the palms and called His Majesty's attention to it. The Maharaja had no option but to be introduced to the president, but Mr. Wilson received more than he gave on that occasion.

On January 1, 1919, the Maharaja was invested with full powers from the King-Emperor as one of the plenipotentiaries for the Conference. The document said: '... in connection with the forthcoming Peace Congress we have judged it expedient to invest a fit person with Full Power to conduct the said discussion on our part in respect of our Empire of India,... that we, reposing special trust and confidence in the wisdom, loyalted, diligence and circumspection of our most trusty and well-beloved His Highness Maharaja Sir Ganga Singh of Bikaner ...'

Along with the rest of the British Empire delegation, the Maharaja left for Paris and took up his abode at the Hotel Majestique. There were three representatives of India at the Paris Peace Conference: the Secretary of State for India (Edwin Montagu), the Maharaja of Bikaner, and Lord S.P. Sinha. The direction of the Conference was in the hands of the 'Big Four': M. Clemenceau (France), President Wilson (U.S.A.), Lloyd George (Great Britain), and Signor Orlando (Italy). Italy, however, after a time withdrew, being dissatisfied with the way in which her claims were met; and thus the real decision rested with three men: President Wilson, M. Clemenceau and Lloyd George. Wilson was a doctrinaire and an idealist, but not a very skilful negotiator; moreover, he could not ensure the acceptance by his country of the decisions reached. Clemenceau, the 'Old Tiger', was very much of a realist, whose chief interest was to make sure that Germany should never again be able to imperil France. Lloyd George, the most subtle-minded of the three, was awake to the importance of making a real and lasting peace, not a mere source of new rancours and difficulties; his hands were tied by the promises he had given in the recent British election (1918) and by the angry temper which reigned among his supporters. Lloyd George, however, never failed to consult the British Empire delegation, and in these consultations and meetings the Maharaja took his full share.

The Peace Conference assembled at Paris by January 12, 1919, and was formally opened on January 18. It was the most widely representative body that had ever assembled in history. It was true that the defeated powers – Germany, Austria, Hungary, Bulgaria, and Turkey – were not included: their part was limited to submitting to the decisions of the rest. The few neutrals were also omitted – Holland, Spain, the Scandinavian countries, and Switzerland. The conference was limited to the 'Allied and Associated Powers'. Almost every other country in the world had joined the Allies in the last stages of the war, and though most of them had taken no part in the fighting they were entitled as Allies to be consulted. The republics of South and Central America, and the Asiatic countries of China, Siam, and Arabia were included. So were India and the British Dominions; and their representation as separate states marked a very important stage in the development of the British Empire.

Never was a conference so carefully prepared for – the large and able staff of experts, the British at the Hotel Majestique; the American, with its large contingent of professors, at the Crillon. All that was lacking in either of these delegations was a simple, clear, complete plan-of-action – which only the French possessed. The work of the conference was largely done in commissions and committees, many of which overlapped in functions and worked in ignorance of each other's decisions. Things moved slowly at first, but after the beginning of April it gathered speed.

India's Inclusion in the League of Nations

One significant question which faced the Indian delegation was the matter of the representation of India in the League of Nations. The contradictory views prevailed regarding the inclusion of India in the League of Nations, as she was neither independent nor self-governing. Lord Sinha had written an excellent note for the Secretary of State regarding India's claim towards the membership of the League. The Maharaja supplemented it with a memorandum of his own, dated February 2, 1919, in which he argued forcibly for the inclusion of India in the League.

While pleading the case of India's inclusion in the League, the Maharaja in a convincing and persuasive manner, said: 'The League should be open to every civilised nation which can be relied on to promote its objects, I would beg to point out that on this ground alone the claim of India for inclusion in the League is unimpeachable ... I would venture to urge with all the emphasis at my command that if the people of India with their ancient civilisation were considered fit to fight in Europe and in other theatres of war side by side with the other civilised nations of the world in the tragic drama which has recently been enacted, then on the grounds of civilisation and the still higher grounds of our common humanity there can be no just or cogent excuse to deny India her admission into the League where other civilised nations are to be admitted ... I would also submit that the exclusion of India from the League of Nations has no ethical, historical or political argument in its favour ... After having borne arms, together with the other civilised nations, in a common cause while civilisation and freedom hung in the balance and after having actually entered the portals of the peace temple, which in itself is a League of Nations, is India to be told to walk out as now no longer belonging to the civilised nations of the world?' The Maharaja was certain that the British Government would never agree to the exclusion of India and was confident that if the prime minister and other plenipotentiaries of the British Empire took up a firm attitude to champion the just cause of India, opposition on the part of other nations, should there be any, would be speedily overcome and the League of Nations thereby made really representative of the civilised world and not of a part of it.

Through the impressive plea made by the Maharaja and other Indian representatives, they were able to accomplish their purpose. The Maharaja's convincing arguments and his bold advocacy gained acceptance, and India was included as a member of the League of Nations, and thus secured for herself an international status. What seemed impossible of achievement in the beginning, was gained successfully by the effort and skill of the Maharaja! There was no question that without Ganga Singh's fervent advocacy of the Indian case, the League of Nations would not have found a place for India.

The Turkish Question

Another complex problem which was faced by the Indian delegation to the Peace Conference related to the future of Constantinople and the Turkish Empire generally. The proposals which the Allied Governments had put forward regarding the partition of Turkey had deeply disturbed the Indian Muslim community. The Muslim opinion in India was greatly inflamed. The Hindu politicians under the leadership of Mahatma Gandhi expressed their sympathy with the Muslims, and the Khilafat Movement became a national problem.

The leading Indian Muslim residents in Europe presented a memorandum to the British Foreign Secretary against such a step. On March 20, 1919, the Maharaja received a long cablegram from Haji Chotani urging that the holy places of Islam should be left to the Sultan of Turkey as also that the Peace Treaty should be such as to reconcile the Muslims to the British. This put the Indian delegation in a very embarrassing situation, specially as all the three delegates were non-Muslim. When Lord Sinha had to return to England leaving the Maharaja alone to represent India, a section of the Indian press hinted that a Muslim delegate should be appointed. The Maharaja immediately wrote to Edwin Montagu and enclosed a copy of the telegram. He urged the Secretary of State to see if a public statement could be made announcing that the Indian Muslim view-point was always being kept in view and that everything possible was being done to press the Muslim case. He also solicited permission to send a telegram in reply and enclosed a draft for approval. The subject was taken up for discussion by the Indian delegation at the meeting of the British Empire delegation on April 3, when both the Prime Minister and the Secretary of State were present. They agreed that though it was unusual to send a reply to such telegrams, a reply could be sent on the lines proposed by the Maharaja in view of the special circumstances of the case. The Secretary of State accordingly telegraphed the Viceroy to make a statement on those lines, but it was never made.

The Indian representatives put up a bold defence in favour of Turkey. The Maharaja while pleading sympathetic consideration to the feelings of Indian Muslims, argued that they had shed their blood and helped with their resources in the defence of the Allied cause. They were, therefore, entitled to claim the principle of national unity and freedom in the case of Turkey, as was being done in the case of the European peoples. He said that the statement of the British Prime Minister that 'we are not fighting to deprive Turkey of its capital' made a vivid impression in India. Repeated declarations, notably on the part of the President of the United States, that the future disposition of Europe would be determined on national lines, had raised hopes among the Muslim communities under the British Crown, that the case of their co-religionists would be decided on the same principle. He emphatically opposed the Allied proposal to deprive the Turk of Constantinople, as it could definitely react on the millions of Muslims who had loyally supported the Allied cause and would create a conviction of unjust treatment which would be a disturbing factor in the world for generations to come. To punish Turkey for the benefit of Bulgaria, to show generosity to the Bulgarian while being vindictive to the Turk would give reasonable ground to Indian Muslims to believe that the war in which they had been engaged was after all an anti-Mohammedan war. He made it clear that he was not pleading for mercy for the Turk, but was merely asking for justice and it should not 'be refused even to those to whom we would not wish to be just.' The Maharaja concluded with an energetic protest stating that the sort of peace proposed was not a peace to which the representatives of India could willingly assent; that the conviction was becoming rife that the British Empire with its large Muslim population 'was embarking on a campaign which was not merely anti-Turkish but anti-Mohammedan.'

There could be no better testimony of the Maharaja's role in Turkish question than the words of His Highness the Aga Khan who himself at the time was in Paris. In a speech at a banquet in London on March 7, 1919, on the occasion of Sir S.P. Sinha's appointment as Under Secretary he said: 'Having been much in Paris of late, I have had opportunities of seeing for myself with what devotion and singleness of purpose the Maharaja of Bikaner and Lord Sinha, in association with Edwin Montagu, have put the Muslim case. I have been told by many friends that though neither of the Indian delegates are Muslims, they have fully realised that on these external questions, Indian interests are Mohammedan interests alone. On one occasion I found them at midnight deep in preparation of a memorandum concerning the Islamic case.'

There were many other problems with which the Indian delegation had to deal, and in every case Ganga Singh played a prominent part in discussions. The two such proposals in which the Maharaja had contributed enormously related to the Japanese proposal for a declaration of racial equality, and the proposal sponsored by President Wilson for the limitation of working hours for labourers.

The first proposal met with vigorous opposition from President Wilson, but unmindful of President Wilson's stand the Maharaja and Lord Sinha, however, strongly supported the Japanese point of view, since they knew the galling restrictions based on race made against their countrymen not only in the colonies but in India itself. The second proposal by President Wilson had evinced a keen interest from the Maharaja, who advocated that so far as the Indian states were concerned, the legislation enacted by British India did not apply, and for the states there 'should be constituted authorities of the various Indian states concerned'. The public statement of this reservation on such a platform was of the utmost importance to the states, and the Maharaja by entering this timely reservation safeguarded in an effective manner the autonomy of the states for the future.

Treaty of Versailles

The *Treaty* was finally presented to the German delegates at a meeting of the entire Conference by M. Clemenceau, the French Premier, who acted as president of the Conference. The final act was staged in the Hall of Mirrors in the Palace of Versailles, on June 28, 1919, where the German delegates were summoned to hear their sentence, not to discuss it. The German delegates, cowed and pale, signed the *Treaty of Versailles*, followed by Allied representatives. In the gardens outside, the fountains played for the first time since the war.

The signature of the *Treaty* which took place at Versailles, in the Galerie des Glaces, was a memorable event. It was the hall where Louis Quatorze set up his motto, *Nec Pluribus impar*, which he decorated with the painted trophies of his victories, in which he received and humiliated the Doge of Genoa, where he proclaimed his grandson King of Spain. In the same room William I, King of Prussia, had been proclaimed German Emperor by the warriors and princes of Germany, fresh from their triumph over France. This was the room where Royalist Germany had recorded her victory, and Republican Germany was to record her defeat.

Tall, handsome, with thick dark moustache glowing with pride over his youthful appearance, the Maharaja of Bikaner, who was wearing a traditional dress, appeared splendid and regal he put his signature on the *Treaty* in the Hall of Mirrors. A.G. Grant and Harold Temperley in *Europe in the Nineteenth and Twentieth Centuries*, have given the account of an eye-witness: 'Today, I saw the Germans sign. The entrance to the Galerie des Glaces was up two lines of stairs, guarded by a line of troopers, with blue uniforms, steel breast-plates, and helmets with long horse-hair plumes, making a splendid appearance ... At three p.m. there was suddenly a tense interval and silence, and, preceded by four armed officers, the Germans appeared. One pale, bowed, with glasses like a student (Muller); the next head erect and hair like an artist's (Bell). Immediately after, I suppose by design, the cuirassiers all suddenly sheathed their swords ... a symbolic and conscious act. The atmosphere of hate was terrible. They advanced and sat down on the fourth side of the square, near the table of rose and almond-wood, on which lay the *Treaty*. In a minute or two Clemenceau got up, and in a sharp, clear, musical voice, like a succession of strokes on a gong, said: "We are in complete agreement. I have the honour to ask messieurs the German Plenipotentiaries to sign." At this point the Germans got up and bowed low. They were asked to sit down again and the speech was translated. After this they came forward and signed slowly amid a tense hush.'

'Then came Wilson (and his plenipotentiaries), Lloyd George, who smiled broadly as he finished, the Colonial Premiers, and the Maharaja of Bikaner, looking magnificent in a pale khaki turban. After that Clemenceau, with Pichon and Tardieu behind him. Then Sonnino, on the last day of his reign, and then the Plenipotentiaries of Minor States. As Paderewski, with his tawny mane and stage-bow, signed, the guns began to boom outside.

'The ceremony ended soon, the Germans were carefully escorted out, and Clemenceau came down the hall slowly, beaming, shaking hands. As he went out the old man reached me his hand, or rather the hand covered as

always in a grey glove. "Felicitations", said I. "*Mille remerciments*", said he ...
A great moment, but I fear a peace without victory, just as we had a victory
without peace.'

The Peace Treaty was at last concluded between the Allied and Associated
Powers and the newly formed German Republic. The Maharaja was one of
the empire statesmen who signed that historic document. With his political
acumen he realised at the time that a treaty which imposed such crushing
burdens upon the vanquished enemy could not be expected to secure a
lasting peace. Nevertheless, he appreciated the honour done, not only to
himself but to India, by his inclusion among the signatories of the *Treaty of
Versailles*.

One significant advantage that had accrued to the Maharaja at Versailles
was that he came in close association with other giant statesmen of the world.
He had developed friendly relations with President Wilson; and worked in
closest intimacy with Lloyd George and M. Clemenceau, who were indeed
great figures on the international stage. With Edwin Montagu and Lord
Sinha, the Maharaja had already developed great personal affection at the
meetings of the Imperial War Cabinet in 1917. It was for the first time at the
Peace Conference that a great Indian Maharaja had worked on terms of
equality with British and European statesmen of the period. That was indeed
an uncommon achievement for the Maharaja, where he availed himself of
every opportunity to display his qualities of statesmanship, and showed the
distinguished diplomats what accomplishments he had. The Maharaja
thereby not only earned acclaim from the people of Bikaner, but recognition
in public life, both in India and the empire. It was this experience which
enabled the Maharaja's extensive friendship with political leaders of British
India and his co-operation with them in furthering India's progress.

During this visit to Europe, the Maharaja was offered the degree of
Doctor of Civil Laws *'honoris causa'* by the University of Oxford, of which his
old friend Lord Curzon was then the chancellor. The Maharaja had accepted
it and agreed to attend the '*Encaenia*' (Convocation) on June 25, 1919, to
receive this distinction, but was unfortunately called away to Versailles, and
was therefore unable to personally receive the degree. The degree was
conferred upon him in absentia.

Peoples' Hero

Ganga Singh's role at Versailles was appreciated by both the states and British

India. The King-Emperor, Prime Minister, Secretary of State for India, Viceroy, and many princes congratulated the Maharaja and wrote to him in terms of high appreciation. In a debate on the Turkish question in the House of Commons on February 26, 1920, Lloyd George spoke: 'We had two delegates at the Peace Conference, both of them representative, able and very influential Indians. One is the Maharaja of Bikaner, who helped us very greatly in the war.' Edwin Montagu said: 'I have to thank you (the Maharaja) for a colleagueship which I value and appreciate.' Lord Chelmsford wrote: 'I know with what remarkable ability and political sagacity Your Highness has performed your task, and India owes to you a debt of gratitude for having so worthily represented her in the greatest gathering of statesmen that the world has ever seen.' The Maharaja of Gwalior in the Princes' Conference held on November 3, 1919, said that the Maharaja of Bikaner had rendered valuable services to India and to the princely order, as member of the Imperial Conference in London and of the Peace Conference at Versailles. 'The language of genuine appreciation is never effusive, and I would merely say that the Maharaja of Bikaner has not only established a claim upon our gratitude, but, what is more important, he has done credit to our Order.'

Steadfast to his principles, the Maharaja's bold advocacy of India's cause, and gaining a place for her in the League of Nations made him famous. He not only became a celebrated statesman, but came out as a nationalist, known or talked about in the four corners of the British Empire. He received a triumphant welcome on arrival in India, and peope of diverse opinions paid generous tributes to his work.

7

The Chamber of Princes

On January 5, 1914, Ganga Singh gave to the Viceroy, Lord Hardinge, a note in which he traced the idea of creating some machinery which could secure sustained and intimate co-operation between the Government of India and the Princes. The Maharaja wrote: 'The Princes have a right, in view of their partnership and their contributions towards the defence of the empire, to be heard in regard to the great matters of Imperial interests, and they also desire to have an opportunity for mutual consultation and for the discussion of matters affecting their own Order.'

Another note submitted by Ganga Singh on July 28, 1916, to Sir Claude Hill, Member of the Council of Governor-General of India, argued for the creation of a Council of Princes.

The first formal Conference of the Princes was summoned in the winter of 1916 at Delhi. The Maharaja of Bikaner, prime mover in the organisation of the Conference, was entrusted the secretarial work of the Conference as honorary general secretary. The Conference was a success because of his untiring efforts and zeal. Jam Saheb of Nawanagar declared: 'We know that this conference owes to a certain extent, if not wholly, its origin to the zeal and political sagacity which the Maharaja of Bikaner has shown for our welfare.'

The next Princes' Conference was held at Delhi in November, 1917. The Maharaja again played a leading part. In his speech, he strongly urged on the Viceroy the necessity of organising a formal Council or Chamber of Princes, and insisted at the same time that the policy towards the states should be liberalised by restoring their treaty position and rectifying the encroachments that had been made in the past. He said that through the establishment of the Chamber of Princes alone the simplification of political relations between the Government of India and the native states was possible. The whole question of direct relations and simplifying the procedure, argued the Maharaja, was essential in order to avoid widespread difficulties and frictions that prevailed at the time. He said: '… it is my considered opinion that no patching up or tinkering with the present system but a drastic change alone on bold and statesmanlike lines, regardless of precedent or sentiment, will do any real good.'

After the Imperial War Conference there was a fresh outburst of activity on the part of the Maharaja for Indian constitutional reforms. When the Secretary of State for India came to India in 1918 to enquire into the best means of giving effect to the Declaration of 1917, the Maharaja was in the front rank of those Princes who submitted the proposal for a Chamber of Princes. His suggestion was incorporated in the *Montagu-Chelmsford Report*, and the Chamber of Princes was officially established.

Lord Chelmsford recognised the Maharaja's contribution and, wrote: 'Your constant efforts, have now been crowned with success, in connection with the establishment of the Chamber of Princes – an event which I feel must ever largely be associated with Your Highness' name.'

The Maharaja as the First Chancellor

The Chamber of Princes was inaugurated on February 8, 1921, by the Duke of Connaught on behalf of His Majesty in the historic audience hall. *(Dewani-i-Am)* of the Mughal emperors in the Delhi Red Fort. The Duke in his address alluded to the importance of the occasion and acknowledged the splendid services rendered by the Princes during the greatest struggle in the history of mankind. In an outpour of his thoughts, the Duke said: 'I am sure that the part will be a worthy one. The British Government has not been slow to recognise the justice of your aspirations; and I rejoice to think that by my share in today's ceremony, I am doing something to promote your wishes and to provide a larger sphere for your public-spirited activities.' Thus was constituted the Chamber of Princes, and by a large vote the Maharaja of Bikaner was elected its first chancellor.

The Prince of Wales, when he visited Bikaner on December 2, 1921, said: 'Your Highness may look with satisfaction on the part you have played in the establishment of the Chamber of Princes, of which you are the first chancellor ...' The Chamber had become a living reality on account of the unending efforts of the Maharaja. As a first chancellor, he had nurtured the organisation very delicately.

The new responsibility was thus cast upon the Maharaja, but on account of his previous knowledge, personal ability and wide experience, he was best fitted for the job. To build up an incipient organisation was a formidable task, but the Maharaja from the beginning kept a wary eye on it. Starting from the scratch, the Maharaja by his incessant toil and energy successfully built the elaborate machinery of the Chamber. He possessed enough will to set up the Chamber in an orderly form, and despite initial hurdles and mutual jealousies among the Princes, the Maharaja did not deviate from the object aimed at.

The Maharaja did not claim to be either the spokesman or the leader of the Princes. He regarded himself as a liaison officer between the Chamber and the Viceroy. He knew more than anyone else that in a body like the Chamber consisting of the Princes of India, where each ruler was conscious of his prestige and position, any claim to leadership would give rise to difficulties of the most serious kind. He therefore went forward with caution, careful not to create enemies.

Though the Chamber had started but neither its powers were defined nor its scope was precisely known, things were either fluid or in a state of flux. The Maharaja with a grim determination – a characteristic feature of his character – moved forward, established its secretariat, commenced informal conferences and formed standing committees. Matters like the princes' rights, based on treaties, engagements and *sanads*, and the counter-claim of the supremacy of the Government of India, were taken up. The problems of the rank and precedence of rulers, and the disagreements over the salute-list were examined. The simplification of political relations between the Government of India and the states were argued.

The Maharaja knew that with the introduction of *Montagu-Chelmsford Report* and the gradual devolution of powers to provincial governments, and at the same time the widening of the bases of nationalist movement in India, the position of Indian states had to be reviewed. He asserted that the time was ripe and there was a need for measures leading to a settled line of action with the goal clearly defined regarding the future position of the states. He thought that it was therefore essential from the point of view of the Princes, that a definite policy, not dependent on personal whims and inclinations of individual viceroys and political secretaries, should be enunciated by the British Government in discussion with them which would safeguard their future position and determine their rights and obligations vis-à-vis the Government of India. As custodians of their states, the Princes had to look to the future, and the future to him did not appear to be bright. The Maharaja took this matter up in personal discussion with the Viceroy in 1922, but the attitude of Lord Reading and his advisers was discouraging. In spite of difficulties in his way the Maharaja did not lose courage or confidence, and whenever an opportunity arose he talked about the basic issue tiresomely.

Despite hindrances in its path, the Chamber was able to settle issues relating to minority administration, ceremonials at the time of installation and investiture, and difficulties in regard to the Indian states forces. Other questions, such as the disabilities of the states in regard to currency, salt, opium, etc., were reserved for expert examination. Questions like the acquisition of private property in British India by rulers and their sons, purchase of residential houses in hill stations, employment of Europeans and other foreigners in state service, the problem of British jurisdiction on lands taken over for railway purposes, restrictions on the power of the states to make grants of mining and prospecting licenses, etc., were also discussed in the Chamber. Despite the Maharaja's efforts for an early solution of such questions, they dragged on inconclusively. The importance of the Maharaja's Chancellorship in this connection was not so much in the decisions taken, but in the problems that were raised for discussion.

The work of the Maharaja as Chancellor was one of careful consolidation and of stabilisation. He knew that the Chamber was in its early stage of growth and there were fault-finders who looked at it with suspicion and distrust. Neither was the Political Department of the Government of India helpful, nor had a few of the more important states shown it favour. Besides, the Princes who had actually co-operated were jealous of his individual relations with the Crown, and did not wish that the Chamber should set itself up as an intermediate body between them and the British Government. In these circumstances, a forward policy in the Chamber was bound to be disastrous. The Chancellor therefore moved with abundant caution in order to sustain the Chamber in its formative stage. The Maharaja was the Chancellor up to 1926, and during these six years he was able to give shape to the organisation. The infancy stage of the Chamber was indeed crucial, but the Maharaja by his wisdom, ideas and suggestions had given its form a distinctive character. The Chamber gradually acquired an appearance where the intentions of the Princes could either find expression or were realised in action. That was indeed an enduring and lasting contribution of the Maharaja.

The Maharaja had devoted all his energies to the building up the organisation and his success was extraordinary. The Viceroy, as President of the Chamber, who had occasion to work intimately with the Chancellor and knew the difficulties and circumstances under which the Maharaja had to labour, was frank enough to express his admiration for the Maharaja's work as early as 1923. The Viceroy declared in unequivocal terms that no future Chancellor 'will ever surpass him in the enthusiasm that he has displayed in the task and in the ability which he brings to bear upon it.'

Several misconceptions prevailed in regard to the aims and aspirations of the Chamber of Princes. Many rumours floated about in various quarters regarding its creation. There was gossip that the Princes wanted to change their constitutional position and political status in the scheme of empire. Refuting these misrepresentations the Maharaja said: 'As one who has for the last five years and more been in close touch with the brother Princes, firstly, as their Honorary General Secretary for the Conferences which were formerly held, and now, as Chancellor of the Chamber of Princes, I claim to speak with some first-hand knowledge when I say that there is not the slightest justification for any such ideas.' The Chamber of Princes, argued the Maharaja, was working to promote the solidarity of the relations between the Crown and the Princes, neither was it a menace to the empire nor to the liberties and the legitimate aspirations of the people of India, including their own subjects, nor clogging the wheels of national progress. What the Princes as a body desired, was to see that their inherent rights and privileges guaranteed by their treaties, and their *izzat* and prerogatives were maintained unimpaired. Also, the machinery governing their relations with the British Government needed revision in the light of experience gained in the past hundred years. They wanted that the Princes be enabled to achieve their just aims and aspirations, do their duty as rulers of their own states, and take their due share in upholding the honour and glory of the emperor. 'I do not believe', asserted the Maharaja, 'that I am biased in saying that what the Princes desire will be found to be both reasonable and capable of attainment within, we trust, without detriment to Imperial interests or those of their motherland, of which, in spite of unfriendly assertions to the contrary, the Princes claim to be as true and patriotic sons as any.' Neither was the Chamber an organisation for stifling the just aspirations of the people of India, nor it was intended to encourage strife and dissension in the country, as alleged by its critics. The Maharaja added: 'I submit that, notwithstanding what our detractors may say, the intentions of the rulers are benevolent towards their people and as hereditary rulers, they have really a very large stake in the well-being of their states and the happiness, contentment and prosperity of their subjects.'

Lord Reading's Tribute

Lord Reading had paid tributes to the Maharaja's work as Chancellor – first, in his opening speech in the Chamber of Princes in November 1921, and, second, in 1926, when the Maharaja had laid down the Chancellorship. In 1921, the Viceroy said: 'The bulk of the work has naturally fallen on the Chancellor, and we are all of us deeply grateful to the Maharaja of Bikaner for the efficient and businesslike manner in which, in spite of ill health, he has discharged his duties. He has set a noble example to those who come after him.'

In 1926, when the Maharaja decided to lay down the Chancellorship, the most striking tribute to the Maharaja was again from Lord Reading who, said: 'It would be difficult indeed for the successor or successors of His Highness of Bikaner to emulate the completeness and the efficiency with which he has discharged the very onerous duties of the Chancellor, and whatever success the Chamber of Princes may have had or may have in the future will be, as some of Your Highnesses have so justly said, in a large measure due to the services of His Highness of Bikaner. He has borne the brunt of all the preliminary work regarding the construction of the Chamber and its constitution. As I have had exceptional opportunities of observing the conduct of the work of the Chamber ... I associate myself most cordially with all that Your Highnesses have said. This vote, accordingly, I have the honour to propose.'

At the state banquet at Bikaner on January 29, 1927, Lord Irwin alluded to the Maharaja's oratory skills in persuasion or appeal to the Chamber of Princes; and said that his complaint against the Maharaja was that he had set such a high standard of eloquence in the Chamber that it might well deter less experienced speakers from entering the arena of debate.

Even after relinquishing the office of the chancellor in 1926, his interest in the organisation did not wane; he continued to be its mentor and guide. He was not only the life-force of the organisation, but served it to the hilt, with utmost fidelity and exactness.

8

Palaces and Public Buildings

*M*aharaja Ganga Singh had a natural love and understanding of beauty, especially in architecture. A born builder with considerable architectural knowledge and artistic ability, the Maharaja took personal interest in all the schemes of public buildings. Many were created by him; others, suggested by the Public Works Department were scrutinised personally from the point of view of artistic harmony and unity with the prevalent style. All his creations were in pink or red sandstone, locally available at Dulmera. The splendour and radiance of the palaces and the buildings built up by him remain matchless even today.

The Palaces of Bikaner – the Junagarh Fort, Lallgarh and Gajner – are unique in India for their blend of the traditional aspects of living with modern practicality and luxury.

The Bikaner Fort

The fort of Bikaner, better known as Junagarh Fort, is the result of building activity of sixteen successive generations of the rulers of the land, beginning from the end of sixteenth century to nearly the middle of twentieth century. As a consequence, it contains antique monuments and excellent *objects d'arts* – such as, the symbolic hands of '*Satis*', seven historic '*Proles*' (gates), nine attractive temples, little shrines of various deities, four deep wells, three beautiful gardens, medieval stables and barracks, old jail, and armoury stores on the ground floor. The most notable are the old palaces, with their porches and pillars, gables and doors, galleries and corridors, added from time to time; which reflect the fine taste of successive rulers who built them. The red sandstone from which the old palaces are built, was brought from the Khari and Dulmera quarries, which were discovered in the time of Raja Karan Singh. There are 15 palaces in the second storey; eight in the third; 11 in the fourth; and five in the fifth. Belonging to different historical periods, the old palaces resuscitate the events and rulers of Bikaner. Made up of different units and designs, the Junagarh Fort is a unique illustration of a composite structure. It is one of the finest and strongest forts in the plains. The mighty fortress was constructed by Raja Rai Singh; its foundation was laid on January 30, 1586, and it was completed on January 17, 1594. In the absence of other natural strong-points, he built it in the sandy plains, with suitable defensive barriers and barricades. According to *khyats*, Raja Rai Singh had, while at Burhanpur, sent instructions to his minister, Karam Chand, for building this fort.

The Junagarh Fort has a quadrangular perimeter of 1078 yards, fortified by a 14.50 feet wide, and 40 feet high strong wall. It has 37 bastions (*burj*) and two entrances, Karan Prole facing east, and Chand Prole, facing west. The Karan Prole is protected by four gates, and Chand Prole by double gates. The gates are fastened with iron gratings, spiky and sharp pointed, which, in olden times, were meant as a stumbling-block for the enemy elephants. The original Fort as built by Raja Rai Singh at the end of the sixteenth century was a small one, forming a regular square with nine bastions on each side and only one east gate. The total area of the Fort is 1,63,119 square yards. It has a moat at an approximate depth of 25 feet, with a width of 15 feet at the base and 30 feet at the top. In medieval times the moat was infested with poisonous snakes and cobras, with cactuses of all sorts. There was a concealed underground tunnel in former days, meant as a means of communicating during the precarious days of the fort's siege. The walls are made up of hard and lime stone. At some places baked bricks are also seen, which were put in repairs done during the period of Maharaja Dungar Singh. The walls are slightly slanting, the bastions are broad and the battlements less prominent than in the preceding centuries, though they are not merely ornament.

The Junagarh Fort is built in the Rajput style of the sixteenth century, which was under the impact of the Gujarati and the Mughal architectural designs. The rulers of Bikaner were in close association with the Mughal court, as such, they adopted the Mughal decorations, which is reflected in stucco, wall painting, and stone inlay works. The mosaic, stone-carving and lattice works reflect the Gujrati impact. The works relating to glass, gold, lacquer and false wooden ceiling, suggest various activities of the period. The confluence of Rajput, Mughal and the Gujrati architectural designs are clearly visible in Junagarh Fort; as a consequence it is one of the precious gems of Indian architecture. Glistening with the blood of heroes, standing upright in undefiled pride, the fort has a reason to boast of the glories of medieval Bikaner.

There are seven *Proles* in the fort. The main *Prole* of the fort, in former days was *Suraj Prole*. This is the only gate made out of yellow sandstone from Jaisalmer, probably to honour Raja Rai Singh's queen who was a princess from Jaisalmer. It is said that the gate of *Suraj Prole* belonged to a fort at village Janglu, 20 miles distant from Bikaner and was brought here by Kanwar Dalpat Singh, son of Raja Rai Singh. Inside the *Suraj Prole*, there is a shrine of Lord Ganesh on the left hand side and on the right a vertical stone slab bears the *Raj Prasasthi* (eulogy) of Raja Rai Singh. In front of the *Suraj Prole* there are statues of two Rajputs on the backs of the stone elephants. The one on the right-hand belongs to Jaimal, the grandson of Rao Dudha, Rao Bika's brother, who fell in a gruesome battle in the fort of Chitor against Emperor Akbar in 1567-68, after performing astounding deeds of valour. The one on the left-hand belongs to Fatta Sisodia, jagirdar of Ameth in Mewar, who was the Kiledar of Chitor and was killed with Jaimal, in the same battle, after offering heroic resistance.

The *Mahals* in the fort reflect three architectural designs. The oldest one is a confluence of Mughal, Gujarati and Rajput architecture. The second is the half-western style of architecture which evolved during the reign of Maharaja Dungar Singh (1872-87). The third has revivalist architecture which evolved specially during the rule of Maharaja Ganga Singh. This is reflected in the new Throne Room, known as Vikram Bilas, which was built in 1936-37 by Maharaja Ganga Singh. The Maharaja was a great protagonist of revivalist Rajput architecture.

The Fort Museum

The fort today is in the possession of a trust called Raja Rai Singhji Trust. It has one of the finest museums in the country. The armoury on display comprises one of the most heterogeneous assemblage of medieval arms. It houses the Ganga Golden Jubilee Museum which has rare terracottas of the early Gupta period. These were found within the territory of former Bikaner State at a place known as 'Rang Mahal', near Suratgarh; a Sarswati of great beauty carved in marble from the tenth samples century; specimen of wood and stone carving; excellent samples of Rajput industrial arts; Persian carpets; historical paintings; old *farmans* issued by the Mughal emperors, and miniature paintings of the Mughal period, collected by the rulers of Bikaner. It has some rare sculptures collected by Raja Rai Singh. It is said that in 1582 the combined efforts of Rai Singh and of his minister, Karam Chand, succeeded in obtaining from Akbar 1050 Jain idols, looted in 1576, during the capture of Achalgarh and the defeat of Surthan Singh of Sirohi, by Tursam Khan, Rai Singh's fellow-commander. These idols, sent to Fatehpur Sikri for melting, comprise masterpieces in bronze, copper and brass, some as old as the seventh century. Other pieces belong to the glorious period of the eleventh and twelvth centuries, and fine examples of the decorative style of the thirteenth to fifteenth centuries, which were brought to Bikaner by Raja Rai Singh. Rai Singh brought home other Gujarati, Jain as well as Hindu, brass idols from his vast fiefdoms in Gujarat and his Subedarship at Burhanpur. When Aurangzeb started his persecution of Hindu 'idolatry', both Raja Karan Singh and Maharaja Anup Singh gave shelter to *murtis* (idols) in danger of desecration. Later when Anup Singh had achieved a compromise with the Emperor and was stationed in the Deccan, he continued to collect Hindu images in the Maratha and South Indian theatres of war. The collection of miniature paintings made by Anup Singh from Bijapur, Golcunda and Adoni is extensive. Many of these can be seen in the Museum at the Fort; including the pure Rajput style which was at its best at Bikaner at the turn of the nineteenth century. The Museum is one of the best in the country and offers a series of masterpieces of Indian art, which can well vie with the treasures of Delhi, Jaipur and Jodhpur, perhaps even surpass them in beauty and splendour.

The Lallgarh Palace

Among a chain of palaces in India, one of the more well-known is the Lallgarh Palace, Bikaner, which was built by Maharaja Ganga Singh, in phases – the first phase was completed by the end of the nineteenth century. It is named after Maharaj Lall Singh, the father of Maharaja Ganga Singh. The palace has four wings – Laxmi Niwas, Shiv Niwas, Sadul Niwas and Karni Niwas. Each building or wing, exterior as well as interior, bears the mark of the Maharaja's expert judgment and impeccable taste. The Maharaja housed the rarest of his treasures, chosen from the connoisseurs of the East and West in Lallgarh Palace. In this red sandstone building, crowned with ornate stone-work, an ideal has been attained. Stern critics have unsuccessfully examined and re-examined its intricate interior decorations with a view to finding a flaw in taste, an inaccuracy in colour tone, or a misdated combination of periods. The uniqueness of the Lallgarh Palace, which still remains a royal home, a hotel and a museum, is a rich tribute to the creative genius of the Maharaja, for its historical importance and artistic worth.

Designed by Sir Swinton Jacob in 1898, the Lallgarh Palace is built around a vast central courtyard surrounded by carved windows of the ladies' apartments. The cupolas, domes, and balconies have been carved by local craftsmen with such delicacy that even today the solid red sandstone has the fragile appearance of lace.

Laid out with the eye of the landscape artist, the palace has long wide verandahs and lofty rooms. Most of the high quality marble, was imported from Italy. The rooms have a tasteful blend of Eastern and Western colour. The palace has all the modern amenities and conveniences.

The Sadul Museum

The art objects which were formerly in the various rooms of the Lallgarh Palace, have now been shifted to the Sadul Museum, established by Maharaja (Dr.) Karni Singh of Bikaner, a Member of the Lok Sabha (1952-77) to commemorate the memory of his father, Maharaja Sadul Singh. The museum is housed on the first floor of the Sadul Niwas and Karni Niwas wings of the Lallgarh Palace, and is a part of Maharaja Ganga Singhji Trust.

The museum depicts the lives and times of the Rajas, Maharajas, Rajputs and the social and cultural heritage of Bikaner State through various artefacts and photographs displayed in 22 rooms of the upper storey of Sadul Niwas building. It houses a unique pictorial record of former princely states which is open to the public.

All the objects in the museum have been arranged and displayed systematically by the strenuous efforts of Princess Rajyashree Kumari Bikaner, Chairperson of the Maharaja Ganga Singhji Trust, and daughter of Maharaja (Dr.) Karni Singh. A life member of Indian National Trust for Art and Cultural Heritage (INTACH), she has been instrumental in the preservation of heritage properties and ancestral forts and palaces of Bikaner Royal House. Her works have also focused on bringing out books related to the history, art and culture of Bikaner.

Crystal Boat

Another attraction of the Lallgarh Palace is a Crystal or Baccarat boat, of the last decade of nineteenth century. There are only two crystal boats of that period available today – one is at the Lallgarh Palace, and the other is at Corning Museum of Glass, Corning, New York, USA.

The boat was made by Baccarat from a prototype sculpted by Vital Cornu at the end of the nineteenth century, probably around 1897-98. The crystal and bronze work was given to the Cristalleries de Baccarat by the store 'Le Grand Depot' which, at that time, sold top quality goods from various porcelain, earthenware and crystal manufacturers, including Baccarat. It was this store that exhibited the boat at the 1900 World Fair, as Baccarat did not wish to participate directly.

This boat was purchased for Rs. 10,000 by Maharaja Ganga Singh, but the year of its purchase is not exactly known. The boat decorated the drawing room of Maharaja (Dr.) Karni Singh for over fifty years; and after his demise in 1988, the boat is now in the possession of his wife, Rajmata Sushila Kumari.

The Director, Corning Museum of Glass and the Archivist, Baccarat France, both were in correspondence with Maharaja Karni Singh, in 1987, and wanted to collect more information from him about the crystal boat in his possession, especially the year and circumstances of its purchase by his grandfather, Maharaja Ganga Singh. Though Karni Singh gathered all possible information, there were no written records, so only conjectures abound about exactly when the boat was purchased.

The first conjecture or opinion is that of Maharaja Karni Singh himself, who in September, 1987, wrote to the Scientific Research Officer of the Corning Museum of Glass, that, 'since a year now, I have been in correspondence with Dwight P. Lanmon of Corning Museum regarding the glass boat reported to have been presented by my late grandfather, Maharaja Ganga Singh of international repute, to the Corning Museum. We have an identical boat in our collections in Bikaner which was inherited by me from my grandfather and this has been brought to the attention of Dwight P.

Lanmon who promised to find out as to how your boat came to America. Which was the original and which was the copy, and were two made at the same time? I am still awaiting information on this rather interesting matter … What I am given to understand from some of the old staff members of my grandfather who are still alive is that Maharaja Ganga Singhji acquired the boat in 1930-31 when he went for the Round Table Conference and the same has remained here since then.'

The second conjecture is of Veronique Nansenet, archivist, Baccarat France, who, in January 1989, wrote to Maharaja Karni Singh : 'We do know from a newspaper article that your grandfather purchased this piece directly at our head office in Paris at the end of 1930. However, other documents mention 1924.' This letter raises a controversy: whether the boat was purchased in 1924 or 1930!

There is the third conjecture, too, prevalent in some quarters in Bikaner that Maharaja Ganga Singh had seen these two boats at the Baccarat shop in 1911, but on account of the high price he did not purchase them at that time. Again, he saw them in 1919, when he had gone to participate in Paris Peace Conference, and at that time, he purchased both the boats – one he kept for himself, and the other he gave as a gift to President Wilson of the USA who was his colleague at the Peace Conference. However, these three opinions are based on incomplete information.

Lately, another dimension was added by George Fernandes, Member of Indian Parliament, who had visited Corning Museum on May 22, 1987; and from there he dispatched a picture card of the boat to Maharaja Karni Singh, with the following note: 'If this magnificent glass boat was prepared for your father's wedding, why don't we bring it into India and keep it in one of our museums.' At the bottom of the picture card, there is a printed line, put by Corning Museum authorities which, reads: 'Table made for the 1878 Paris Universal Exposition, Baccarat, France; cut glass boat plateau added in 1924 for the Maharaja of Bikaner, India, OH, 167 cms.'

The Gajner Palace

Gajner, a historical retreat, located 20 miles from Bikaner, is famous for its beautiful palace, pleasant lake, and fabulous grouse-shoots. In the midst of the desert, Gajner, with plenty of water and trees is indeed a heaven in the sand with delicate and aesthetic architecture.

The history of the Gajner is quite old. The place was first selected by

Maharaja Gaj Singh in 1746, who named it as Gajshinghpura, which in due course of time came to be known as Gajner. Maharaja Gaj Singh had also built a palace here, known as Jalmahal with a small garden. It was a place for hunting and recreation for the rulers of Bikaner.

The Gajner Palace in its present form was built by Maharaja Ganga Singh in the first decade of the twentieth century. The work had started in 1908 and completed by the end of 1910. Colonel Sir Swinton Jacob was the architect. All the luminaries who visited the state during Maharaja Ganga Singh's reign stayed here for longer periods than in any other of the palaces.

Many royal visitors, viceroys and dignitaries, enjoyed splendid game at Gajner. Prince of Wales in 1905, described it as 'one of the wonders of Bikaner'. Lord and Lady Minto spent their 'happiest days' in the shady bower of Gajner. Lord Hardinge was fascinated with the charm of oasis in a desert. Lord Chelmsford, who stayed at Gajner in November, 1920, said: 'A bracing desert air to rest and refresh at Gajner ... In Bikaner the days fly fast and I can hardly believe that nearly a week has passed since we arrived here.' M. Clemanceau of France, visited Gajner in 1922, and later on wrote to the Maharaja that he had to explain to his friends 'what is Gajner, its beauties and the high feats of the Maharaja of Bikaner'. 'At Gajner, it seemed to me', wrote Lord Reading in 1922, 'that I was in the land of imagination, of the fairies of whom I read and heard in my youth.' In January, 1922, Countess of Reading, wrote: 'I have tried to write home and tell my son all about Bikaner and Gajner, but I find it will fill volumes, and I had exhausted my adjectives on the first page.' 'No passage of time can efface the memories of Gajner', said Prince Arthur of Connaught in January, 1925. 'The memory of my shoot at Gajner', said Lord Irwin, 'will remain with me as a red-letter day in my calendar of sport.' John Hope, who had accompanied Lord Linlithgow, during the latter's visit to Gajner in January, 1938, wrote: 'The trip did me more good than any doctor could have done, and my old friend the jaundice has gone!'

Lord Mountbatten, the first Governor-General of free India, who visited Bikaner in January 1948, for the Investiture of Maharaja Sadul Singh with G.C.S.I., had stayed at Gajner Palace. His Public Relations Officer, Alan Campbell-Johnson in *Mission With Mountbatten*, gives a vivid description of the place: 'Gajner is a beautiful spot, where stands a marvellous Palace of the Maharaja, all of red stone carved with lattice-work, reflecting exquisite workmanship and great excellence. The palace roads are over-arched with trees; and the lake is over-flowing in the treeless desert all around. Here a great artificial oasis, with a lake nearly a mile long, has been built out of the Rajputana desert, which provides the Maharaja with a paradise for shooting – his great hobby in life.'

The Public Park

A remarkable creation of Maharaja Ganga Singh, as early as 1912, was the Public Park. The idea of a Public Park in Bikaner, originated in the Maharaja's mind in a novel way. It had its roots in the history of the state. The valorous deeds of Raja Karan Singh and his two brave sons – Kesri Singh and Padam Singh; followed by Maharaja Anup Singh, the eldest son of Raja Karan Singh, the hero of Golcunda, made the bravery of the Bikaner warriors famous. As a result of their services the Mughal emperors had granted a small district of Purejat, which the rulers of Bikaner held for 239 years. In 1904, the district of Purejat was ceded by Maharaja Ganga Singh to the Government of India for cantonment purposes, in exchange for a certain cash compensation and two villages adjoining Bikaner – Babalwas and Rattakhera – over which the Imperial Government transferred full rights to Bikaner.

The Maharaja feared that the historical importance of the Purejat district would be lost sight of in course of time, and in order to keep alive this precious memory, he built the Public Park. In its centre he created a permanent monument in remembrance of Purejat district. It was while selecting a suitable site for this memorial that the idea of a Public Park first occurred to the Maharaja. Gradually he enlarged the scheme, and a spacious park covering an area of about 35 acres was built.

The most striking monument in the park is the big central tower designed by Colonel Sir Swinton Jacob which is constructed of marble and red sandstone and stands 66 ¼ feet high. Round this tower an ornamental water tank is built, and on the tablets of the tower, in addition to the history of the Purejat, are inscribed feats of arms of the Bikaner State, its rulers and men, covering a period of 447 years since the state was founded. On the four sides of this tower, which is called *Kirti Stambh* or the Tower of Glory, are war memorials, and on them are recorded the names of the soldiers of Bikaner who fell in the Mutiny in 1857, in China in 1900-01, and in Somaliland in 1903-04. Space was left to record future campaigns. The Tower of Glory or *Kirti Stambh* is exclusively a monument to commemorate the memories of Raja Karan Singh, Rajkumar Kesri Singh, and Rajkumar Padam Singh; of Purejat district, which was once a part of Bikaner. It also records the historic victory of Golcunda in which Maharaja Anup Singh played a leading role.

The Public Park was inaugurated by Lord Hardinge, the Viceroy, on November 26, 1912. He was greatly impressed by the Maharaja's step of combining together the Public Park and the history of Bikaner; and said: 'The idea of commemorating the historical association of the district of Purejat by a monument (*Kirti Stambh*) in your capital is one in which Your Highness must have the sympathy of all who know the value of old traditions and the important influence, they bring to bear upon the formation of character.'

Public Buildings

Maharaja Ganga Singh converted the city of Bikaner from a medieval Indian town of narrow streets and bazaars, of mean-looking houses and unimposing public buildings, into a modern capital with good infrastructure and all the amenities of life. He had been, from his earliest days, a great builder. He recognised from the first the necessity of transforming his capital into a modern town and himself planned noble edifices, public parks, convenient and architecturally beautiful public offices. Wide highways replaced the narrow lanes of old Bikaner; one by one buildings of public utility were designed and erected. Commemorative statues adorned important positions.

The Hardinge Municipal Hall, Victoria Memorial Club, Kote-Darwaza and King Edward Memorial road, Walter Nobles' School, Irwin Legislative Hall, Secretariat Offices, the High Court, Lady Elgin's Girls School, Maharani Nobles' Girls School, Railway Office, Vikrampur Cantonment, Bijey Bhawan, Dungar Memorial College, Public Library, King George V Stadium, and other edifices gave dignity to the capital and made it a modern city. Prince Bijey Singh Memorial Hospitals (Men and Women), constructed in 1935-36, with a number of wards and operation theatres, had been a unique achievement in the field of public health. Its opening ceremony was performed by Maharana Bhopal Singh of Udaipur on March 11, 1937. This was the first well-equipped hospital in Rajasthan, and in north India. In design and layout, the hospitals represented not merely a distinguished addition to the architecture of Bikaner, but had the qualifications, latest equipment and scientific infrastructure to enable the Maharaja to provide his subjects with first-class medical attention.

In addition, Ganga Singh built the Government Press, Golden Jubilee Club and School, State Hotel, King George V Infirmary, Princess Chand Kanwar Orphanage, Ganga Theatre and Cinema, Wellingdon Technical Institute, temples, Ganga Golden Jubilee Museum, and other structures which transformed the face of the capital. The Maharaja had taken a personal interest in all schemes for public buildings and maintained their harmony. He never allowed any plan for an important building in the city of Bikaner to pass without the closest scrutiny. In fact, he was his own 'master-builder'.

As a consequence the complexion of the city changed; its appearance gave a new look, different from the haphazard growth of most Indian capitals. There was nothing incongruous, nothing jarring to the taste. Everything was in harmony, and looked like the conception of a master mind, who slowly worked out and filled in the details planned years before. 'Comparatively speaking,' writes Dr. Gaurishankar Hirachand Ojha in *The History of Bikaner State* that, 'Maharaja Ganga Singh alone had built far more public utility buildings in Bikaner, than all the previous rulers, put together, had done during the course of 350 years.' His building activity was a clear-cut testimony to his benevolent rule, benign heart, and deep attachment to his people.

The monumental work of the Maharaja was seen in the palaces and public buildings in the capital city of Bikaner where every wall and every inch of the ground bore the testimony of his genius and perseverance. The modern institutions of public utility, splendid palaces, beautiful parks and gardens, and rich foliage appeared like a 'fairy land' to the casual visitor. 'The entire structure of this state', said Maharajah Scindia of Gwalior in 1937, 'is the workmanship of that dynamic master-mind whose energy, thought and spirit pervades every sphere of the lives of the Bikaner people'.

9

Glory to Bikaner

Maharaja Ganga Singh, after his Silver Jubilee and more after the years of the First Great War had successfully broken the isolation of Bikaner. By his unusual initiative and drive, he was able to open up many prospects for the state. Like an inquisitive explorer he was searching for new possibilities for Bikaner's progress.

The Maharaja had realised that the two essential requirements for breaking up the isolation of the state were the development of irrigation and railways. The construction of the Gang Canal from the Sutlej Valley water works at Ferozepur was a stupendous undertaking, described later which the Maharaja completed in 1927.

Almost equal to this as a measure of far-reaching consequence, was the advent of the railways which broke the insularity of the state. The distance was the main obstacle in the development of the state. The hardships of travel in the state at the fag end of the nineteenth century had been graphically described by the Maharaja thus: 'When fifty years ago, I became Maharaja of Bikaner (1887), Lord Dufferin was the Viceroy of India. In those days Bikaner was very difficult to access. I well remember the long and tedious journeys of some one hundred and forty miles which as a little boy I had to undertake. In great heat or cold we travelled in a camel carriage, with brief halts in little rest-houses, to and from the nearest railway station.' As such the Maharaja, after assuming ruling powers in 1898, had undertaken the improvement of communications which was imperative for the gradual modernisation of the state. The nature of the country precluded the economical construction of long-distance roads, because any metalled road across the desert would without constant vigilance of a large body of labourers be frequently made impassable by dust storms, which would deposit large quantities of sand on the road surface. The only suitable means of so long distance communications in such a country were railways.

The Maharaja knew the vital importance of a well-planned railway system in connecting distance parts of the state with the capital and bringing the whole area into direct contact with neighbouring provinces and states. He devoted his attention to the construction of extensions of the existing Bikaner railway system. The construction of the railway in the form of a loop from Hanumangarh through Ganganagar, Karanpur, and Raisinghnagar to Suratgarh, before the opening of the Canal in 1927, was a great achievement of the Maharaja. The total length of railway to serve the tract was 160 miles. The second extension scheme of railway line, was from Sadulpur (Rajgarh) to Delhi, with a branch to Rewari, which opened the State of Loharu, and connected the Bikaner system with the railway headquaarters at Delhi. The third extension scheme, was from Sadulpur to Hanumangarh, with the object of opening out an important tract in Bikaner territory lying between these two stations. In 1898 the total mileage of the Bikaner state railway was only 85.15 miles; whereas it measured 883.05 miles, at the time of the Maharaja's death in 1943. Bikaner was now easily accessible to the outside world and Bikaneris could reach Delhi, Bombay or Calcutta by express trains. The creation of an effective network of railway communications had undoubtedly contributed to the marked improvement in the economic life of Bikaner. Through both of his great undertakings – the Canal Scheme and the Railway System, Ganga Singh had successfully opened up the state and heralded the dawn of a glorious chapter in the history of Bikaner.

Benares Hindu University

A significant event that took place in the Maharaja's life was the laying of the foundation stone of Benares Hindu University in 1916. The founder of the university, Pandit Madan Mohan Malaviya, a veteran statesman and a great nationalist leader, was a close and trustworthy friend of the

Maharaja. The Maharaja had rendered substantial financial help, not only at the initial stage of the university, but in subsequent years too. The foundation stone of the Senate Hall of the university was laid by Lord Hardinge and the Maharaja of Bikaner on February 4, 1916. On this occasion the Maharaja had placed two sets of coins – 2 silver and 2 copper coins – of the Bikaner State below the foundation stone. A lengthy inscription on a large copper plate fixed on the wall of the Senate Hall of the university in 1916, says: '... the high-minded and valiant Ganga Singh, the Ruler of Bikaner.'

Mahatma Gandhi was also present on the occasion. At that time he was not an important figure in the national movement. He met the Maharaja after the function was over. It was the first meeting of the Maharaja with Mahatma Gandhi.

The Silver Jubilee Convocation of the Benares Hindu University was held on January 21, 1942. Dr. S. Radhakrishnan, later on the President of India, was the Vice Chancellor at the time; and the Maharaja was the Chancellor. The convocation address was delivered by Mahatma Gandhi. Though the Maharaja did not attend the convocation on account of his illness, but his welcome address was read in absentia. In that address, while alluding to Mahatma Gandhi, the Maharaja wrote: 'I had the pleasure of first meeting Mahatma Gandhi 25 years ago when the university was founded and he came here to bless it. Today when we celebrate its Silver Jubilee, I, as its Chancellor, am privileged to welcome him again. The Mahatma is widely held to be one of the greatest sons that India has ever produced, and is undoubtedly a world figure.'

The Nawab of Bhopal

The years following the Peace Conference were significant in the history of Bikaner. Apart from the development of irrigation and railways, the state now became a hub of Princes, Viceroys and dignitaries. The Princes thronged from time to time to witness the new progress obtained in the state and at the same time to establish a rapport with India's leading Maharaja. Nawab Hamidullah Khan of Bhopal who visited the state in January 1923, had carried the happiest memories of the traditional Rajput hospitality. He characterised the Maharaja as 'the most charming and predominant personality amongst our Order'. So great was the regard for the Maharaja that the Nawab of Bhopal always addressed him as 'Dear Dada' and paid great attention to his advice. The Nawab wrote: 'I value each word of your advice.'

Lord Chelmsford's Visit

Another important visitor to Bikaner was Lord Chelmsford, the Viceroy, who stayed for a week in November 1920. He was greatly impressed to witness the progress achieved within the state, and said, 'Fortunate is the state where the administration has nothing to fear from public scrutiny and where changes come as a gradual development from within and not by an unwilling surrender to the superior force of public opinion.' He applauded the personal interest taken by the Maharaja in the great Sutlej Canal Project and, said: 'If outside your state Your Highness is best known for your services to the empire, your own subjects will in time to come perhaps remember you best as the Maharaja who brought the Sutlej water to their land.' Lord Chelmsford then referred to the splendid hospitality of the Maharaja. 'Future viceroys will find in Bikaner, as I have, a perfection of hospitality to welcome them, a game bird that is no respecter of persons to test their skill, a bracing desert air to rest and refresh them, a harmony between Prince and people and in the ruler a valued friend.'

Prince of Wales' Second Visit

The most important event of the period was the visit of Prince of Wales (King George V) who honoured Bikaner for the second time. The King-Emperor arrived on December 2, 1921, and stayed in Bikaner for six days. In the entourage of the Prince of Wales, Lieutenant Lord Louis Mountbatten was also there. Nobody had imagined at the time that he would some day be the Crown Representative and the first Governor-General of free India. The main function was held at the old Fort Palace, where, at a state banquet, Prince of Wales, said: 'I have been looking forward keenly to this visit to Bikaner from many motives. In the first place, I desired to renew and strengthen my deep personal friendship for Your Highness by a visit to you in your home; in the second place, I wished to have the privilege of seeing the capital of this Rathore State and try to judge myself what is the magic of this desert environment which makes loyalty to my House flourish like an evergreen.' The Prince of Wales further said that the Maharaja was the embodiment of 'friendliness and goodwill', 'a great sportsman and an excellent host. The Polo ground has known you and amid your numerous preoccupations you have found time to score a century against the tiger, your own grouse and duck can testify to a keenness of eye, which no swiftness of flight can elude. As a host Your Highness is an expert in all that hospitality can do to interest and entertain.'

After the brilliant ceremonies, including a wonderful review of state troops and the celebrated Camel Corps, the Prince went out to Gajner on December 5, and there he spent a quiet week-end shooting. The Prince and the Maharaja both left Gajner by motor car for Bikaner on December 6. On way, near Kotra village, the Prince shot a chinkara. The same day the King-Emperor left Bikaner by special train.

After leaving Bikaner, the Prince of Wales on December 7, wrote: 'Nothing could have been more delightful than my visit to Your Highness' state. I was much impressed with Your Highness' desert city and with the very warm welcome which Your Highness' subjects gave to me ... I must congratulate you on the wonderful organisation which made everything run so smoothly and so pleasantly... I shall long remember Bikaner.'

Lord Reading's Visit

Another distinguished Viceroy who paid Bikaner a visit of six days, from December 28, 1921, to January 2, 1922, was Lord Reading. He was one of the foremost of Britain's gifted statesmen, who had to his credit a brilliant record of service in the interests of the Empire. As Viceroy, he had a reputation for sagacity, an exceptional knowledge of human nature, and combined in himself a rare strength of character with a deep sense of justice, tact, sympathy, and imagination. The Maharaja's personal friendship with Lord Reading started when both were associated together in England at meetings of the Imperial War Cabinet and later on in Paris during the Peace Conference.

Lord Reading had to face extraordinary difficulty during the beginning of his period in 1921. The Non-Cooperation Movement launched by the Indian National Congress was at its height, and the long shadow of the Jallianwallah Bagh Tragedy (1919) had cast a terrible gloom all over the country. The establishment of the Chamber of Princes (1921) was viewed with grave suspicion in British Indian quarters. Lord Reading had dealt with the situation in British India with tact and firmness, but he got very little time to attend to the affairs of the states. The Maharaja considered his visit to Bikaner significant, for it gave him an opportunity, being the Chancellor

Maharaja Ganga Singh of Bikaner performing 'Puja' at the opening of Gang Canal on 26th October 1927.

Maharaja Ganga Singh with Girija Shankar Bajpai, ICS (right), who was the secretary to the Indian delegation to the League of Nations.

Maharaja Ganga Singh with his grandson, Prince Karni Singh.

Maharaja Ganga Singh at the Round Table Conference held at London in 1930.

Maharaja Ganga Singh on his visit to London for the Silver Jubilee celebrations of King George the V.

Maharaja Ganga Singh and his grandchildren as cadets. L to R: Granddaughter Princess Sushil Kanwar, Prince Karni Singh and Prince Amar Singh.

The Maharaja with other members of the delegate to the League of Nations at Geneva in 1930.

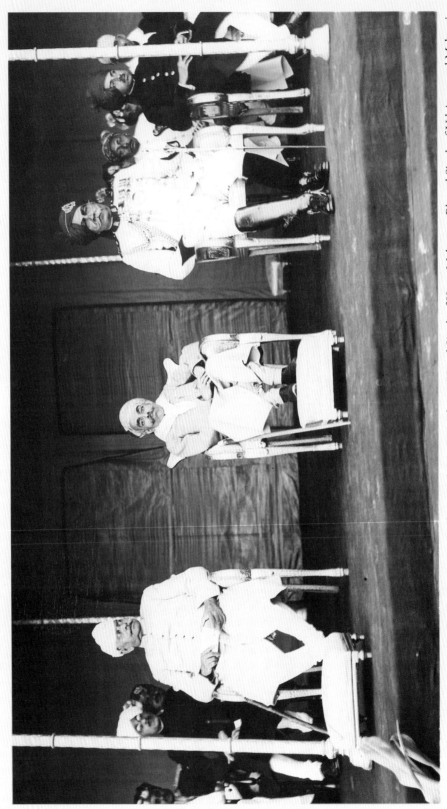

At the opening ceremony of Prince Bijey Singh Hospital in 1936. L to R: Maharao Umed Singh of Kota, Maharana Bhopal Singh of Udaipur, and Maharaja Ganga Singh.

Maharaja Ganga Singh (centre) with six grandchildren at Gajner Palace, Bikaner. On his right is Lord Willington, the Viceroy; and on his left is Lady Willington.

Maharaja Ganga Singh (standing third from left) and Prince Sadul Singh (standing fifth from left) at a lion shoot in the Gir forest.

Maharaja Ganga Singh sitting on throne in the Vikram Bilas Durbar Hall at Fort, Bikaner during his Golden Jubilee - 1937.

Maharaja Ganga Singh on elephant proceeding to Laxmi Nathji temple from Bikaner Fort, as part of the Golden Jubilee celebrations.

Maharaja Ganga Singh with Lord Linlithgow, the Viceroy, and Lady Linlithgow, near Hazoor steps, Bikaner Fort in 1937.

of the Chamber of Princes, to acquaint the Viceroy with the real nature of the Chamber.

At the banquet on January 2, the Maharaja spoke frankly about the misconception that prevailed with regard to the aims and aspirations of the Chamber and the Indian states. He refuted the sinister aims and unworthy motives that were attributed to the Chamber of Princes by various obviously hostile quarters. He stated that the Princes were the true well-wishers of the country, and they would never be a party to any policy of repression or to any attempts at stifling the just aspirations of the people of British India.

Dressed in a black tail coat decorated with his medals, Lord Reading replied cautiously but with warmth. He alluded to his friendship with the Maharaja and said: 'I then learned to value not only the sagacity but the broad outlook and the wise judgement of His Highness. There were sown the seeds of a riper friendship which found its response in one of the first messages sent to me from India when I was appointed Viceroy.' He went on: 'The quality of the eclectic is well marked in Your Highness; you have displayed it in extracting from the West the special knowledge of the West and applying it wisely and judiciously to the special environments of the East. In itself this is a notable accomplishment.' He added that the Maharaja, was 'gifted with an extra sense, and was indeed a proud and resplendent figure, and yet with the consciousness of responsibility ... I thought today as I saw him approach, here is a presentation in the twentieth century of Rajput chivalry.' As a ruler and administrator, his achievements had been outstanding. He said that it was his firm conviction that whatever might happen in the future, Bikaner would be true to its traditions and be staunch and faithful to the Crown.

M. Clemenceau's Visit

In 1922, the Maharaja was privileged to entertain M. Clemenceau, whom he had met at the Versailles Peace Conference, where as Premier of France he presided over the deliberations of the Conference. Due to his radical ideas and fundamental reforms in the political system of France, M. Clemenceau, was popularly known as 'the old Tiger'. His qualities of unbending courage and grim determination to a cause were greatly appreciated by the Maharaja. Faithful to his ideals and whole-heartedly devoted to the interests of France; clever at producing convincing arguments, and sticking to them until his objective was realised; these qualities of Clemenceau appealed to the

Maharaja. The sturdy old man had dominated the Conference by his uncompromising role and cynical contempt for the platitudes of President Wilson. Clemenceau had proved his mettle and shown his accomplishments at the Peace Conference. According to the Maharaja, there was no one like Clemenceau.

The Maharaja's aristocratic bearing, outstanding talent, and charm appealed equally to Clemenceau. 'At a private party in Paris the Maharaja suggested to him that if he came to India, the Maharaja of Bikaner would be pleased to introduce the French tiger to the tiger of the Indian jungle. These words, spoken no doubt in jest, were remembered by Clemenceau when after a tour in the Far East he decided to visit India.'

From Indo-China Clemenceau wired to the Maharaja that he looked forward to meeting the Indian tiger. The Maharaja planned his whole tour in India and was very pleased to entertain his old friend. A fine tiger shoot was arranged in Gwalior, the Maharaja himself accompanied 'to watch the meeting of the tigers'.

In Bikaner the distinguished guest was shown all the courtesy to which he was entitled. At the banquet which was held in his honour the Maharaja recalled his own pleasant associations in Paris and the historic events in which both of them had taken part. Clemenceau spoke about Indian and international affairs; he was frank and critical of Englishmen. He spoke with affection about Ganga Singh. 'No doubt, our host is descended from a distinguished line of ancestors. It is something to be descended from a long and distinguished line. It is more important what one has made himself to be. To be both is indeed a matter of great honour.'

What he had seen of the Maharaja himself and his achievements 'endeared him to his heart', and Clemenceau took back with him a high regard for his host. He often remembered his visit to Bikaner, and especially that of Gajner, where he derived the 'greatest pleasure', and wrote that it would not be forgotten. Clemenceau, spoke to his friends affectionately about the high feats of the Maharaja of Bikaner, or 'his great Bikaner friend', and humorously wrote to him: 'Wherever you are, if you do not write a line or two I shall call you a great Prince but a very wicked boy.'

The League of Nations

In 1922, when the Maharaja was in England on a holiday, he was requested by Lord Peel, then Secretary of State for India, to be a member of the Indian delegation to the League of Nations. For personal reasons he was then unable to accept that invitation. The same invitation was renewed in 1924. As one of the statesmen who had signed the Covenant which had brought that body into existence, the Maharaja felt attracted by the invitation to observe its actual work at close quarters. His colleagues in the delegation were Lord Hardinge, with whom the Maharaja had for many years been on terms of close friendship, and Sir Mahommed Rafique, an eminent jurist and scholar from the United Provinces. The Maharaja had as his chief secretary, Sir Stanley Reed, and the heir-apparent accompanied him as a substitute delegate.

The League Assembly of 1924 was an exceptionally important one. It was called upon to deal with the Italian occupation of Corfu, which had been carried out in violation of international treaties and obligations. The League of Nations which had been established to guard over the sanctity of treaties and the security of the weaker nations from aggression by the stronger, was called upon to assert its authority. This was the first of many occasions when *Treaty* violations were brought before the international court of the League. At that period the Powers supporting the League were still sufficiently strong and resolved to avert a recurrence of the calamity of war. When the Assembly met it was clear that a very difficult task lay ahead for which it would have to use the untried weapons of collective force against Italy, a country that was itself a member of the League. The situation contained a serious danger: if the League ordered Italy to withdraw from Corfu, and the order was disobeyed, the statesmen at Geneva would be left with the choice of seeing the authority of the League shattered in the eyes of those who had put their trust in it, or of unleashing the horrors of war which the League had been established to prevent. It was a similar dilemma, (though on a smaller scale,) to that which broke up the League of Nations as ineffective in international authority eleven years later when Italy attacked Abyssinia, flouted the orders of the League and threatened with war any power that would attempt to carry those orders out.

It is well-known how the League of Nations succeeded in 1924, (as it failed in 1935), in compelling the aggressor to surrender its loot. Italy had to withdraw from Corfu.

The Maharaja took his full share in the work of the Assembly. Apart from the question of Corfu that body had to deal with a draft treaty of mutual assistance which was to link disarmament with guarantees for the security of states. The British Government considered the proposal indefinite and vague, and the guarantees which the draft treaty contained illusory. The Maharaja who spoke on behalf of India during the general discussion agreed with the principle of arbitration in international matters but indicated that any reduction in armaments in India would have to be proportionate to the special geographical position and frontier problems of India. The Maharaja was criticised in the Indian press for opposing reduction of military forces in India, although the allegation that he had taken a militarist attitude was without any foundation. He merely pointed out that against the menace of frontier tribesmen, who were well supplied with arms and ammunition imported from Europe, neither economic sanctions nor arbitration would be sufficient to guarantee the safety of India.

The impression created by the Maharaja's appeals at Geneva had been described by Wickham Steed, the famous publicist and former editor of *The Times*, who was present at Geneva as an interested witness to the proceedings of the Assembly.

> The Assembly of the League of Nations at Geneva, September 6th, 1924. The President, Mr. Motta, announces: 'The Maharaja of Bikaner, delegate of India, will address the Assembly.' Complimentary applause from the Assembly. The same tall, soldierly figure as at the Peace Conference, but dressed in a simple well-cut lounge suit, ascends the tribune, bows to the President and begins to speak. Reminiscent of other British oratory, the Assembly resigns itself to an expected flood of 'up-lifting' exhortation. Its resignation quickly gives place to attention, and attention to admiration. Clear, brief, to the point, matter-of-fact yet elevated, the Maharaja soon convinces his hearers that he knows what he is saying, means what he says, and says what he means. Ten minutes later he descends from the tribune – amid rousing applause and markedly different in quality from the initial greeting. He had made the best of all the English speeches at the Assembly.

Maharaja Ganga Singh's work in the Assembly of the League of Nations received due appreciation from Lord Reading who in a cable expressed his gratitude to the Maharaja for his labours on India's behalf.

Prince Arthur of Connaughts' Visit

Prince Arthur of Connaught, who had visited Bikaner for the first time in 1903, again came on December 29, 1924 and stayed for a week. The visit to Bikaner of any member of the Imperial House of Windsor was always a matter of extreme gratification for the Maharaja.

The Prince found excellent sport at Gajner and Hanumangarh; at the latter place he held the record of having bagged the biggest black buck shot in the Bikaner State during the past quarter of a century and more – 'an exceptionally fine trophy unequalled in most parts of India'.

At the state banquet on January 5, the Maharaja said: 'We shall always cherish the memories of the happy days during the visit to Bikaner of Their Royal Highnesses in 1903, of which the main Gateway of my new palace, the Connaught Arch, will remain a lasting memorial.' The Maharaja also spoke about the distinguished services of the Prince to the empire in many fields, both in peace and in war; and thereby contributing to knit closer together the bonds that united the various component parts of the empire; and added, 'for your being a soldier Prince and a good sportsman – qualities which we Rajputs share and admire in a special measure in common with the English people.'

In reply, the Prince of Connaught said that he was not a stranger but rather as one who was renewing the recollections of his youth, re-forming old friendships, and realising by closer association the love for India which he had inherited from his father and in which he was proud to had his share. 'I am not exaggerating,' he said, 'when I describe my friendship with Your Highness as a life-long one, both in peace and war.' 'Equally at home in the clamour of war or at the council table, Your Highness's sound judgement and personality have been relied upon by all.'

The Prince who had seen a review of the Bikaner troops was greatly impressed by it. 'No one could have witnessed the magnificent spectacle,' he said, 'without being impressed by the soldierly bearing and steadiness under arms of all ranks, while history so recent as to be within the memory of us all records the fact that, in the hour of need and stress, your troops played their part with bravery and distinction.'

The Prince was greatly delighted by the Maharaja's hospitality. He said: 'Our stay in Bikaner has been for us all too brief. You have given us the best of sport and the best of times, and in the short period at our disposal we have seen many and varied places in your state. But whether among the beautiful trees of Gajner, or on the spacious plains of Suratgarh, or in the forests of Hanumangarh, or in the magnificent surroundings in which we are assembled tonight, the same kindliness and wonderful hospitality has prevailed, the same sense of sportsmanship and comradeship has been present. I can assure you, the Princess and I carry away with us tonight feelings of the deepest gratitude, and a recollection of friendliness which no passage of time can efface.'

From year to year a large number of guests from all parts of India and abroad arrived in Bikaner.

In 1923, Lady Montagu Butler, wife of the Governor of Central Provinces, visited Bikaner. After the completion of her visit, the Governor, on December 2, wrote: 'My wife Iris returned yesterday full of your hospitality and kindness generally. It is very good of your Highness to have given them such a splendid time.' Later on, Iris Butler in *A Viceroy's Wife* writes: 'Sir Ganga Singh … occupied a great position in Indian politics and social life. A man of striking personal beauty, charm and great ambition … A very cosmopolitan, a very sophisticated man, but one who never forgot his Rajput past. He was a wonderful host and did not ignore old friends even if they were quite unimportant people. Neither did he ever fail to keep contact with friends old and new who were very important people …'

Mirza M. Ismail, who was Chief Minister (Dewan) of Mysore at the time, and later on became Dewan of Jaipur in 1942, visited Bikaner in October 1926. Greatly impressed by the unbounded hospitality of the Maharaja, and on October 12, he wrote: 'The trips made in your Highness's company to various institutions, beautiful palaces, culminating at Gajner – a truly delightful spot, will remain a very pleasant memory with me for the rest of my life.'

The Duke and Duchess of Sutherland visited Bikaner in 1928, and on February 8, from Udaipur, the Duchess wrote: 'We can never thank Your Highness enough for our most enjoyable visit … I shall always remember Gajner and be very proud of the fact that I have shot myself in the famous Bikaner sand-grouse shoot; and it will be something to remember and no doubt boast about all my life. We both of us enjoyed every moment of our visit.' The Duchess of Sutherland, in another letter dated March 22, which she wrote from Dholpur, stated: 'I loved every moment of our time at Bikaner. Every new place we go to in India and every day that passes only makes me long to come back soon to Bikaner.'

Harcourt Butler, again visited again Bikaner in February 1928, and wrote: 'We were simply amazed at your hospitality extended to us not only at Bikaner and Gajner, but also on the train in coming and going. We are all greatly impressed with what we saw at Bikaner, the progress and excellent clock like regularity of everything. It was a wonderful experience and we shall never forget it. I can't tell you what a delight it was to me to visit Bikaner again and make the acquaintance of the Imperial sand-grouse.'

Interesting Anecdotes

Lord Irwin had succeeded Lord Reading as new Viceroy in April 1926; the Maharaja of Bikaner first met Lord and Lady Irwin, at the gathering of the Princes in Simla. The impression which the Maharaja of Bikaner had created upon them was described by Lady Irwin, thus: 'suave, Europeanised, and a man who had exalted snobbery to the realm of genius. One would not have taken him at first sight for an Indian Prince. He might have been a European diplomat of some distinction who spoke English and French perfectly and was clearly on easy terms with the great in London and Paris, as one could tell by his casual references to their Christian names.'

The Maharaja had extended an invitation to Lord Irwin to visit Bikaner, and the Viceroy on July 13, 1926, responded: 'I have heard and read so often of the delights of a Bikaner cold-weather that I shall be bitterly disappointed if I cannot experience it during my first year in India.'

In another letter dated August 11, the Maharaja mentioned an interesting tale of an old Jat peasant to Lord Irwin. 'It will, I think', he wrote, 'also interest Your Excellencies to hear that the other day, when riding out to a temple and tank not far from here, I came across an old *Jat* (a farmer from the predominant agricultural caste in the state) who was 112 years old ... He was still pretty hefty and, apart from a train journey, walked out in two goes the 15 miles from the capital to Kodamdesar in order to make sure of meeting me and seeing me at close quarters there, where I often go to see the extensive alterations to the temple and tank which I have been carrying out as thanks offerings out of my own pocket. He had seen five of us, the first being Maharaja Surat Singhji – my great grandfather – who made the treaty with the British Government in 1818; and, of course, he very clearly remembers the Mutiny and the guns rattling by his village, when my grandfather was hastening with his troops to render what assistance he could to the British in the adjoining districts of the Punjab. I sent him from here to Bikaner where he saw the rest of the family and specially my grandchildren; so that he has now seen what in the ordinary course of events will, please God, be seven generations. Although the weather will be rather severe then, I shall try to have the old gentleman present in Bikaner during Your Excellencies greatly looked forward to visit next January.'

Lord Irwin was glad to read the contents of the Maharaja's letter and, on August 28, replied: 'I was most interested to hear your story of the old *Jat*. For a man of 112 years old, he must be remarkably hale and hearty and I hope that he will be able to be present in Bikaner during our visit next January. I shall be most interested to hear his first-hand stories of your illustrious great great grandfather.' Lord Irwin visited Bikaner in January 1927, met the old, peasant, and derived immense pleasure from the fascinating tales he heard.

Black Buck for Warwickshire

A old personal friend of the Maharaja was Sir William Birdwood, General Officer Commanding-in-Chief, Northern Command, Rawalpindi, who, in 1921, had expressed a desire to the Maharaja, for two black bucks for the Warwickshire Regiment, which Ganga Singh graciously dispatched. On February 3, Sir Birdwood wrote to the Maharaja: 'I have seen the two black bucks, you so very kindly presented to the Warwickshsire Regiment. The regiment is now at Landi Kotal, at the head of the Khyber Pass, and I have recently been spending three days up there inspecting. You will, I know, be glad to hear that they appreciate your present enormously, and I think I may say that all ranks take the greatest pride in their two bucks. It was a horrid cold when I was there – in fact, snowing hard – but this did not seem to affect the buck, who were given any amount of warm bedding and were looking extraordinarily fit and happy.' The Maharaja was happy to read Sir Birdwood's letter and, exclaimed: 'Lucky pair! How nice it is to be fortunate in life'!

Sir William Birdwood, later on, had become Field Marshal and Commander-in-Chief of the Indian Army. He had a great admiration for the Maharaja and enjoyed his time with him on a number of occasions. He and Lady Birdwood both came again to Bikaner in January 1929; and on January, Sir Birdwood wrote: 'One very seldom meets a man, who is that, but you have that very rare and delightful faculty of putting everyone at their ease from the moment they enter your house – the faculty not only of an Indian Prince, but of an English gentleman!'.

The decade following the Peace Conference was significant in the history of Bikaner for a number of reasons. The state had become the hub of Princes;

dignitaries came in flocks to see the progress; and the viceroys were eager to meet the leading Prince of the day. The Gang Canal had started cultivation in 1927 and it steadily transformed the barren tract into fertile gardens, giving an enormous fillip to the economy of the state. The growth of the railway system had opened up the state; and ushered in a welcome change. The Maharaja's life was entirely given to work; he had endeared himself to everyone. A Prince with endless patience and firmness of purpose, the Maharaja not only made a reputation for himself but also lived up to his reputation; and in the course he had emerged as an important statesman of the country and the empire. He devoted all his energies to the task, gained his purpose, and put Bikaner, on the map – undoubtedly, a great accomplishment – which gave a feeling of exaltation to every resident of Bikaner. Though the achievement of success was a source of inspiration and hope to the Maharaja; but he was not contented with what he had gained, he wanted to push the state further into the limelight.

10

The Gang Canal

*T*he greatest achievement of Maharaja Ganga Singh, and the one that gave him an undying fame in the history of Bikaner, was the bringing in of the Gang Canal in the northern portion of the state, which for centuries had remained thirsty for water. To bring the canal in the vast and sandy expanse of Bikaner was not an easy task. Located in the middle of the Indian desert, the tract was the driest and most arid in the country. There was no river; water sources were few and far between; sand-dunes that covered the land in unbroken monotony added to the barrenness of the expanse. For generations it had been the ambition of the rulers of Bikaner to bring a sustained source of water-supply within the scope of their territory, with as much land as possible under irrigation. Self-sufficiency of the state was always their primary concern.

The idea of canal irrigation was first mooted by a far-sighted engineer, Colonel Dyas, as long ago as 1855, but no practical steps were taken towards this end. During the reign of Maharaja Dungar Singh efforts were made in 1884 for the extension of the Abohar Canal into the Bikaner territory, but the Punjab Government turned down the proposal on the plea that the canal had already been completed and that only surplus water could be released through the canal; but it was seldom available. The question was again unsuccessfully raised by the Bikaner State Government by taking it up with the Political Agent in 1887.

With Maharaja Ganga Singh's coming of age in 1898, one of the urgent and complex problems which he had to face was how to improve the lot of the people, minimising the evils and the dangers resulting from recurring famines and scarcities. He had faced acute trials and ordeals during the famine of 1899-1900, which was the worst of its kind during the last hundred years. The experience also showed him the necessity of immediate action. It was critical that means of regular irrigation be found through a big canal from a river like the Sutlej. His efforts to secure irrigation for the state met with many reverses and set-backs. The Maharaja did not admit defeat; and on more than one occasion he asserted that 'if success is to be attained it is only by perseverance and by the working up of all the necessary facts and figures and by putting forward one's case in such a clear and cogent manner as to render it unassailable as far as lies within human power.' In 1903 the Maharaja asked the Government of India to help him by lending the services of an irrigation expert. Due to the sympathies of Sidney Preston, the then Secretary to the Government of India in the Public Works Department, the matter of the Sutlej Canal Project was pushed forward, and the Maharaja was able to secure competent help. In November 1903 A.W.E. Standley, demonstrated the perfect feasibility of irrigating Bikaner lands from the river Sutlej. Ganga Singh, later on, in 1921, remarked 'he (Standley) might, as far as we in Bikaner are concerned, be called the Father of this Project, that is, the Gang Canal.'

At the early stage of the formulation of the scheme of Gang Canal, Lord Curzon had rendered great help. He recognised that the grim spectre of famine could never be exorcised as long as the *ryot* was dependent on a precarious and often capricious monsoon. His efforts led to the preparation of the first Sutlej Valley Project in 1905 by R.G. Kennedy, then chief engineer of the Punjab.

In 1905, when R.G. Kennedy drew up the first Sutlej Valley Project, Ganga Singh who was anxious not to lose this opportunity, had gone to Simla to explain his case personally to Lord Curzon. He was uncertain of the attitude of the Viceroy. He feared strenuous opposition to any claims on behalf of Bikaner from the officials of the Punjab. He hoped, however that the Viceroy would be sympathetic. It was in the hope of converting the Viceroy and, with his help, of persuading the Punjab Government that the

Maharaja went up to Simla. There he met with a pleasant surprise. Far from meeting with opposition from the Punjab and the Government of India, the Maharaja found that, thanks to the policy of Lord Curzon, the scheme, as drawn up in outline and approved by the Government of India, included a considerable area in the north of his state. The Maharaja returned 'full of hope, knowing that his long-cherished ambition would one day be realised.'

The opposition to Bikaner's share in the benefits of any irrigation scheme was made by the Bahawalpur state. The main objection raised by the Bahawalpur state was that Bikaner had no riparian rights as it had no frontage on the river, and was not entitled to share in the waters of the river. The Maharaja refuted the Bahawalpur's objection; and simultaneously, won over the sympathy of Sir Denzil Ibbetson, then Governor of the Punjab, who himself was guided by high ideals and lofty principles in the matter.

Though the decision to have a Sutlej Valley irrigation scheme was originally taken in 1905, it was not till 1912 that a definite scheme was accepted. For the Maharaja, who had come back in 1905 with high hopes that the work would be finished in seven or eight years, this delay was a source of great anxiety and alarm. In 1912, when the scheme was accepted, he thought that now at last the work would proceed. Again his hopes were dashed to the ground. The progress of the project was hindered by the Great War of 1914-18; and long and interminable arguments on the merits and demerits of different projects between the Government of India and the Punjab Government. Eight long years lapsed since 1912 and finally during the regime of Sir Michael O'Dwyer the project made considerable headway. During the Governorship of Sir Edward Maclagan in September 1920, an agreement was finally signed, between the Punjab, Bahawalpur and Bikaner under which the Sutlej Valley Project was taken in hand in 1921.

Once the agreement was signed the difficulties of the scheme became apparent to the Maharaja, but he had in his service a highly competent and dedicated officer – G.D. Rudkin, who had been the Revenue Commissioner, and later from 1912, Revenue Member of the Maharaja's Council. Gifted with unusual energy, great foresight, and a great attention to detail, G.D. Rudkin, made the irrigation scheme his own special concern. He laid down the entire colonisation policy, the way in which the capital cost was to be met, and the immediate and future requirements of the tract. His sole objective was to make the irrigation scheme as efficient as possible.

The question of financing the project was examined by G.D. Rudkin in depth. The original estimate of Rudkin was for Rs. 2, 01, 21, 121; and his revised estimate came to 3 million rupees. The financing of the project was a serious problem. The Maharaja did not like to take loans from the Government of India as that ordinarily involved political control. Neither could he meet the expenditure from the revenues of the state. The sale of the waste land in the canal colony was one source of income, but that was insufficient to meet the entire cost. The Maharaja adopted the policy of raising a loan. Since the credit of the state was so high the financiers, both from inside and outside the state, came forward and advanced the necessary funds as short term loans at rates which compared very favourably with the rates paid by the Government of India itself. The total amount so raised for the actual work of the canal and subsidiary projects was just under two and a half million rupees.

Since the Maharaja did not demand any type of financial aid from the Government of India, Basil Blackett, Finance Member of the Viceroy's Council, wrote, to the Maharaja in November 1924: 'My congratulations are due to you on solving the problem of how to finance the Bikaner portion of the Sutlej Valley Scheme. You have relieved me of considerable difficulties by so successfully making your own arrangements in the matter.'

Foundation Stone Laying Ceremony

The foundation stone to commemorate the construction of the (Bikaner) Gang Canal at Ferozepur was laid on December 5, 1925, by Maharaja Ganga Singh; Sir Malcolm Hailey, Governor of the Punjab; Sir Shadi Lal, Chief Justice of the Punjab; E.R. Foy, Chief Engineer, Irrigation Works, Sutlej Valley Project; and other dignitaries were present.

The Maharaja in his speech said that the canal would usher in 'an era of great economic development and all-round progress of Bikaner', and future generations. Sir Malcolm Hailey, who presided over the function said that the desert dwellers of Bikaner would see the water which would open to them a new life and would guarantee a prosperity 'which is now but a fable and a dream'. The benefits to Bikaner would be immense, and the Bikaner people would never have achieved it, but they were fortunate to possess a ruler of 'foresight, energy and strength of purpose'.

The actual work of construction started on December 5. It was an epoch-making event in the history of Bikaner. The Maharaja's long-felt hopes were heading towards fruition.

The Gang Canal Project

The canal was named after Maharaja Ganga Singh. The length of the main canal from the headworks to Shivpur was 84 1/2 miles. The additional length of the feeder and distributaries was 568 miles. The capacity was 2,144 cubic feet of water per second.

The detailed survey of the tract was started in 1921 and completed in three years. The whole area was divided into squares of 25 bighas each (1 bigha is 5/8 acre), the length of each side of a square being 825 feet.

The area was divided up into 913 *chaks* or water-courses, of which 495 *chaks* were given to the old inhabitants in proprietary right. Their holdings, which averaged 98 bigahs in size, were consolidated by squares on those water-courses. The average size of each *chak* was 50 squares.

The area irrigated by the Gang Canal was 620,000 acres. The total area of irrigation commanded under the scheme was 910,000 acres, but due to insufficient water supply 290000 acres was excluded from irrigation.

Except in the first five miles near the river, the main canal down to Shivpur, a distance of 80 miles, had been lined with concrete in order to conserve water and prevent water logging. The lining work was carried out by the Punjab Irrigation engineers – E.R. Foy and Hadow – who were at one time superintending engineers in the Bikaner State. The Gang Canal at the time was the longest lined canal in the world. This had enabled an area of 44,500 acres to be added to the irrigated area.

The new tehsils were formed at Karanpur, Raisinghnagar, Padampur and Anupgarh. Mandis were planned and completed at Ganganagar, Kesrisinghpur, Karanpur, Gujsinghpur and Raisinghnagar, and new towns founded at these places. Ganganagar was kept as the headquarters of the new district.

A branch of the Bikaner Railway was built in the form of a loop from Hanumangarh through Ganganagar, Karanpur, and Raisinghnagar to Suratgarh. A branch line to Anupgarh along the Ghaggar bed was also built. The total length of new railway to serve the tract was then 160 miles.

Opening Ceremony of the Canal

The entire work of the canal was completed by the autumn of 1927. On

October 26 the Viceroy, Lord Irwin, came in person to open the Canal which was named after the Maharaja, the Gang Canal, and the occasion was celebrated in a manner befitting the importance of the event in the history of Bikaner. October 26 was also the closing day of the Hindu festival of Diwali – the Festival of Lights – always held as auspicious for new beginnings. His Majesty King George V himself was pleased to send a cablegram to the Maharaja, which said: '... I heartily congratulate you on this memorable achievement and on the success of the efforts which have surmounted all difficulties to ensure the benefits of irrigation to a portion of your territory...'

Many princes and dignitaries came from far and near to rejoice in the completion of this feat. The Rathore Princes had gathered in strength. Among them were the Maharajas of Jodhpur, Kishengarh and the Raja of Sitamau. The Maharaja of Jammu and Kashmir, to whom the Maharaja referred as 'one of the brilliant budding Princes,' was there on the occasion. The Maharao of Kotah, a wise and popular ruler, a personal friend of the Maharaja, and soon to be allied to the House of Bikaner; and the Maharaja of Datia, whose hospitality the Maharaja had often enjoyed, were present. The Maharaja's valued and dear friend of thirty years, Jam Saheb of Nawanagar, came to congratulate the Maharaja on this historic day. The presence of the Nawab of Palanpur, whose personal charm and magnetic qualities had won friends all over India, visited with his heir-apparent. Other dignitaries were: the Maharaj Rana of Wankaner, Rao Saheb of Alipura, Raja of Sangli, Rana of Danta, the Nawab Regent of Loharu, and the heir-apparent of Benares. Among the Ministers – Colonel Haksar, Rushbrook-Williams, Qazi Azizuddin Ahmad, considered among the best brains in the Indian states were present.

A number of guests from British India also participated in the celebrations. The venerable Pandit Madan Mohan Malaviya, a trusted friend of the Maharaja, the famous nationalist leader, and the founder and Vice-Chancellor of Benares Hindu University; Sir Bhupendra Nath Mitra, a man of outstanding merit and ability, who later became High Commissioner for India in London; and S.R. Das, the Law Member of the Government of India, applauded the successful culmination of the Maharaja's efforts.

The British officers did not go unrepresented. Ganga Singh's valued friends of many years – Sir Malcolm Hailey, the Governor of the Punjab; Sir Geoffrey de Montmorency, Chief Secretary of His Majesty; Sir Clement

Hindley, the President of the Railway Board; and C.C. Watson, Political Secretary to the Government of India; L.W. Reynolds, Agent to the Governor-General in Rajputana – were present.

The Maharaja's greatest friend and his dear old tutor and guardian – Sir Brian Egerton – actually booked his passage, gave up the last minute on grounds of health. The Maharaja fondly remembered him and said: 'I know that his thoughts will be with us today, and I am certain that no one in Bikaner could be more pleased at the advent of this Canal than Sir Brian Egerton.' Though Sir Brian Egerton could not come, but his family was represented by Sir Philip Grey-Egerton, his eldest son, who had come to Bikaner for the purpose of attending the function. Sir Philip Grey-Egerton had a genuine affection for Bikaner, and the Maharaja called him 'an old Bikaneri'.

Colonel Windham, Major-General Sir Charles MacWatt, Colonel Watson, Standley; and the state officers, engineers and the members of the Maharaja's council attended the function.

Lord Irwin accompanied by the Maharaja arrived at Shivpur, the site of the opening ceremony, at 4.30 p.m. There was no Viceregal flag or the Union Jack on the motor car; the Bikaner Standard Flag was flying in spree, because 'it was far more courteous for the Viceroy not to fly his flag when in an Indian state'. The Maharaja delivered his speech, in which he characterised October 26 as a 'great and joyous day', 'the proudest moment of my life'; when after nearly 29 years of striving and strenuous endeavour his 'ambition of a lifetime' was fulfilled; or one of his 'most cherished dreams realised'. On this memorable event, the Maharaja expressed his indebtedness to Lord Curzon, during whose vigorous and stimulating viceroyalty a practical scheme for a big irrigation canal in Bikaner was first conceived in 1905; Lord Chelmsford, during whose viceroyalty a definite agreement regarding the Sutlej Valley Project was signed; Sir Denzil Ibbetson, who, true to the best Imperial instinct, held and worked on the principle that nature's gift of water should be used to the best advantage of the country; Sir Michael O'Dwyer and Sir Edward Maclagan for their equal fair-mindedness and sympathy; and to his old and valued friend Sir Malcolm Hailey, who gave ready help; and finally, that of the Punjab Government throughout the period of construction.

The Maharaja recalled with great pleasure the names of Sidney Preston, R.G. Kennedy, Sir Michael Nethersole, A.G.C. Fane, T.B. Tate and F.H.

Burkitt; while Bikaner, he said, would never forget A.W.E. Standley. He expressed his gratitude to the state officers – G.D. Rudkin, revenue minister; F.C. Glass, the senior irrigation engineer; Rustomji, the finance minister; and J. Fearfield, the manager of Bikaner Railway.

Brimming over with high spirits, the Maharaja said: 'I have humbly endeavoured in all earnestness to live up to the ancient Hindu ideal of Kingship. Etymologically a Raja is only he who pleases his people and keep them well content…'

Turning towards Lord Irwin, the Maharaja said that the Viceroy could therefore well imagine his emotion and his joy at the propitious advent of life-giving waters from the Punjab to irrigate Bikaner's arid plains. 'Your Excellency will thus release water today not into an uninhabited waste, which is to be colonised in the future, but into a tract where, so to speak, each man is waiting at the corner of his field watching for the water to arrive to enable him to cultivate it.' Both by the tradition set up by his ancestors and by his own upbringing, the Maharaja had been taught to live for his people; their hopes and aspirations had been his prime ambition and their well-being his supreme reward.

'Your Excellency,' proclaimed the Maharaja, with of joy, 'today is the closing day of our Hindu festival of Diwali – the Festival of Lamps – always held as auspicious and a good omen for man in his longing for greater and greater light. Today Your Excellency will be lighting a new light, opening to my people a new life of Hope and Faith with the opening of the sluice gates here at Shivpur. May the flood gates you open, open the door to the perennial flow of plenty and prosperity to my state!'

In the presence of the distinguished gathering, and amid loud applause and hand-clapping, Lord Irwin opened the flood-gates, and released the perennial flow of plenty and prosperity to the state. When the sluice was opened and the water flowed into the concrete-lined Canal, it gave a new lease of life to the desert land which had not known running water for hundreds of years. In a flash the Gang Canal had made history. The peasants greeted Lord Irwin and the Maharaja with shouts of: 'Long live Lord Irwin'; 'Long Live Maharaja Ganga Singhji of Bikaner.' Loud, victorious cries of: *Jai Jangal Dhar Badshah*, reverberated in the atmosphere heralding the beginning of a new era of prosperity, never known or seen, in the dry and parched desert of Bikaner. The Maharaja and the Maharani both ploughed the field with pearl seeds in the great tradition of 'Raja

Janak'. That plough is still preserved and is on display at the Sadul Museum of Bikaner.

The Gang Canal which was opened by Lord Irwin is the greatest tribute to the Maharaja's efforts to bring rich benefits to his people. In the words of the Viceroy: 'It is a memorial for generations to come for a ruler to whose foresight and enthusiasm in the progress of his state they will surely owe much … I offer you our most heartfelt congratulations on the consummation of this great achievement.'

Two days after the opening ceremony, Lord Irwin wrote: 'I shall always deem it a great privilege that you should have invited me to be associated with so memorable a day in the history of your state, and, as I think you know, there is no one who wishes more warmly success to you in this great project now completed than I. It was a wonderfully stimulating day and occasion for us all.'

After the completion of the opening ceremony, a banquet was held at Ganganagar. Lord Irwin, in his brief speech, alluded to the Maharaja's unbounded hospitality, and admired his magnificent organisation by which he had been able to entertain such a large number of guests on so lavish a scale at a considerable distance from the capital of Bikaner State. The welcome was fully in accordance with the princely traditions of Bikaner. Lord Irwin said: 'His Highness' hospitality is proverbial; so also are his fidelity and devotion to his old friends; and I am gratified to learn that among those present to-night there are several old Bikaneris and friends of the Maharaja who have travelled all the way from Europe especially in order to be here on this occasion.'

At the banquet the Maharaja had expressed his gratefulness to Lord Irwin, and concluded by saying: 'The Gang Canal is the result of the grace of God.' At that moment Pandit Madan Mohan Malaviya humorously remarked: 'Perhaps not by the grace of God, but by the grace of the Imperial sand-grouse.'

Lord Linlithgow, the Viceroy, when he visited Bikaner in 1937, correctly said: 'Even had Your Highness no other achievements to your credit, the Gang Canal would be a lasting memorial of your rule.'

When in the same year, Maharaja Scindia of Gwalior visited Bikaner, he was filled with surprise and admiration: 'The first impression I had on entering the borders of Bikaner was that the whole country must be a dry desert but when I first beheld the serene flow of the Gang Canal and the beautiful results it had produced in such a short time I had nothing but admiration for the Maharaja of Bikaner's genius. The canal has raised flourishing cities where villages could not thrive and reared up a countrywide garden of rich verdure and cultivation in regions where even common grass and shrubs found it an impossible struggle to survive.'

The Legislative Assembly which met in session on January 16, 1928, unanimously applauded the memorable achievement of the Maharaja, and gave standing ovations to him. The House said: 'We know not why God Indra bore so much resentment against this land, but our Maharaja Ganga Singh, humbled his pride by alighting, like Bhagirath, the Ganga at the doors of Shivpur ... The advent of Gang Canal cannot be said to be less in importance in any way than the advent of Goddess Bhagirathi. Just as Bhagirathi liberated the sons of Sagar and gave them a new life, so also this Gang Canal shall pour a new life in the people enduring the terrible hardships of the desert.'

The people of Bikaner were filled with admiration for their Maharaja, who had 'converted a barren plain into flourishing fields, teeming towns and busy markets.'

The Sikh community of the state called October 26 a 'red-letter day in the history of Bikaner.' The Settlers of the Gang Canal Colony hailed the Maharaja's successful implementation of the Project with 'great enthusiasm'. The Jain Swetamber Terapanthi Sabha, Calcutta, called the advent of the Gang Canal 'a glorious step which would be remembered for ages to come.' Similarly, the Marwari Chamber of Commerce, Calcutta, boldly announced that the success of the Project reflected the 'true spirit of patriotism' of the Maharaja. The Jat Sabha of Bikaner called the event 'the beginning of a new life – a life of prosperity and plenty.'

The Muslim subjects of the state, said that the Maharaja had changed the desert – from one form into another; and prayed by repeating the laudatory words, composed by a Urdu poet, Sa'adi:

May God grant you good fortune
And may prosperity ever smile upon you;
May the Rose of Your glory bloom for ever
And may you be a thorn in the eyes of Your enemies. Amen.

The *Times of India* pointed out in its editorial columns on the occasion of the inauguration of the Gang Canal: '... There has lately been much debate about the increasing dependence of British India and the Indian states upon one another and on the question of the future handling of affairs of common interest to them. Bikaner, led by the wise statecraft of Maharaja Ganga Singh, has brought co-operation of that kind down from the clouds of discussion and crystallised it in practical fact.'

11

The Round Table Conference

After attending the session of the League of Nations in 1924, Ganga Singh resumed his duties as Chancellor of the Chamber of Princes. Shortly afterwards in 1927, the Government of India appointed a Committee, known as Butler Committee. It was set up to enquire into the position and rights of the Princes *vis-à-vis* the British Government. The members of the committee visited Bikaner and were hosted graciously. The Maharaja discussed the case of the states with the visitors. The *Butler Committee Report*, published in 1929, was not satisfactory to the Princes. The Maharaja expressed his reaction in a private letter to his friend Field-Marshal Sir William Birdwood. He wrote: 'The *Report* like the curate's egg is good in parts. Some of their holdings and recommendations are of great importance to us and favourable, and others otherwise; and the *Report* is very halting and superficial in most cases; but we must explore the avenues left open to us and turn them to our advantage by diplomatic and political action and negotiations with the Viceroy and the British Government.'

Soon afterwards Lord Irwin, the Viceroy, announced that all Indian interests would be summoned to London at a Round Table Conference. The proposal was warmly welcomed by the Maharaja. He was also nominated as one of the representatives on behalf of the Princes to participate at the conference. Before the Maharaja began his work as one of the delegates to the

Round Table Conference, however, he received an invitation to lead the Indian delegation to the League of Nations Assembly. The Secretary of State for India, W. Wedgwood Benn, wrote: 'It is the first time that the task of leading the Indian delegation at Geneva shall be shouldered by an Indian Prince; and I can think of no more worthy of this distinction or more fitted to uphold the dignity and the traditions of his Order in this capacity than the Maharaja of Bikaner.' He proceeded to Geneva where he played an active part in the Assembly discussions.

Hardly had the League of Nations closed when the Maharaja was nominated as one of India's representatives at the Imperial Conference, which met in October 1930 in London.

Out of the Conference emerged what came to be known as the *Statute of Westminster*, the new *Magna Carta* of the Empire. Although this problem immediately concerned only the British Dominions, the Maharaja recognised its vital role in the future development of India as a part of the empire. His contributions to the deliberations of the conference were gratefully acknowledged by all the leading delegates, and the Prime Minister, Ramsay MacDonald, in a letter, sent at the close of the conference, paid a handsome tribute to him as the 'doyen amongst the representatives present from every quarter of the empire'.

The Round Table Conference

Next on the agenda was the Round Table Conference in November, 1930, in England. It was inaugurated in the House of Lords by the King-Emperor on November 12. The object of the Conference was summed up by the King in his opening speech: 'To discuss the future system of government for India and seek agreement for the guidance of his Parliament as to the foundations upon which it must stand.'

After the ceremonial opening in the House of Lords, the Conference met at St. James Palace under the chairmanship of the Prime Minister on November 12. 'The gathering was in every way unique. The big drawing-room of that ancient palace could never have witnessed a conference of equal variety and magnificence.' There were three parties to the Conference – British representatives, British Indian representatives, and the representatives of the Indian states. The British delegation had Ramsay MacDonald, the Prime Minister; Lord Sankey, Lord Chancellor; Lord Reading, a brilliant ex-Viceroy; and Sir Samuel Hoare. The British Indian representatives were: the

Aga Khan, the spiritual head of the Ismaili community and the leader of the Muslim delegates to the Conference; Mohammed Ali Jinnah and Sir Mahommed Shafi, the Muslim representatives; two women delegates, Mrs. Subbarayan and Begam Shah Nawaz; and two Hindu delegates, Sir Tej Bahadur Sapru and the Rt. Hon. V.S. Srinivasa Sastri. The Indian states delegation consisted of the Rulers of Baroda, Bhopal, Bikaner, Alwar, Dholpur, Kashmir, Nawanagar, Patiala, Rewa and Sangli; and their ministers, namely, Sir Prabhashankar Pattani, Sir Manubhai Mehta, Sardar Sahibzada Sultan Ahmed Khan, Nawab Sir Muhammad Akbar Hydari, Sir Mirza M. Ismail and Colonel K.N. Haksar. There were a total of 84 delegates – a striking gathering of rulers, statesmen and of leaders who had achieved distinction in various walks of life.

Among the British Indian delegates there was a very strong feeling that the representatives of Indian states would stand against the claim of British India and join hands with the British Government in denying self-government and Dominion status to India. The situation was fraught with suspicion and distrust. The Indian states representatives were in a state of discomfort and anxiety. 'The task therefore, of safeguarding the special position of the states', writes (Dr.) Karni Singh, 'and yet supporting the righteous claims of British India was by no means easy and it fell to Maharaja Ganga Singh's lot to do so.' Because of his experience and wisdom, the Maharaja alone was suited to meet the difficult situation that had arisen. He had the right qualities to take a definite stand at a critical moment. He had the background, given that he had put forward the conception of a federated India as a solution of the problem of the two Indias as early as 1914, before such an idea was even conceived by anyone else. His astute statesmanship led him to draw up a programme which, 'while maintaining the states in their rights for the present, would also safeguard them in the future.' The discussions in this connection were carried on at the Carlton Hotel, where the Maharaja was staying, and which became the scene of great activity. He also invited Indian leaders with differing opinions and held long discussions with them. Out of these discussions he formulated his plan of action.

The proceedings of the Round Table Conference opened with due solemnity on November 17, 1930. At the plenary session of the Conference, Sir Tej Bahadur Sapru opened the case for India, and strongly pleaded that 'freedom within our own borders as integral part of the British Commonwealth of Nations' should be granted to India. He made an appeal, clear and convincing, to the Princes to come forward to form a united India, each part of which would be autonomous, enjoying absolute independence within its borders and regulated by proper relations with the rest. His speech caused a strong and sudden burst of emotion. The whole conference was for a moment awed into silence before applause burst forth from all quarters. Hardly had the echoes of the reverberating cheers died down, when the stately Maharaja of Bikaner, rose to voice the views of the princes of India.

The first and foremost question was: what would be the fate of the conference? Everyone thought it would depend, quite certainly, upon the way of feeling and thinking of the princes on this occasion. For the Maharaja it was an important and decisive day. It was for him to say whether the princes would help in the creation of an All-India federation, or adhere to by the letter of their treaties. A feeling of uncertainty, and curiosity pervaded the atmosphere. The Maharaja however, did not allow the conference to remain long in doubt. Clearly expressing his opinion, he welcomed the idea of federation, and affirmed the faith a that in the greatness of India lay the greatness of her princes.

The Maharaja explained that the princes were not opposed to political progress in British India. He argued that while, in a political sense there were two Indias – British India and Indian states, the country was a single geographical unit and 'we are all members one of another'. The princes were Indians – 'we have our roots deep down in her historic past … everything which tends to the honour and prosperity of India has for us a vital concern. Everything which retards her prosperity and shakes the stability of her institutions retards our own growth and lowers our stature. We claim that we are on the side of progress.'

The Maharaja declared the states' keeness to participate in promoting the greater prosperity of India as a whole. 'I am convinced that we can best make that contribution through a federal system of government composed of the states and British India … An All-India federation is likely to prove the only satisfactory solution to India's problem …' The Maharaja concluded decisively, 'the Indian states would join a federation, making of India a United land.'

It was indeed a notable speech; the Maharaja's declaration was far-reaching and far-sighted. He had committed himself to a 'Federal India' as the common ideal. His plea in favour of an All-India federation as the only 'satisfactory solution', was like an unexpected heavy blow on the head of the conference and the Conservative members, but British India was happy. The reactionaries in England who had pinned their faith to the Princes were startled and amazed. The Maharaja's bold advocacy of 'federated India' gave a shock of surprise to many, who were under the pretension that the princes would throttle the conference. This declaration changed the whole situation — 'revolutionised', as Ramsay MacDonald, the Prime Minister said; and added: 'What the Princes have said has at once not only opened our vision, not only cheered our hearts, not only let us lift up our eyes and see a glowing horizon, but has simplified our duties. The princes have given a most substantial contribution in opening up the way to a really united federated India.'

The Maharaja's role at the Round Table Conference was greatly applauded. The *Morning Post* (November 18, 1930) styled the Maharaja as a 'stalwart' and 'an effective and eloquent advocate of his country'. Lord Irwin congratulated the Maharaja for his 'admirable' speech and the 'lucid and graphic' picture which he had presented of India's place and future in the empire. 'I wish', he wrote, 'I could have heard you delivering the speech at the Round Table Conference.' C.Y. Chintamani, a nationalist leader, on November 25, wrote that the Maharaja had demonstrated 'uncommon ability and unquestioned patriotism'. Sir Akbar Hydari characterised the Maharaja as 'a statesman whose knowledge has been ripened by contact with so many statesmen of the empire.'

The conference had accepted the concept of federation. The task of working out its details was assigned to a committee known as the Federal Structure Committee, with Lord Sankey as chairman. The members selected from the Indian delegation to serve on this Committee were – Maharaja Ganga Singh of Bikaner, the Nawab of Bhopal, Sir Akbar Hydari and Sir Mirza Ismail. The Maharaja of Bikaner played a prominent part in putting the views of the states before the committee and received the appreciation of Lord Sankey for the 'great part' which he had played, both in the Committee and Round Table Conference. Lord Sankey said 'from first to last the Maharaja gave us all a splendid lead' and added that his own work as the chairman of the Federal Structure Committee 'would have been doubly difficult but for the Maharaja's assistance and advice'. The Secretary of State for India said, 'there was no one who could fail to recognise the conspicuous part played by him or be blind to the transcendent importance of the decision which he took; and induced his brother princes to take the path of federation as the true road for India to follow.'

By this time Ganga Singh had risen in stature so much that the *Bombay Chronicle,* dated December 3, 1930 cited him as among the probables who could be asked to succeed Lord Irwin as His Majesty's Viceroy in India. On December 18, Peterborough, a journalist, of the *Daily Telegraph*, who had a long talk with the Maharaja, wrote: 'I found no difficulty in understanding how it is that his name is generally mentioned when any discussion arises as to the possibility of appointing an Indian as His Majesty's Viceroy.'

Rejoinder to Winston Churchill

An important development that took place after the Maharaja had chosen the path of federation was the speech delivered by Winston Churchill, the Tory fire-brand Member of Parliament, at the Indian Empire Society in London on December 11, 1930. Churchill was averse to federation or Dominion status to India. His speech was filled with invectives to the Indian cause; the purpose of which was to break the conference. He did not favour the grant of Dominion Status to India. He proclaimed that the Round Table Conference had no authority to frame a Constitution for India. He called the Round Table talk 'airy'.

Maharaja Ganga Singh read every word of Churchill's speech with minutest care, which was published in all the prominent newspapers. The Maharaja was not a person 'to pocket any insult, and more so when it was an affront to his nation.' He prepared a statesman-like statement and released it to the press. It was ably worded, with a graceful but pointed defence. He vindicated the logic and need of the Round Table Conference, and systematically demolished Churchill's speech. The opening lines of the Maharaja's rejoinder was couched in refined diplomatic language: 'Mr. Churchill is a brother soldier and an old personal friend of mine. But for my heavy official pre-occupations, I should have welcomed an opportunity of discussing the Indian problem with him, not that I am vain enough to think I could persuade him to change his views, but to clear the air. I have no intention of crossing polemical swords now; but the issues raised by his last speech are of such tremendous importance that I feel it incumbent on me to say something from the standpoint of the Empire and of India.' He said that the greatest work which the Round Table Conference could do at the time was to strive for a peaceful, contented, and prosperous, India. The stark truth of the matter was that India could no longer be held in subjection by a policy of blood and iron. India, he said, 'is an articulate country and will express and struggle for its just rights and demands'. The Round Table Conference was a good beginning, declared the Maharaja towards the building up of a 'new and free India'.

The Maharaja's reply was an appropriate rebuttal to Churchill. He received much appreciation, and letters of congratulations poured in from his well-wishers and admirers. A member of the British Parliament, Q. Hankey, wrote to the Maharaja: 'Many congratulations on your statesman-like reply to Winston Churchill. It is one of the best things that has been said or written about the Round Table Conference.' S.B. Patterson, an old friend of the Maharaja, congratulated him for his 'admirable reply to Winston Churchill's deplorable speech'. Colonel E.I.D. Gordon from South Africa, on December 18, wrote: 'I am glad that you severed Churchill's speech of 11 December so promptly and so trenchantly ... my heartiest congratulations.'

Meeting Mahatma Gandhi

The first Round Table Conference had adjourned in January 1931, to meet again in September. The delegates returned to India. The Maharaja was not happy that the premier political party, the Indian National Congress, refused to participate in the first Round Table Conference. Congress leaders, some of whom, including Mahatma Gandhi, were his 'personal friends' and for whom he had great regard, were unfortunately in jail. The Maharaja genuinely felt that without the participation of the Congress the outcome of the discussions of the Round Table Conference would not be fruitful. Together with some of his British Indian friends, he left no stone unturned to impress upon the government of importance of seeking the participation of the Congress. The Maharaja started his efforts as soon as he landed in Bombay on February 5, 1931. The main question that exercised his mind was what the response of Mahatma Gandhi, Jawaharlal Nehru and the Congress on the issue of their participation in the next Round Table Conference was likely to be. Shortly before the Maharaja reached Bombay on February 5, he had an informal meeting in his cabin with Sir Tej Bahadur Sapru, V.S. Srinivasa Sastri and M.R. Jayakar to consider how best to proceed 'to combat the Congress in the event of their not being amenable to reason'. To them it seemed that Mahatma Gandhi's attitude was on the whole 'hopeful'. Immediately after landing at Bombay, the Maharaja held discussions at his residence (Devi Bhawan) with Sapru, Sastri, Sir Phiroze Sethna, Ramnik Lall Mody, Sir

Chimanlal Setalvad, Sir Purshotamdas Thakurdas, Sir Chunnilal Mehta and Seth Lalji Narainji – they held the view that the Viceroy be requested that the political prisoners who were not guilty of serious offences should be released, so that the conducive atmosphere for negotiations with Mahatma Gandhi could develop. The Maharaja on February 6 wrote to Lord Irwin: 'I hope that wiser counsels may prevail, specially after Mahatma Gandhi and Jawaharlal Nehru have seen Tej Bahadur Sapru today, who left Bombay for Allahabad, and, I hope, also Sastri and Jayakar in the near future.' The Maharaja's aim was that the great achievements already gained by the Round Table Conference should be brought to fruitful conclusion, and that could be possible if the Congress abandoned its path of 'obdurateness'. Dr. Karni Singh writes that 'in the end, these efforts succeeded; the Congress leaders were released, a meeting took place between the Viceroy and Mahatma Gandhi and ultimately the Congress decided to participate in the deliberations, selecting Mahatma Gandhi as its sole representative.'

Even then there were hitches at the time of Mahatma Gandhi's departure to England; 'but at every step the Maharaja did his best, by informal discussions with the Viceroy, Mahatma Gandhi and other personal friends of his in the Congress as well as others, to ensure Congress participation in the Second Round Table Conference.' According to Dr. Karni Singh, 'Gandhiji paid a visit to Devi Bhawan, the residence of Maharaja Ganga Singh in Bombay, on June 10, 1931, and the two had a long heart to heart talk. During these talks the Maharaja offered to look after the passage arrangement for Gandhiji's visit to England and Gandhiji jocularly called the Maharaja the purveyor of steamer passages. The passage was later actually arranged through the Maharaja's Household Department with special accommodation for Gandhiji's kitchen on the after-deck on *S.S. Mooltan*.'

On July 22, 1931, the Maharaja wrote to Mahatma Gandhi expressing his pleasure at finding his name included amongst the new members of the Federal Structure Committee of the Round Table Conference.

Second Round Table Conference

The Second Round Table Conference commenced its work in September 1931. The main task of constitution-making was with the Federal Structure Committee which now also included Mahatma Gandhi and Pandit Madan Mohan Malaviya.

The meetings of the Federal Structure Committee were presided over by its Chairman, Lord Sankey, the Lord Chancellor. In the absence of Maharaja Gaekwad of Baroda and the Nawab of Bhopal, the Maharaja of Bikaner expressed words of welcome to the new members of the committee, and particularly to Mahatma Gandhi, who represented the most important political party in India. Similarly he welcomed his old friend, Pandit Madan Mohan Malaviya. He pleaded that his faith in the federation remained unaltered, and he considered federation the only alternative which could help India at that juncture. Federation, for him, was the ideal for British India and the states. His motto was: 'Federation with honour and safety to the states.'

The Maharaja was in agreement with the views of Mahatma Gandhi who had said that no one had the right to dictate to the states what they should do, or what they should not do. There should in all matters between British India and the states be a spirit of reasonable give-and-take; otherwise, in the absence of it, ultimately fruitless quarrels would arise and 'we shall not be able to come to any definite scheme of federation'.

Though the Maharaja attended the Second Round Table Conference, his contribution was not as conspicuous as in the First Round Table Conference. With the help of Maharaja Bhupendra Singh of Patiala, he succeeded in achieving unity among the princes at the Delhi Conference of princes and ministers early in 1932. This conference, which led to complete agreement between the two parties, laid the foundation of a consistent policy on the part of the princes by defining the essential safeguards under which they were prepared to enter the federation.

The Government of India Act, 1935

The main task having been achieved and principles adopted, it was not essential for the Princes to take part in the third Round Table Conference, held in September, 1932. For the Joint Select Committee, important ministers of the states visited England and among them was Sir Manubhai Mehta, the Prime Minister of Bikaner.

The White Paper relating to the proposed constitutional reforms, which emanated after nearly two years' deliberations, was published in March, 1933. The Princes felt that the scheme envisaged in the White Paper was greatly at variance with the one contemplated at the Round Table Conference. A rift had occurred, meanwhile, amongst the princely order on the question of representation on the Federal Legislatures. The British Government had also strengthened its position and hardened its stand against the Indian National Congress and the Princes. The British Government adhered to the view that if the decisions regarding the form of federation were to be fair to all parties, they could not accept the view of any one particular section and that 'His Majesty's Government were concerned only in obtaining a fair and reasonable settlement.' The result was the *Government of India Act, 1935*, and the revised draft of the *Instrument of Accession*.

The *Government of India Act 1935*, was put into practice partially in 1937 – only the provincial part of the constitution was implemented, and the federal part was put into abeyance. The federation as envisaged by the *Act of 1935* had belied the hopes of the Maharaja. Etched with limitations and restrictions, the federal scheme fell short of the Maharaja's expectations. The *Act* contained many financial, administrative and other provisions which were contrary to the spirit of a true federation. The Congress was also dissatisfied with the scheme of federation as laid down in the *Act*. In addition, the attitude of some important Princes was lukewarm. The result was the constitutional impasse.

The Maharaja's faith in the imperative need of ordered political growth remained unshaken. Reiterating his belief in federation, the Maharaja said: 'I have for many years been a staunch believer in a federal constitution for India, which would unite as equal partners the states of India already sovereign, and the British Indian Provinces recently made autonomous. To that faith I adhere today.'

The lofty vision of a United India, each state true to itself and to British India as well, welded and fused together in a comradeship in peace and war, one 'Federated India' – that was the vision that flit before the Maharaja's mind's eye. No wonder he was the first and staunchest supporter of the new-born ideal of a new age. He had acclaimed with conviction, his unshaken faith in the cause espoused. He had chosen the path of a true federation, of which, he was a great architect – his massive designs of federalism, developed so assiduously by him, shall ever be remembered in the constitutional history of India. Appreciating the Maharaja's role, the Maharaja of Nepal in May 1935, wrote: 'Sir Ganga Singh is a great man whom the empire, the nation, and his friends shall never forget.'

12

Momentous Occasions

$\mathcal{G}$anga Singh resolved to settle down to the work of internal administration. He now concentrated his attention on his own state, and initiated wide-ranging building and developmental programmes. Simultaneously, a number of administrative reforms were also undertaken. The land revenue and taxation was reorganised. Medical relief and education received his special attention. The criminal investigation and police departments were reconstituted in 1934. The Maharaja opened a chain of schools, hospitals, police stations and other public institutions in the canal area. The economic resources of the state were further developed. More powers were given to local bodies and the Legislative Assembly in order to strengthen peoples' participation. The judicial system was brought up to modern standards. The state indeed showed a remarkable transformation; it changed beyond recognition. When the Nawab of Palanpur visited the state in March, 1934, he wrote: 'What a change I saw in Bikaner as I had not been there for sometime! Comparing with what I saw 22 years ago, it has become a very fine and big city now.'

The Family

Maharajkumar Sadul Singh, the heir-apparent, had come of age on September 7, 1920. The Maharaja had associated him directly with the administration; and appointed him chief minister and president of the state Council. The Maharajkumar had worked as chief minister for five years (1920-25). This provided him enough administrative training.

On April 18, 1922, Maharajkumar Sadul Singh was married to Princess Sudarshan Kumari, the daughter of Maharaja Vankatraman Singh and the sister of Sir Gulab Singh, the ruler of the state of Rewa. On April 21, 1923, Yuvrani Sudarshan Kumari gave birth to a daughter – Princess Sushil Kanwar. The following two children were sons – Prince Karni Singh born on April 21, 1924, and Prince Amar Singh on December 11, 1925. Princess Sushil Kanwar married Maharajkumar Bhagwati Singh of Udaipur in 1940. The Maharaja was delighted at this matrimonial alliance of his granddaughter and, said: 'I am so happy that relations which had existed between our dynasties for generations have once again been revived in our life time.'

The Maharaja had a great affection for his grandchildren, especially Prince Karni Singh, whom he gave a pet-name 'the soldier boy'. He had lavished his love and affection on his grandchildren, and in turn was loved by them. To their education and training he devoted infinite care, especially to the proper upbringing of Prince Karni Singh, the elder son of the heir-apparent. The Maharaja found great happiness in watching his grandchildren grow up in the true traditions of his house. This happy domestic life provided him with the necessary counterpoise for the hard work which had so occupied his attention.

A Tragedy in the Family

The year 1932 had opened badly for the Maharaja. His second son, Prince Bijey Singh, a young man of outstanding ability, drive, and exceptional promise, died 'as a result of a mishap from a gun'. It was a great tragedy which touched the Maharaja deeply, because 'the Prince was one cast in the very image of his father and held in especial affection by him'. For many years he had been the Maharaja's constant companion and had accompanied him to the League of Nations, the Imperial Conference, and the first Round Table Conference. He had been adopted by the Maharaja's mother into the family of Maharaj Lall Singh, 'when by giving both its sons in succession to the royal family had been threatened with extinction.' His death was a great shock to the Maharaja, who could not reconcile himself for a pretty long time of this irreparable loss, but his 'stern sense of duty gave him courage to continue.'

Maharaja Ganga Singh of Bikaner in his ceremonial dress.

Maharaja Ganga Singh and the Princes at the Huzoor steps awaiting the arrival of the wedding party, of the marriage of his granddaughter, Princess Sushil Kanwar.

Maharaja Ganga Singh on the occasion of his granddaughter's marriage, is seen here with the bridegroom, Maharaj Kumar Bhagwat Singh of Udaipur.

Maharaja Ganga Singh bidding farewell to Maharana Bhopal Singh of Udaipur and the wedding party after the marriage of his granddaughter.

Maharaja Ganga Singh (sitting second from left) on the occasion of conferring of the Honoris Cause' Doctorate by the Osmania University, Hyderabad.

Maharaja Ganga Singh delivering the Convocation address at the Benaras Hindu University in 1940

Maharaja Ganga Singh with Prince Karni Singh, Kr. Jagmal Singh of Bagseu, A.D.C., Kr. Rawat Singh of Rampura, A.D.C., and others, at Cairo, in 1941.

Maharaja Ganga Singh on his visit to London for the coronation of H.M. King George the VI.

The world-famous Bikaner Camel Corps (Ganga Risala), ready for a Military Review.

Maharaja Ganga Singh at the Shivpur Head, Gang Canal. His grandson, Prince Karni Singh, took this photograph.

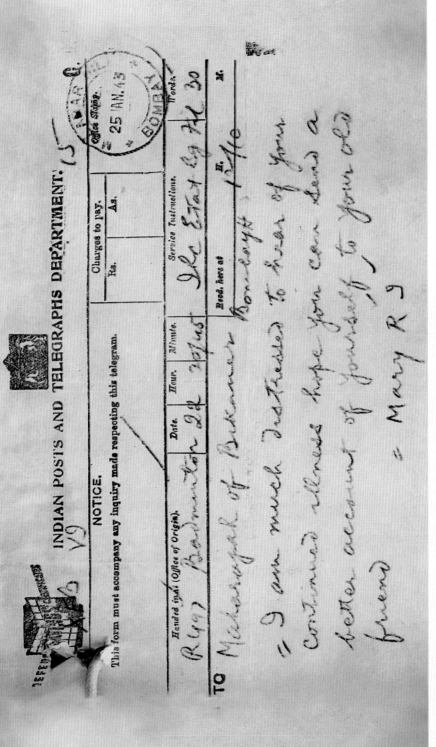

A facsimile of last telegram from Queen Mary to Maharaja Ganga Singh sent on 25th January 1943.

A view of the Lallgarh Palace, Bikaner.

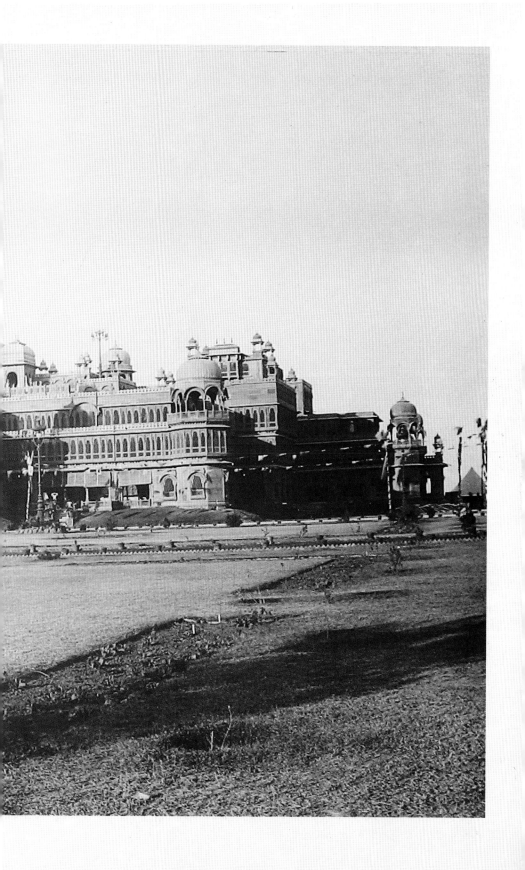

Maharaja Ganga Singh leaving Cairo for India after his trip to Middle East War theatre, 3rd December 1941.

The Silver Wedding Anniversary

1933 witnessed the completion of 25 years of married life for Maharaja Ganga Singh and Maharani Bhatianiji Saheba, his only surviving wife. Maharani Bhatianiji had rendered great service – unostentatiously and unceasingly – to the state and its people, and particularly its women and children. She was widely known as the 'First Lady in Bikaner'. She maintained the high standards and fine traditions of the ancient House of Bikaner, and was also the true embodiment of a Rajput Princess. A model wife and mother, she proved herself a worthy helpmate, consistently sharing the responsibilities of the state. She was always by the Maharaja's side, cheering him on in times of difficulty and stress and anxiety, providing a constant source of inspiration and encouragement.

Maharani Bhatianiji was famous for her philanthropy. She made substantial offerings from her own money at sacred shrines and places of pilgrimage. Her numerous charities and bounties to the poor were well known. She gave donations towards the construction of public parks, hospitals, etc.; and undertook welfare activities for people, within and outside the state, out of her own privy purse. As vice-president of the Girls Guides Council for Rajputana and Central India, with a genuine interest in women's health and education, she frequented girls schools and women's hospitals. She was the main driving power behind the establishment of Maharani Nobles Girls School, which started in 1927.

During the terrible floods at Gajner in August 1933, when great devastation was wrought in the Magra district and in the adjoining tracts of the state, Maharani Bhatianiji, who at the time was at Gajner, was indefatigable in her personal exertion and efforts to save lives. She had herself directed rescue operations from early in the morning of the August 8, when the floods were at their worst. She was personally instrumental in having rescued several people who were marooned on the house-tops, surrounded by deep water – operations which, in the face of a terrific gale and strong current of flowing water, were frought with danger.

Maharani Bhatianiji had a great sense of duty. During the period of the world-wide financial, agricultural and trade depressions, she had declined, for a number of years, to draw any increase in her civil list allowance, sanctioned to her in 1928.

There was yet another important trait in the character of Maharani Bhatianiji which earned for her profound admiration and respect, extending far beyond the boundaries of the state. The Maharaja's first wife, had died in 1906, leaving behind two motherless children – Princess Chand Kanwar born in 1899 and Prince Sadul Singh born in 1902. The Maharaja's mother had expired in 1909. He had married Bhatianiji in May 1908, and within 20 months of his marriage, he was able, with the utmost implicit confidence, to entrust the full charge of his motherless children to Maharani Bhatianiji – in spite of her having sons of her own. This sacred trust Bhatianiji had faithfully discharged up to the time of the heir-apparent's coming of age.

The married life of the Maharaja and Maharani had been one of exceptional happiness. The silver wedding anniversary was therefore a day of great and genuine rejoicing. The celebrations were conducted without ostentatios display in a spirit of profound thankfulness. At the banquet in honour of the occasion, the Maharaja broke through his ordinary reticence in matters connected with his family life and paid a generous tribute to his consort. 'She had been a safe repository of my confidence', said the Maharaja, 'and she has shared with me to the fullest extent all my great burdens and responsibilities. And in all this she has, whilst emulating the example set forth by my beloved and revered mother of not interfering or meddling in state affairs, nobly seconded my efforts in suppressing political intrigues and party factions in the state and at our csourt.'

The British Government also in due time recognised the exceptional position of Maharani Bhatianiji among the consorts of Indian Rulers, and His Majesty awarded her the much coveted decoration of the Crown of India, an order which was given but rarely and only in cases of outstanding merit or achievement. Since this order was instituted by Queen Victoria in 1878, there were only seventeen Indian recipients – of these fourteen were Indian princesses and the remaining three were British Indian ladies of distinction. The Maharaja was very proud of his wife's public recognition by the Imperial Government. She was the second of the wives of the rulers of the premier states of Rajputana to have this honour ever since the institution of this order.

Another honour of great distinction that Maharani Bhatianiji had received in 1938 was the degree of Doctor of Letters, *honoris causa*, conferred upon her by the Benares Hindu University. In honouring the Maharani, the university had taken consideration of her eminent position, high attainments and the interest she had taken in the advancement of women education.

Health Problems

In 1933 Ganga Singh developed a cyst in his throat for which he was operated upon at Bombay in June. A regular board of doctors had examined him. The board consisted of the Bikaner State doctors, and besides them, Dr. Bacha, a surgeon, and Dr. Bharoacha, the physician, at Bombay. On June 23, the Maharaja wrote to Colonel G.D. Ogilvie, Agent to the Governor-General in Rajputana that 'till yesterday I had reluctantly to imitate Mahatma Gandhi to a certain (forced) extent; and was absolutely on liquid diet – infernally hungry the whole time; and still am so! – getting semi-sloppy food since then; and don't know when I shall be allowed decent food again.' However, the operation was successful, and with malignancy ruled out, the Maharaja arrived home in Bikaner on July 4.

A Statue of the Maharaja

The people of Bikaner decided to appreciate the work of their ruler. They wanted to create an equestrian statue of the Maharaja who had brought the Gang Canal and bestowed manifold benefits on them , in the Public Park. The funds for the statue were subscribed by the chiefs and nobles, the *seths* and *sahukars*, and other classes and communities.

The statue – 9 feet 8 inches high – was the handiwork of the well-known Italian sculptor, Professor Carestiate of the Royal Academy of Venice. Its total height, together with its pedestal of Bikaner pink sandstone, was 18 feet. The background was designed by H. Foster King of the firm of Messrs. Gregson, Batley and King, Architects, Bombay. The Maharaja is depicted in the well-known uniform of his Camel Corps, the famous Ganga Risala. The statue stands facing the fort and immediately opposite the principal entrance to the public park. The total expenditure on the statue, including its transportation and installation, came to Rs. 55,737 and 9 annas.

On February 24, 1934, Lord Willingdon visited Bikaner personally to unveil the statue. Sir Manubhai Mehta, Prime Minister of the state, in his speech on the occasion recounted the varied achievements of the Maharaja and said that his greatest work was the construction of the Gang Canal, which had brought down the waters of the distant Sutlej to the arid plains of Bikaner. It was in this connection especially that 'his name and fame would go down to future generations as the modern 'Bhagirath', who once again brought down the celestial Ganga from the heavens above to this terrestrial region down below.' With the hereditary instinct of a prince and the military traditions of the Rathore House behind him, the Maharaja was a born soldier. Sir Manubhai Mehta called him 'the soldier-statesman', and fittingly quoted the following words of the eminent poet, Wordsworth:

He holds no parley with unmanly fears;
Where duty bids, he confidently steers;
Faces a thousand dangers at her call,
And, trusting in his God, surmounts them all.

Sir Manubhai Mehta then requested Lord Willingdon to unveil the statue. 'May this fine piece of art ever stand out as a beacon transmitting the fame of this benevolent ruler as an echo and a light unto eternity.'

At the unveiling ceremony, Lord Willingdon praised the Maharaja's outstanding services to the people of his state. The state possessed a vista of fine buildings and public gardens – well-kept roads, widespread electrification, many works of domestic, commercial and economic value; hospitals, schools, administrative blocks, palatial residences and neatly laid-out bungalows – and, above all, a great canal system. He asked the assembled audience that 'as you note this evidence of one man's rule, you will perhaps turn your eyes with me to that Fort which stands before us'. 'The spirit that lives in that fort', said the Viceroy, 'must surely know that His Highness Sir Ganga Singh of Bikaner has not betrayed his ancestors, nor the glories of the past; that, that fort, steeped, in its slumbering beauty, in the great traditions of bygone years, does not lie humbled by the surroundings of a later day: that what went into the building of that fort was not in vain. Such, Your Highness, is your monument.'

The Maharaja was a man, said the Viceroy, who had played a prominent part in guiding the destinies of the good ship-India-through the dangerous channels of the past 20 years. There had been times when she was driven from her course and was tossed on the tempestuous seas, but the Maharaja was able to guide her course through that stormy passage. 'When the harbour is reached and we lie in calm waters, the name of Sir Ganga Singh of Bikaner will ever be remembered.'

Lord Brabourne, the Governor of Bombay, a good friend of the Maharaja, along with Lady Brabourne visited Bikaner in December, 1934. In a letter of thanks to the Maharaja on December 31, Lord Brabourne, wrote: 'The more I look back on our stay with you the more pleasant memories do re-appear – the shooting which was the greatest possible though it left me with the certain knowledge that I can't shoot. All your beautiful things in Bikaner – thank you a thousand times.'

From Bikaner, Lord and Lady Brabourne had gone to the State of Palanpur, where the Nawab was their host. On January 1, 1935, the Nawab of Palanpur wrote to the Maharaja about their visit to his state. He stated that Lord and Lady Brabourne as soon as they arrived and before they shook hands, 'first gave me Your Highness' messages.' They had spent nearly an hour in the Palace and took a keen interest in studying and seeing everything. In the big dinning hall Lord Brabourne saw the oil paintings of the Nawab's ancestors. The Nawab wrote: 'We began to talk about the sword given by Emperor Akbar. I was at first surprised as to how he knew it; but then he told me what all Your Highness had told him. What a kindly act of great affection! Could anybody else in the world do that? I was so tremendously touched and now I can't express half of what my feelings were then. This is not the first occasion. Your Highness has been continuously manifesting your magnanimous heart in a variety of ways. And so I often give out to people that I am what you have made me. All my education is received from that wonderful college of Lallgarh.' The Nawab of Palanpur had a great faith in the Maharaja and he regarded him as his elder brother, and Bikaner as his 'second home'.

Ganga Singh's phenomenal capacity to cultivate friends resulted in many visitors annually. His cordial warmth and hospitality were legendary. In March 1935, the former ruler of Greece – King George visited Bikaner. He characterised Bikaner as 'a progressive state' whose ruler had worked a lot for the 'enlightenment' of his people.

October 1935, Colonel George Ogilvie, Agent to the Governor-General in Rajputana, visited the state. On his arrival in Bikaner, he was indisposed and very well looked after by the Maharaja. After leaving the capital Ogilvie wrote: 'I can never forget the Maharaja's kindness and sympathy with me in my afflictions … I could not have found a more comfortable place than Lallgarh Palace to take care of me …'

The Maharaja of Travancore who came to Bikaner in March 1936, said that 'the single-minded devotion and unparalleled energy' of the Maharaja had transformed the state in every respect.

Silver Jubilee of King George V

It was in July 1930, that Stanley Baldwin, acting prime minister, announced in the House of Commons, that the king had approved of the prime minister's recommendation that the 25th anniversary of His Majesty's accession falling on May 6, 1935, be fittingly celebrated as the Silver Jubilee. King George V had expressly desired that the celebrations should be as simple as possible, avoiding all undue expenditure. That was the first occasion in English history when the King had celebrated his Silver Jubilee. The Secretary of State for the Home Department had intimated the king's desire that celebrations should be on a local basis and that His Majesty's subjects should, wherever practicable, observe the occasion near their homes. The Bikaner Legislative Assembly in March had passed a resolution; tendered a message of congratulations to Their Majesties on the occasion of their Silver Jubilee. The jubilee was celebrated in Bikaner with a royal salute, parade of the State Army, and thanks-giving ceremony at the temple of Sri Lakshmi Narayanji, with traditional forms of entertainment. The jubilee celebrations were performed in London from May 6 to 18, 1935. No military detachments from overseas were invited in order to minimise expense. The Maharaja of Bikaner left for England in April, 1935, along with an entourage of five. He had been the honorary aide-de-camp of the king for close upon thirty-three years at the time. No Indian princes other than those attached to the staff of the king were invited. The Maharaja took part in all the ceremonials connected with the jubilee. His participation in the celebrations, apart from being an official honour, was also an act of personal homage and thanksgiving, especially as the Maharaja had the feeling that in view of King-Emperor's failing health 'he might not in this life have a further opportunity of seeing his emperor'.

Demise of King George V

The demise of King George V in 1936 was a great shock to the Maharaja. The Bikaner Legislative Assembly expressed their sympathy and profound sorrow at the sad demise of the King-Emperor George V, who had become a personal friend. The King-Emperor in his correspondence with the Maharaja had always addressed him as 'My dear friend', and on the envelope always wrote: 'To my friend, the Maharaja of Bikaner.'

Coronation Ceremony

In May 1937 the Maharaja went again to England to take part in the coronation ceremony of their Majesties King George VI and Queen-Empress

Elizabeth. The Maharaja's coronation present to the king was a miniature statue of Rao Bika, the founder of the Bikaner State; and to the Queen Elizabeth, it was a mauve enamel and gold mounted strut clock. On behalf of the Maharani of Bikaner, the Maharaja had presented to the Queen a jade and a silver stationery stand. The King-Emperor re-appointed the Maharaja as his honorary aide-de-camp. After his return from England the Maharaja got engaged in his Golden Jubilee, an ensuing event of great historic importance for himself and for the people of Bikaner.

Ties with the Royal Family of Great Britain

The Maharaja of Bikaner had developed strong ties of friendship with the royal family of Great Britain. His connections with King Edward VII and Queen Alexandra had started from 1902. King Edward VII had a high appreciation of the Maharaja's command over English – both written and spoken.

Prince and Princess of Wales (afterwards King George V and Queen Mary) both were close friends of the Maharaja. They had first visited Bikaner in 1905 after which their friendship had blossomed and they were in regular correspondence over a wide range of subjects. After his first visit to Bikaner in 1905, the then Prince of Wales, on November 27, 1905, had written to the Maharaja: 'How extremely happy the Princess and I have been in the enjoyment of your charming society and most kind hospitality!' The Prince acknowledged that the friendship between him and the Maharaja had been 'firmly cemented'. Again, on March 1, 1907, the Prince wrote: 'I had received the framed photographs of yourself and your children which the Princess and I are delighted to possess, and for which we are most grateful.'

On occasions, Prince of Wales, in his letters to the Maharaja, used to express his views, very frankly, on Indian political situation as it existed then. His faith in the Maharaja is revealed from his letter dated February 11, 1910, in which he stated: 'I will try to confine any references I make on political affairs to separate sheets, which I hope you will always destroy when read.'

The exchange of correspondence between the Maharaja and King George V had multiplied after his coronation in 1911. King George V paid a second visit to Bikaner in 1921. He had a great admiration for the Maharaja and highly valued his friendship.

The coronation of King George VI and Queen Empress Elizabeth was held in May 1937. Maharaja Ganga Singh maintained the same level of friendship with Their Majesties. When the Maharaja fell ill and underwent an operation in January 1943, the Queen Empress was greatly worried about his health. On January 25, 1943, she sent a telegram which stated: 'I am much distressed to hear of your continued illness, and hope you can send a better account of yourself, to your old friend.' The royal family of Great Britain had always regarded Maharaja Ganga Singh as their trusted friend.

The tradition of friendship between the Royal House of Bikaner and the Royal Family of Great Britain was duly maintained by the successors of Maharaja Ganga Singh, namely, Maharaja Sadul Singh and Maharaja Karni Singh; and now Princess Rajyashree Kumari Bikaner – the great grand daughter of Maharaja Ganga Singh. When Princess Rajyashree Kumari Bikaner sent a message of congratulations to Her Majesty on the occasion of her Silver Jubilee in 1977, the Private Secretary to the Queen of England in his letter dated March 24, replied: 'The Queen remembers your great grandfather very well and, as a child, greatly admired him.' This illustration is quite useful as it demonstrates nearly a century old ties of friendship between the Royal House of Bikaner and the Royal Family of Great Britain. This, indeed, is a chapter of sincere friendship, and unflappable, between two glorious royal houses – one of the East and the other of the West.

13

The Golden Jubilee

The most memorable event of 1937 was the Golden Jubilee of Maharaja Ganga Singh. The 15 anniversary of his accession to the Throne of his ancestors, according to Hindu *Samvat,* a Hindu calander, was on September 18. Long before the event there was a thrill of anticipation as the people of Bikaner prepared to give to their Maharaja due homage. A public meeting, representing all classes and creeds, was held at the Ganga Theatre in the Capital on September 3, 1936, which was presided over by Raja of Mahajan, a premier noble of the state. This meeting decided to celebrate the golden jubilee in a most befitting manner. Colonel Maharaj Bhairon Singh was selected as President of the Peoples' General Committee; and Major Mandhata Singh, Finance Minister as Chairman of the Executive Committee. The Executive Committee was given the direct charge of all arrangements which were chosen by the General Committee. In addition, G.T. Hamilton Harding was appointed the Director of Golden Jubilee arrangements so far as the state functions and entertainments were concerned. This was different from the celebrations and arrangements which were made by the Peoples' Golden Jubilee Celebration Committee.

The state treasury gave Rs. 500,000 for arranging a series of festivities throughout the state and entertaining in the capital the Viceroy, the

Maharaja's friends, and many other distinguished guests from all parts of India. At the same time, the Peoples' Committee had invited contributions to a Golden Jubilee Fund. No sooner had the fund been opened than money began to pour in from all sides. Knowing the character of their ruler the people knew well that he would never make use of the money thus voluntarily offered to him for other purposes than to benefit the people themselves. In fact, although the money was handed over to the Maharaja to do with it as he liked, not a single pie of it was used as a contribution to the cost of the jubilee celebrations; the whole of the fund was enlarged by grants from the state treasury and from the Maharaja's privy purse. It was utilised to finance a number of important public charities.

While wealthy men contributed considerable sums, ordinary people, not to be outdone, sent in modest contributions. The fund-raising demonstrated the people's devotion to their king.

At one time it appeared as if the festivities would have to be called off, owing to a prolonged break in the monsoon. Throughout the month of August there were no rains. The situation was precarious, distress seemed imminent. The Maharaja was considering abandoning the jubilee celebrations; he began to make the usual preparations for fighting the dreaded calamity by measures of relief. Relentless rain throughout the state, at the beginning of September, saved the situation. The Maharaja fixed September 18 for the beginning of the state Jubilee celebrations; in haste preparations for the jubilee were resumed.

The people from the rural areas thronged to the city. The population of the capital was more than doubled by the arrival of nearly a hundred thousand visitors, both from the districts of the state and from neighbouring states and provinces, who had come to witness the great event and take their part in the festivities. The city was transformed into a fairy realm with elaborate decorations. There were victory arches erected everywhere. One arch built by the Army was decorated with rifles, swords, shields and daggers. It bore the arresting motto, 'Ever Ready, Ever Loyal'. Two arches, erected by the merchant community of Bikaner, were inscribed with mottos studded with gold sovereigns; the silver frames were built with rupee coins. One of the leading mercantile families had erected an arch covered with panels of solid silver, showing in relief various scenes of local activity. All the crafts and trade had constructed their own arches. 'The jewellers' arch was covered with gold and silver ornaments; and that of the green-grocers was decorated with the choicest fruits and vegetables. The arches presented a fine spectacle, never seen before in the parched sands of the Thar.

The main streets and public places were lined with banners and flags in red and orange, the state colours, celebrating the glorious traditions of the House of Bikaner. Many private houses were adorned with streamers, and carried such mottos as: 'Long Live Our Gracious Maharaja', 'Silver Leads to Gold and Gold to Diamond', 'May We Celebrate Diamond Jubilee'. In the evenings the principal buildings and monuments were brilliantly illuminated by coloured lights, nearly sixty thousand lamps had been specially installed for this purpose. At night, flood-lighting threw into prominence the magnificent architectural detail of the redstone palaces and public buildings, the ancient fort and palaces rose as magnificent silhouettes against the sky. Brightly coloured fountains played in the garden of Lallgarh Palace, seat of the Maharaja, in all public places great lotus flowers, carrying crimson and golden lights, floated in placid pools of water.

In the gardens of both the Fort and Lallgarh Palace the trees were decorated with thousands of lamps of yellow, green, red and deep blue. Visitors and locals thronged the city, barefoot and on decorated *ekkas*. Many villagers rode on camels, decorated with ornaments. Indigenous Bikaneri regalia and pomp was at its peak.

The Maharaja's Message

The first stage of Golden Jubilee celebrations of the Maharaja had started on Saturday, September 18, 1937. It was for the first time in history that the Golden Jubilee of a Rathore ruler was celebrated. The celebrations opened with the Maharaja's personal message of love and good wishes to his people of all creeds, classes and communities. He said that from the time he came of age, he had placed his duty to his state and to his subjects above everything else. The peoples' well-being had occupied the foremost place in his thoughts and deeds. He prayed three times a day for peoples' welfare, happiness and prosperity and that they be spared the ravages of famine, scarcity and pestilence. He thanked God for his long years of service to the state over which he had been ordained to rule. The Maharaja said: 'All my efforts have been directed to doing everything that was possible, and within the resources of our state, for advancing your moral and material interests, for your education and health and for further improving your economic conditions, especially through irrigation and the network of railways which now traverse the state.'

King-Emperor's Message

The same day the Maharaja had received a cablegram from the King-Emperor George VI in which he conveyed his warm congratulations. 'I gladly avail myself of this notable occasion', said the King-Emperor, 'to send my sincere wishes both for your own welfare and for the future prosperity and happiness of your state which I know that Your Highness has so much at heart.'

The Viceroy's Message

Lord Linlithgow, the Viceroy, summed up the great and varied services that the Maharaja had rendered to his sate, to India, and to the Empire. He wrote, 'during that long period Your Highness has manifested in the highest degree the qualities of a ruler, soldier and statesman and I know well how deeply indebted Bikaner is to you for the unfailing devotion which you have shown to the interests of your state.' The Viceroy's evaluation was widely shared. *The Times*, London, in its editorial wrote: 'Among the Maharaja's wide circle of friends those who know him best will most concur in Lord Linlithgow's judgement that the Maharaja has manifested in the highest degree the qualities of ruler, soldier, and statesman.' Among Ganga Singh's many achievements, his statesmanship had a marked influence on the shaping of constitutional reforms. He was 'the moving spirit' in shaping the Chamber of Princes. His success in making Bikaner 'a modern and model state' would be ever remembered. Similarly, *The National Call*, Delhi, in its editorial wrote that the Viceroy's summing up of the varied achievements of the Maharaja were 'judicious', and in any way, not an 'over-statement' of the case. The editor commented: 'We believe we are not doing an injustice to any other Indian Prince, when we affirm that the Maharaja of Bikaner, in virtue of his individual achievements, stands head and shoulders over the average run of Indian rulers.' The editor wished the Maharaja would be spared for many more years to rule wisely and well over a progressive Bikaner.

Of the same sort was the comment of *The Leader*, Allahabad, whose editor stated that Maharaja Ganga Singh could be 'compared favourably with some of the best and greatest ruling princes of the last hundred years'. He had a 'larger patriotism' and served the motherland as a 'true-hearted' son. The editor added: 'A student of the past and the present of Bikaner, the past going back to some hundreds of years, would find it impossible not to give his admiration freely to Maharaja Sir Ganga Singh for the tremendous progress he has been instrumental in effecting in the condition of the state. A man of tireless energy, a fertile brain rich in constructive ideas, an idealist who takes constant care never to forget that he must be practical, … His Highness has failed nowhere and at no time to leave the impress of his dynamic personality on every person with whom he came into touch.'

The jubilee celebrations of the Maharaja's beneficent reign was heralded by the firing of a royal salute of 101 salvos from the batteries posted in all the four sides of the capital. In accordance with custom, religious ceremonies started the celebrations. In the morning a state procession marched from the Fort to the temple of Sri Lakshmi Narayanji. The leading elephant carried the state flag. It was followed by Units of the Bikaner Army, the Camel Corps, the Mounted Lancers and the Infantry, all in their magnificent full dress uniforms. There were also three elephants which carried the *Mahi Maratib* – the insignia conferred by the Mughal emperors on the rulers of Bikaner, which signified the great territorial sovereigns of the country. Other elephants followed with the state regalia; after the thirteen musical instruments, the silver palanquins, bullock chariots and led horses had passed, the Maharaja's own party followed on more elephants. The Maharaja was on a magnificent ten-foot elephant, bedecked in blue and silver velvet and a variety of jewels and ornaments. The Maharaja himself, seated in the golden *howdah*, wore a white *Durbar* Coat, a saffron-coloured turban, all his Orders, decorations and war medals.

The streets were lined by a dense crowd, and along the entire route of the procession, a distance of over five miles (both ways), every window, balcony and house-top was occupied. The progress of the ruler was accompanied by remarkable outbursts of enthusiasm. All classes of people – Hindus, Muslims, Sikhs and Christians – gave the Maharaja a standing ovation. Women sang songs of rejoicing and blessings. Flowers were showered on Ganga Singh, who was evidently moved by the enthusiasm of his people.

The large courtyard of the temple was filled with thousands of men, women and children. Here the Maharaja alighted and entered amid deafening cheers, to perform the religious rites. As he stood in front of the Image of Sri Lakshmi Narayanji, thoughts and memories of the past 50 years flitted through his mind. He offered his prayer and deep gratitude to the family deity for the love, loyalty and attachment of his people.

Next followed the *Tuladan* ceremony in which the Maharaja, according to ancient custom, is weighed against gold for purposes of charity. The weighing took place in a pair of huge scales set up in the *Yagyashala*, a fine building of red stone which stands in the grounds of Lallgarh Palace. The Maharaja's weight was 2 *monds* and 22 *sers* (14 st., 8 lbs). To this was added the weight of his *poshak* (dress), jewellery and sword, which was 5 *sers*. As such 2 *monds*, 27 srs of gold was required. The price of gold at the time was Rs. 35 a *tola*.

To the chanting of Sanskrit hymns by the priests, the Maharaja took his seat on one of the scales, while ingots of pure gold from the state treasury were slowly piled upon the other. The scales balanced when gold to the value of Rs. 3,02,912 or approximately £ 25,000 had been heaped up.

Then the Maharani and the Prince each were weighed in silver. The silver was valued at Rs. 11,658 for the Maharani; and Rs. 3,608 for the Prince. The amount spent on the gold and silver *Tuladan* was substantially from the Maharaja's privy purse. Both sums were added to the Jubilee fund, which was used for charitable purposes.

On the *Tuladan* ceremony, the *Daily Herald*, London, commented: 'Worth his weight in gold – yes, really – is the Maharaja of Bikaner, just celebrating the golden jubilee of his rule… He looks the perfect Maharaja: dark, handsome, moustaches waxed.'

The Peoples' Jubilee Committee, during the course of ten days, from September 18 to 27, organised a number of functions. A series of open air cinema and dramatic performances were organised.Each day there was a display of fireworks on the *maidan* opposite the Victoria Memorial Club which was also attended by the Maharaja. School children were feted everywhere in the state. Sports meets and wrestling matches were organised. Flag hoisting ceremonies were held throughout the State. There were illuminations and fireworks in all the towns.

The first stage of jubilee celebrations came to an end with a banquet given by the Maharaja at Lallgarh Palace to some 230 *sadhus* – ascetics – who at the close of the feast gave their benedictions to the Maharaja and the Royal House.

The Maharaja had donated Rs 3,00,000 from his privy purse for religious purposes, such as the construction of new temples on the bank of the sacred lake at Kolayat, to the fitting of golden gates to the temple of Dwarka, an eminent place of Hindu pilgrimage in Gujarat, and for various other important places of worship of the different religions in the state.

Soon afterwards the Maharaja had left for Simla on a visit to the Viceroy and there was an interval in the celebrations.

Dusserah

The Maharaja returned in time for the Dusserah festival which though was not the part of jubilee celebrations but fell within the festive period. Dusserah is the anniversary of the victory of the great King Rama over Ravana. It is regarded by all Hindus, especially the Kshatriya caste, as the greatest holiday of the year. The Maharaja's birthday fell on Dusserah Day and was raised in significance by the special importance of the Jubilee.

The Maharaja held a review of the State Army, followed by religious ceremonies. He held a birthday *durbar* in the old Throne Room of the Fort. The Dusserah ceremony in Bikaner had remained essentially unchanged for centuries. The Maharaja, while acknowledging the value of modern innovations, knew also that the spirit of the people needed the firm foundation of ancient traditions and symbols.

The same day the Maharaja rode in an elephant procession to a sacred tree outside the city where the actual Dusserah ceremonies took place. In many parts of India there is a mimic battle ending in the beheading of an effigy of Ravana. In Bikaner, after the religious ceremonies under the sacred tree were over, the Maharaja walked to a platform, where a life-size portrait of the legendary fiend had been erected, and shot an arrow into its heart from a great bow, amidst great cheering.

The second stage of the Golden Jubilee celebrations opened on October 26 and lasted up to November 30. A number of distinguished guests arrived to take part in the celebrations – some stayed for a few days, others for a longer period. Lord Linlithgow, the Viceroy had arrived on November 4, and stayed for six days. Over 120 highly distinguished guests from outside the state had come. These included Princes, political agents, members of the Governor-General's Executive Council, judges of the Federal Court, journalists, nationalist leaders, Chief of the General Staff, friends of the Maharaja, etc. Many guests were accompanied by their wives. The chiefs and nobles of the state, escorted by their retainers on camels or horses, had arrived in the capital. In addition, prominent citizens, including the Maharaja's new subjects in the canal area, had been invited as state guests.

The chiefs and nobles gave a banquet in honour of the Maharaja on October 27 in the gardens of the Fort. The Peoples' Fair was held at the new stadium in which the Maharaja himself took part. The Bikaner Camel Corps performed a torch-light tattoo with splendid precision and artistic sense.

The Jubilee Durbar

The most interesting ceremony was the Jubilee *Durbar* that took place on October 30. *The Times of India* (October 30, 1937) commented: 'There are few more colourful sights in India than a Rathore *Durbar*.' It was a public *durbar*, where apart from the chieftains, army officers, ministers, and officials, prominent citizens had also gathered. The crowd assembled on the open spaces in the Fort. After the completion of traditional rituals, the Maharaja addressed the audience. He reviewed the principal events of the period and laid stress on his deep conviction that he was the first servant of his people. In that spirit he set up various institutions with the donations which they had generously contributed to the Golden Jubilee Fund. He announced the introduction of numerous reforms, and grants to all associations, and every class of subject in his state.

As he addressed the assembled audience, he referred to all his subjects, who were scattered over the 23,000 square miles of his territory. He said: 'They alone are the judges whose verdict on what I have tried to do for them can guide me in my future labours.' He assured his subjects that he would always be devoted to promoting their happiness and to furthering the cause of their state. 'The Jubilee Fund', he said, 'which my people raised of their own free will, and to which they handsomely contributed according to their means, I regard as a monument more to their constant devotion to the state than to my individual self.' He declared that the entire fund collected by the people would be utilised for their benefit. The public *Durbar* thus came to a close.

The Viceroy in Bikaner

The Golden Jubilee celebrations reached their climax on November 4 with the state arrival of Their Excellencies the Viceroy and the Marchioness of Linlithgow. There was no finer setting for traditional pageantry than the 'rose red city, half as old as time; nowhere was the art of ceremony better

understood than in Bikaner. As the white viceregal train drew into the
station the Maharaja in a wonderful coat of blue brocade glistening with
jewels and Orders stood beneath a golden canopy to receive his guests. The
Yuvraj and ministers and nobles were behind him, dressed in a dazzling
range of colours from the palest of rose pink satins gold. They far outshone
even the scarlet uniforms of the aide-de-camp's and the grey morning coat
of the Viceroy on which glittered only a single Order, that of the G.C.S.I.

From the station the Viceroy moved in procession. In the procession
alone there were 28 elephants. The elephant on which rode the Viceroy and
the Maharaja, was an enormous beast caparisoned in royal purple and silver
with a gold *howdah* and anklets of silver bells. It was preceded by a long
column of elephants carrying the standard of Bikaner and the gold fish and
other insignia presented to the rulers by the Mughal emperors. In the column
were also two pairs of magnificent oxen draped in blue and silver, their horns
silvered, drawing the two *raths* or carriages, as well as 12 caparisoned horses,
two platoons of the Sadul Light Infantry in scarlet and blue with white
gaiters, a section of the Camel Battery, two troops of Lancers – one in French
grey, the other in bottle green – and various bearers of gold sticks, gold and
silver maces, spears and umbrellas. The whole of this advance party moved in
perfect formation through the crowded streets to the music of the bagpipes.

On the second state elephant was the Marchioness of Linlithgow and the
Resident for Rajputana, A.C. Lothian. Her Excellency was in great spirits,
and smiled so happily and charmingly that she received a special cheer from
the swarms of people upon the roof-tops.

Against the sharp blue of the desert sky and the pale pink of the
buildings, the most varied and strident colours met and mingled. Add to this
the moving background of saffron and scarlet *pugrees* which everyone in
Bikaner was wearing for the occasion – the entire spectacle was enchanting,
like a page in the folklore of Rajasthan.

In front of the old Fort the procession halted and there the elephants
were abandoned for motor-cars. The Viceregal party drove along the long
avenue which led, under the triumphal arches, decorated entirely with
muskets, bayonets, spears, and banners shaped like crusaders' shields, to the
Lallgarh Palace.

During the course of his stay, the Viceroy attended a review of the
State Army. He showed particular interest in the Camel Corps, a kind of
force that was rarely seen elsewhere. He visited buildings of special

interest, including the two new hospitals. He visited the fort, the old palaces, armoury and Sanskrit library, Law courts, the public library, the Legislative Assembly Hall, the Victoria Memorial Club, etc. The Ganga Golden Jubilee Museum was inaugrated by the Viceroy. The Peoples' Jubilee Committee had erected this museum as a memorial to the Maharaja's rule. It is an imposing structure of indigenous style of architecture. It contained pictures and emblems of Bikaner history, as well as specimens of arts and crafts. In his opening address the Viceroy said: 'The Museum is a right place to value and reverence the prowess of the Bikaner Rathores of the past. No country can claim finer and more chivalrous warriors than they, and their example should be an inspiration to the youth of today and tomorrow. It is my earnest wish that this Museum, which constitutes your single proof of the loyalty and devotion to their ruler of the people of Bikaner and which commemorates an anniversary of such importance in the history of this illustrious state, should long serve to remind the people of Bikaner of the glories of the past and of the great contributions which during the long period of his rule His Highness has made to its prosperity and well-being.' The Viceroy opened the gate with a golden key. A lofty entrance hall showcased three fine portraits of the Maharaja. Other paintings depicted the Paris Peace Conference showing the Maharaja among the Empire and international statesmen, and a series of paintings on Bikaner's heroic tradition. There was a magnificent collection of state heirlooms, including the ceremonial silk robe which was a present from Emperor Jehangir; a gold insignia of *Mahi Maratib*, which was three times granted to the rulers of Bikaner by the Mughal Emperors; the famous Sandalwood Throne of Rathore Emperors brought from Kanauj in 1212 A.D. to Marwar; the splendid specimen of Bikaner carpets, lacquer work and artistic brassware.

The Maharaja's Plea for United India

The state banquet on November 6 was an important historic occasion. The Maharaja alluded to the visits of previous Viceroys to the state, and the many schemes he had devised for the industrial and agricultural improvement, as also the great schemes of irrigation, including the Gang Canal. He spoke about the issue of federation and, said that 'to that faith I adhere today'. 'My vision of India is a federal government, or a United States of India, which would embrace both British India and the Indian states.'

The Viceroy's Speech at Banquet

Lord Linlithgow referred at length to the achievements of the Maharaja during the past 50 years of his rule. 'The Ruler of one of the most conspicuous and progressive states in India', he said: 'the Maharaja of Bikaner has achieved for himself an outstanding position in India and the Empire'.

At the close of his address Lord Linlithgow made a dramatic announcement, which roused the gathering to frantic applause. 'It is a source of profound satisfaction to me to-night', he said: 'to be able by the command of His Imperial Majesty the King-Emperor to announce that His Majesty has been graciously pleased on this auspicious occasion to recognise the eminent record of the Maharaja of Bikaner alike in peace and war as ruler, as soldier and as statesman by the promotion of His Highness from the rank of Lieutenant-General to the rank of General.' The announcement of this honour, which was unique among the Princes of India, was a fitting close to the official celebrations. To the Maharaja ... Maharaja who was a soldier first and foremost, this testimony of Royal favour, was probably the most touching of all the tokens of appreciation which had been showered upon him on his golden jubilee.

On November 10, Lord Linlithgow, wrote: 'I write at the first possible moment to thank Your Highness for your delightful hospitality. As I write, my last three days spent in Gajner are uppermost in my mind, and I feel that I need scarcely tell you how my wife, I and my daughter enjoyed ourselves there. You showed us most excellent sport, and the arrangements made under Your Highness' direction were really perfect.' Lord Linlithgow had also referred to the elephant procession which 'pleased' him 'most'. He added: 'The enthusiastic reception with which I was greeted touched me very much, and I was immensely impressed by the dignity and the splendour of the procession itself.' Lord Linlithgow's daughter, Lady Doreen Hope, on November 12, wrote: 'It really was the most magnificent spectacle I have ever seen, and the colour of it all quite unbelievable ... I loved every moment of the visit and was sad when it all came to an end.'

Sir Henry Craik, Member of the Governor-General's Executive Council, who accompanied the Viceroy, wrote: 'I have not seen anything so marvellous as the elephant procession since the Curzon *Durbar* of 1903.' 'Looking to the last few memorable days', wrote another member of the Viceroy's entourage, 'my feeling is one of wonder rather than of anything else. I have seen and experienced so many things which still remain in mind

– the splendour of the pageantry and ceremonial, the perfection of the display, amazing organisation and Your Highness' generous hospitality. I shall never forget the days in Bikaner.' Patricia Betham, wife of Colonel G.L. Betham, Political Agent for the Southern Rajputana Sates, said: 'I have never enjoyed any visit more in my life and don't think I ever shall again.'

Gathering of the Princes

Towards the end of November, a large number of princes had gathered in Bikaner for the final stage of festivities. The rulers of Gwalior, Udaipur, Jodhpur, Jaipur, Patiala, Kotah, Palitana, Palanpur, etc., were there on the occasion. The brilliant gathering was enlarged by the presence of a number of heir-apparent of various states, many distinguished Ministers of states, and eminent guests from British India. Pandit Madan Mohan Malaviya, Vice Chancellor of Benares Hindu University, and a reliable friend of the Maharaja was there. Some Europeans and journalists were also present. The Maharaja had welcomed each of his distinguished guests individually.

The most remarkable function of the Princes' visit was a state banquet, which took place on November 30 in the *Durbar* Hall of the Lallgarh Palace. The eminent rulers with their princes, sardars, and officials had made a brilliant picture in their colourful dresses and turbans; and the significance of the occasion was heightened by the knowledge that it was an unprecedented gathering of so many Rulers at the table of one of their Order. The Maharaja made a brief but impressive reference to the great problems that confronted each state. He appealed to the princes, especially the young generation of princes, to promote close relations with their people.

Replying on behalf of the guests, Maharajah Scindia of Gwalior, referred to the lavish hospitality of the Maharaja, hereditary friendship between Gwalior and Bikaner, and the marvellous progress that had taken place in the State of Bikaner. He said: 'There are comparatively few among us, Your Highnesses, that can point to a career, more remarkable for its untiring devotion to duty, more single-heartedly given to the prosecution of one great aim and the one great ideal of life, than that of the Maharaja of Bikaner. As a Ruler and a statesman, as a scholar and a sportsman, as a leader and a soldier – what is more – as a man among men, the Maharaja of Bikaner has achieved renown everywhere. His is an example as remarkable for its varied interests and great achievements as for the depth and compass of his mind and the steadfastness of his determination.'

The festivities ending, Bikaner returned to its normal activities. The events of the jubilee, however, left a lasting impression on the minds of the people. The celebrations had showcased Bikaner as a place where medieval glory and modern progress co-exist in harmony. It had demonstrated the traditional splendour of a state under a benevolent, far sighted ruler. It had opened the eyes of British Indian people and proved what an Indian Prince could do for his masses.

14

The Maharaja as Sportsman

*M*aharaja Ganga Singh in a life of hard work and few holidays, used shikar as his only relaxation. A magnificent shot and a lover of wild life the Maharaja had made his state particularly famous for the game of wild duck and grouse and buck and chinkara heads. The Imperial sand-grouse shoot at Gajner during the Christmas season had become one of the major events in the Maharaja's social calendar. Sometimes the Maharaja invited as many as 100 guests from all parts of India for this great event. Not only Gajner with its beautiful lake, but its adjoining tanks of Sugansagar, Chandesagar, and Kodamdesar as well abounded in bird life. There were duck, demoiselle crane, and the great Indian bustard which were shot at different seasons of the year; and when the pressure of work permitted the Maharaja used to spend a day or even a few hours in the country with his gun.

The sand-grouse arrived every year in Gajner on their October migration. This was also the season when the heat eased, the cold weather began, and the tired, 'sun-dried' officials of British India recovered enough of their energies to think about recreation. Maharaja Ganga Singh recognised the diplomatic potential of these birds.

They were not ordinary sand-grouse. They were known, appropriately, as the 'Imperial sand-grouse', and were reckoned by some gourmets to be the tastiest game-bird in the world. The Maharaja made them the centre-piece of a great Imperial social occasion. Itineraries of visiting princes were often rescheduled to fit in the Bikaner sand-grouse shoot, and Viceroys had often put aside the business of empire in order to attend. However, sand-grouse lasted barely three hours, so the Maharaja had appended a chase after bustard and black buck, often conducted from a rolls-royce, thus making hunting an enjoyable and a memorable sport.

In the erstwhile states, indiscriminate *shikar* was never permitted. Nobody could do *shikar* without an appropriate license. A limit as to the number, in case of big game shoot, was prescribed. No sportsman was allowed to shoot more than four tigers a month in one area. The breeding seasons were avoided. Poaching was not at all permitted, and the forest guards vigilance prevented poaching. There were strict forest laws and rules were strictly adhered to.

The Maharaja's delight in *shikar* was commented upon by Lord Chelmsford in 1920, when he said: 'I am reminded of a serious omission in this impressive list of Your Highness' activities by a ghostly whisper from the spirit of your 100th tiger that you are no believer in the doctrine of all work and no play.' The Maharaja liked to enjoy a holiday and rest from work in magnificent jungles. In October 1925, he wrote to Montagu Butler, the Governor of Central Provinces, that 'I really do not get rest anywhere except in the jungles during my annual holiday.'

The Maharaja was a keen enthusiast of tiger shooting. As Bikaner had no tigers of its own, he had to make arrangements with other states more fortunately situated in this respect, or in the provinces of British India. He had shot his first tiger in 1898 in the forest of Deoli, Tonk state. His bag of tigers was over 150, chiefly in the jungles of Kotah, Gwalior, Bhopal, Datia, Central Provinces, and other parts of India; and he had been one of the few Indian rulers invited by the Government of Nepal for the splendid shoot which the Terai of that country alone could provide.

In one of his 'diaries', Ganga Singh has recorded the details of a ten foot long tigress he shot in the forests of Nepal in 1920: 'The tigress looked so immense in actual life that when I saw her – and I had a good view of her for several minutes in very low grass where we saw her continuously for several hundred yards coming towards us – I felt sure it was a big tiger and I have now seen a good many tigers shot and can generally spot at once whether the animal is a tiger or tigress – and it was only on seeing her head at close quarter, when she was lying dead, that I suspected her of being a tigress after all.'

The Maharaja had shot his first lion in 1916 in the Gir forest of the Junagarh State. He wrote: 'This was my first lion – a fine animal with a very fair mane.'

The Maharaja bagged his first Arna buffalo in 1920 in the forests of Nepal. In a letter to Lord Stamfordham, the Private Secretary to the King-Emperor, on May 27, the Maharaja wrote: 'This was my first Arna buffalo and I was very pleased to secure such a fine new trophy.'

In the Jungle of Deo Bar (Benares State)

It would be worthwhile to give some extracts from the Maharaja's shooting 'diaries'. These extracts indicate some of his famous big game shoots and his hunting prowess.

In 1921, the Maharaja had gone to Chakia in Benares State for stag and cheetal shooting. He started in the early morning for the jungle of Deo Bar, where by the time he got there the stag had gone up the hill. Climbing up, he saw a magnificent stag walking across half a dozen hind, at a distance of about 100 yards. His mannlicher struck the stag in the shoulder and it dropped to the shot, picked itself up, staggered on a bit and died. It turned out to be $37^1/_{16}$ inches in length. It was the Maharaja's biggest cheetal stag which he got in a single shot. When the Maharaja was coming through the forest of Deo Bar, he saw an unforgettable sight. The herd gave way as a panther, who was sitting alone on the path, sprang on a young stag. When the Maharaja came round on that spot he saw the hind leg of the stag in the panther's mouth and a regular tug of war going on. The Maharaja wanted to shoot the panther, but a cowherd boy had began to shout loudly 'Cheetah! Cheetah!' The panther was disturbed, it let go the stag, having broken the hind leg, and hurriedly went down a cave under a ledge of rock. Darkness had fallen and it was too late to send anyone after the panther. The Maharaja returned disappointed.

In the Forests of Gwalior

One of the Maharaja's excursions was in the forests of Gwalior State – Ochhapura, Hirapur and Budhera – in April-May 1904, where in ten days the Maharaja procured tigers.

In the Budhera forest, a tigress came out 40 yards off from the Maharaja's tree on beat. The jungle was very thick, and the Maharaja could not see her head, shoulder or heart. Since she was standing, Ganga Singh took a shot at her lungs and she galloped away without even a growl. 'I could not understand how I missed her. After beat was over we found lots of blood and found her dead some 100 yards behind my tree.' After the beat, great excitement arose among beaters who swore another tiger was about and had gone under some rocks in a small cave. The elephants could not go up that hill, so the Maharaja walked up and found beaters all around. It was a tricky position, with the tiger above him on a slope. He went up to within 12 yards from the mouth of the cave and saw distinctly two eyes glistening inside; and he could just see the head. It was pitch dark inside the cave. '... tiger seemed of fair size and I could not understand why he did not charge out on us as he could see us. I took a careful and steady aim at his head and fired killing him dead, hit just under his left eye. Unfortunately when he was pulled out, it transpired to be the cub of a small size, which if I had known, I would not of course had fired at. The experience was exciting while the drama lasted, my only regret being that the tiger was not a full grown one.'

In the same forest the Maharaja got out to the jungles at dawn, crossed a *nullah* and just got to a cave when he saw a fine female bear with a cub on her back, was coming towards him (perhaps she had not seen him). The Maharaja walked towards her, and when she was 50 yards off, he tried his new 450 cordite at her, carefully avoiding her cub; she went over at once and was up again, when a couple of shots from the gun finished her off, and 'he (the Maharaja) caught her cub yelling blue murder'. Just then he heard a growl and a yell from a man some 400 yards behind him. He ran up but was too late. A male bear went for the man, who had jumped down. He was not hurt but bear had gone down the *nullah*. The Maharaja saw him running along on the other side of *nullah* from 250 to 300 yards off at least, so he brought his mannlicher into play. He hit him first shot, and the bear went to the left straight up the opposite bank. 'A lucky shot in the back made him drop some 50 yards and he rolled down to the bottom where I killed him. Both fine bears.'

Sport in Amira Preserve

In March, 1922, the Maharaja went for a big shikar in the Amira preserve of Hyderabad State. The *Hyderabad Bulletin* on March 7 published the news: 'This is no ordinary excursion, the Maharaja of Bikaner, for he is out to lay low a mighty monarch of the forest who has fooled the best of sportsmen in the Mudanpalle jungle for eight years. A perfect monster of an animal, said to exceed 10 feet, he has peculiar characteristics. Driven till forced to break before the guns, he pauses, roars, a flesh-creeping thunderous roar – and then comes at a gallop towards the *machan* at such a pace that he has been missed a dozen times or more. But fierce as this beast is, he has no terrors for Bikaner, who is perhaps the most experienced big game hunter in India today, – he is determined to bag this brute before he leaves Mudanpalle.'

The Maharaja's party consisted of Prince Sadul Singh, Maharaj Kumar of Bikaner, the A.D.C's., and Sir Philip Egerton, the guest of the Maharaja, and Captain Kirkbride, the Personal Assistant to the Resident in Hyderabad. His camp was at Mudanpalle. The Amira preserve was five miles away from the camp. For five days the Maharaja sat in his *machan*. He did not lose his patience. Every day a trap was laid, with fresh bait. Everyday, the cunning tiger came, killed the animal and hurriedly went back into jungle. Seven times, the tiger broken out, despite the shots, and seemed 'to think that his safety lies in galloping past the *machans*'.

At last, the mighty beast appeared; it was a grand sight. As he emerged he emitted such a roar that the earth seemed to tremble; he then leapt high into the air and came at terrific speed towards the Maharaja's *machan*, and at that moment the Maharaja discharged two rounds, the first hit him in the head and the second the shoulder, and the mighty tiger rolled over and fell in. The Maharaja at last had bagged the monstrous tiger – the mighty monarch of the Mudanpalle jungle.

In the Forests of Central Provinces

The Central Provinces jungles were very famous for big game shooting, especially the Kholsa block. In April 1926, the Maharaja and the Maharani, along with their two sons – Prince Sadul Singh and Prince Bijey Singh – had gone for big game shooting in Central Provinces forests.

On the Moharli excursion an unfortunate incident had happened. One day, when the Maharaja went out for a drive accompanied by the two Princes and the Princess in the hope of coming across a good cheetal stag, the party suddenly came on a herd of bison, of which they had no news whatsoever, and consequently the last thing the party expected was to come upon any bison. The light was then failing; the herd was standing in high grass, which was half way up their shoulders and body. After a careful look at the herd and after deliberate whispered consultations the party came to the unanimous conclusion that one of the animals was a fine bull bison. It was an enormous animal with horns, and stood out conspicuously amongst the whole herd; the Maharaja took deliberate aim and shot at the animal . There was not the faintest doubt that it was anything but a big bull; and it was only when the party were examining the dead body that all concerned were horrified and surprised to find it was not a bull but a bison cow.

The Maharaja's great regret was that through a most unfortunate accident he shot a female bison. He therefore wrote a letter to the Divisional Forest Officer, and to Sir Montagu Butler, Governor of the Central Provinces, and explained to them the circumstances relating thereto, and conveyed his 'sincere and unqualified regret' at this accident. The Maharaja further insisted on his paying the full penalty, which was fifty rupees and which he sent to the Divisional Forest Officer, Chanda, for 'having accidently shot a bison cow and unwillingly infringed the forest laws' which he had always been most anxious to respect.

Trophies

The Maharaja's trophies formed an interesting collection, specially in view of the fact that they had not been collected, like some other collection of this kind, in the spirit of a big game hunter, who went from country to country for game. The trophies, bronzes, pictures of wildlife are today all there in the Lallgarh Palace, Bikaner.

There is a notion prevalent in some quarters that the decline of the tiger population in India is mainly on account of the big game shooting by the former Princes. This notion is erroneous. Despite the fact that the Princes accounted for a large proportion of all the tigers shot in India prior to independence in 1947, they were hardly responsible for the rapid decline in numbers. The Princes on the contrary were the greatest protectors of tigers in the country. The number of tigers in 1930 was 40,000; and in 1946 it was 30,000. While the number of tigers in British India dwindled, in princely India the numbers were the same.

The worrying fall in the tiger population in post-independent India is on account of varied factors such as, large-scale development and mining projects, damming, industrialisation, expressways and ports, and urbanisation. In addition, the poaching on preserves, and misuse of positions of trust by forest officials for personal gains, have contributed to the extinction of tigers in India. One can only hope that the Government of

India and other voluntary organisations are able to take some stringent measures to counter this problem.

Polo

Apart from his exploits in the field of *shikar*, the Maharaja in his younger days was devoted to the royal game of polo. His skill in the game was superb. His tutor, Sir Brian Egerton had recorded: 'During the few years of my tutorship I had seen the Maharaja develop into a tall young man, of striking appearance, a brilliant polo player, a marvellous shot, and a keen pig-sticker.' Similarly, in 1921 when the Prince of Wales (King George V) had visited Bikaner, he especially said: 'But my account would be incomplete without a reference to Your Highness as a sportsman. The polo ground has known you ...'

15

The Man Behind Bikaner

*O*ver six feet tall with an impressive figure, broad chest, graying hair, piercing eyes, bushy eyebrows, a big upturned moustache, and a complexion tanned by long exposure to the Bikaner sun – that was Maharaja Ganga Singh of Bikaner. A majestic figure, the Maharaja evoked admiration and homage even from a listless onlooker. Even when simply clad, he stood out in any company. In the uniform of his Camel Corps, with a great turban, glittering decorations, he was, as Lloyd George wrote in his *Memoirs*, 'a magnificent specimen of the manhood of his great country'.

In November 1913, G.P. Jacombhood had drawn a painting of the Maharaja, wearing his Camel Corps dress and being invested with the Order of G.C.S.I. by His Majesty. Her Majesty the Queen had it brought to Buckingham Palace to look at it. 'What a charming picture!' said the Queen and commissioned Jacombhood to paint her a repetition of it for herself.

In 1930, Peterborough, a journalist, who interviewed the Maharaja in London, wrote that he surely had the most compelling personality. 'Splendidly built with the carriage and manner of a soldier, the Maharaja of Bikaner might easily be taken for the finest type of English General but for his darker skin.' In the National Portrait Gallery, London, there is Sir James Guthrie's picture 'Statesmen of the Great War', placed in 1930, in which the Maharaja is 'one of the finest figures'.

Ganga Singh's rule had been marked by achievements of the greatest benefit to his state. These achievements were almost entirely the fruits of his own labours. Lord Linlithgow in 1937, said: 'Indeed I know of no ruler of an Indian state in modern times who has by his individual efforts done more for his state and his subjects than the distinguished Maharaja of Bikaner.'

As a ruler, the Maharaja possessed in an extraordinary degree the qualities of beneficence, untiring industry, unfaltering courage, quickness of apprehension and decision. Leaving nothing to chance, he was convinced that careful preparation and attention to detail were the secrets of successful action. He was a stern task-master. He had no patience with those who were haphazard in whatever work they did. The system, orderliness and method of arriving at a decision was more important for him than using one's imagination. He was dashing, brilliant ruler, full of swagger and high principles but neither sentimental nor theatrical. There was always something that he wanted to do. He once said: 'That life was short and the list of his dreams long.' He held that it was his duty and his right to give his best to his people. In alluding to himself as the first servant of the state as well as its sovereign, he gave expression to something in which he profoundly believed. Highly cultured, embracing both eastern and western learning, the Maharaja was credited with being one of the most progressive and able rulers of the Indian states. He had a long record of distinguished service, in the field, as a Prince, as an administrator. D'Witt Mackenzie of the Associated Press of America, London, who had interviewed the Maharaja, when he was only thirty-six, called him 'one of the greatest of the Ruling Princes of India.' In 1939, when the Osmania University, Hyderabad, conferred the degree of Doctor of Laws, '*honoris causa*', on the Maharaja; its Vice Chancellor, Nawab Mahdi Yar Jung Bahadur, said: 'as a Ruler, the Maharaja of Bikaner is among those Princes whose reputation is not confined to India but extends beyond its boundaries.' Charles Allen in *Lives of the Indian Princes*, writes: 'Among all his contemporaries, who were highly intelligent and commanding personalities in their own right, none could match Maharaja Ganga Singh of Bikaner.'

The Statesman

The Maharaja had broken the isolation of his state in the years following his Silver Jubilee in 1912. Thereafter he sat down to think of the state's position in the Commonwealth. The first requisite was to give to the states an organisation, so he took a leading part in the formation of the Chamber of Princes of which he was the Chancellor for six fruitful years. Called to the Imperial Council and Cabinet of the Empire during the First Great War, he was referred to as 'one of the wise men that came from the East.' When the War had terminated he was appointed by the King-Emperor as one of the Plenipotentiaries for signing the Peace Treaty, and in that capacity he was one of the signatories of the *Treaty of Versailles*. At the critical fifth Assembly of the League of Nations in 1924, the Maharaja found himself amongst the leading statesmen of the world. On more than one occasion the Maharaja represented India with distinction at the Assembly of the League of Nations.

At the Round Table Conferences, Ganga Singh spoke of the Indian states forming a federation, earning much applause. A key influencer of the constitutional history of India, his statesmanship received critical acclaim worldwide.

Nothing satisfied the Maharaja; he always wanted to do 'something more' for the people of his state. He stopped at nothing, allowed no feelings of doubt, no procrastination to hinder him. He stuck to his resolution of Bhakra Dam, remained determined to fulfil his great ambition for the benefit of the people. When his old friend, Sir Sikander Hyat Khan, Premier of the Punjab, visited Bikaner, in March, 1939, the Maharaja disclosed his mind. He said: 'We are also most interested in another project of the Punjab which will, benefit the Bikaner state, the Bhakra Dam. And I hope, under his able and vigorous rule of the Punjab this scheme will for us, before long, be a settled fact and that Bikaner will receive another plentiful supply of water for the plains which only want more water to make them fertile.' Sir Sikander Hyat Khan replied, 'So far as I am concerned, I can assure you that you can always rely on me and I will be at your beck and call whenever you need me... We are, as you are aware, closely connected by links of the Sutlej Valley Project; and let us hope that even a bigger link would be forged soon when the Bhakra Dam becomes a fruitful proposition. I hope I shall not be divulging a secret; but I see signs of that scheme maturing at an early date.'

Sir Sikander Hyat Khan, struck by the magnificent works of public utility in the Bikaner state, said: 'I think that those people who malign the Indian states without rhyme or reason and mostly those who do not know anything about Indian states, are doing the greatest disservice to their motherland and to our country. Your Highness has got an administration which – I am not exaggerating when I say – is second to none.'

The Maharaja's devotion to his religion was intense. Though he had a great respect for the traditions and customs of the Hindus, but that did not prevent him from pursuing the path of secularism in the conduct of the affairs of the state. To this end, he had enacted the Religious Tolerance Act in 1928. The Aga Khan in a speech at a banquet in London on March 7, 1919, while testifying the harmonious relations between the Hindus and the Muslims in Bikaner state, said: 'I will mention as a ready example appropriate to the occasion that our esteemed Chairman (Maharaja Ganga Singh) has ruled the state of Bikaner for 30 years, and that 20 have passed since he attained his majority. In that long time, throughout the 23,000 square miles of his territory ... the two communities have lived for generations side by side on terms of the greatest amity and goodwill.' Secularism had been the key-note in the policy of the ancestors of the Maharaja, since the foundation of the state in the fifteenth century.

Essentially a soldier, statesman, and administrator, the Maharaja did not share the literary tradition of the Royal House of Bikaner, and books attracted him mainly for their utility. His collection of wild-game paintings was probably unique, and the modern sculpture of animals today decorates the Lallgarh Palace Museum. He had a deep and abiding interest in architecture, which was quite in harmony with his temperament and activity. Being a great builder himself, he was fitted for architecture – a field in which his knowledge of the details of design and construction was flawless

The most notable characteristic of the Maharaja, was his dislike of any overt display of wealth and extravagance. His entertainments both in Europe and India reflected this trait. A man of moderation and good taste, he entertained like a connoisseur. In his private life he was a simple and unaffected gentleman. In summer he wore a *banyan* (vest) and a *pyjama*, but in winter he used to dress himself formally. Every day, after a bath, for at least ten minutes, he set his moustache with a very fine elastic netting; and on occasions, he would give dictation to the stenographer as he dressed. One of his courtiers recorded: 'After he had put on his clothes he would go to the room where the shoes were all in a row, and there was a long pointer like you have in school, he would just touch one of the shoes with it, and that pair would be polished and brushed. Then in the lobby, there was his collection of walking-sticks, and he would pick out one. Then a tray containing cigarette cases, one of which he would select. So he was very particular.' The Maharaja did not like his officers to look shabby. They had to dress well, and be clean-shaven, otherwise they could not dare to go before him. And he was very insistent that they always took note-books with them and a pencil. 'Don't trust your brain, write it down', the Maharaja used to say.

Neither by resplendent dress nor by the display of wealth and ceremony did he attract attention. Though his personality and bearing marked him out in any company as a great Prince and as one accustomed to command, there was no external paraphernalia that proclaimed to the world his rank or position. Despite his modesty, pomp and ceremony could not be excluded from the life of an Indian prince. On such occasions the Maharaja did what was expected of one in his position. Where display and ceremony was required to be observed for the prestige of the state or family tradition, he always complied. Strict court etiquette prevailed on such occasions. On the Dusserah *durbar* and similar occasions the traditional oriental ruler displaced the modern king. The Maharaja maintained that in a state which had long established and unbroken historical tradition, the etiquette which surrounded the ruler on formal occasions should be fully observed and maintained. In ordinary life, however, he avoided unnecessary display, and preferred the life of a private gentleman.

There were other peculiarities. The Maharaja was probably the best-dressed Prince, whether in European or Indian style; and he was perhaps the only Prince who could tell a story with a cockney accent. His conversation, chiefly anecdotal, never failed to be interesting; aristocrats sat round in attitudes of admiration and submission as he narrated his tales. He was a precise speaker and carefully maintained all protocol.

The Maharaja's Daily Routine

The Maharaja's hours of work and daily routine were regulated by his own conception of duty. He used to devote nine hours for regular work, apart from field inspections. His normal working day began at eight o'clock whether he was in Bikaner, Gajner or Bombay. 'To see the Maharaja sitting at his office table surrounded by his numerous stenographers and secretaries and pouring over files and correcting drafts is to have a new notion of what an Indian Maharaja can be', writes K.M. Panikkar. In the earlier days of his reign, when typewriting had come little into vogue, the more important drafts were often written in his own hand. No important letter was ever issued either from himself or from his government without the Maharaja correcting it himself. 'Seated at the head of his table with a number of red and blue pencils of gigantic size on either side, he began his dictations to the assembled stenographers.' It could be an important letter to the King-Emperor, or the Secretary of State for India, or the Viceroy, or to a brother Prince, or a comprehensive memorandum on some important public question, or a routine note on a file; but each one was dealt with by the Maharaja with 'meticulous care'. Reading daily newspapers, seeing important press cuttings, disposal of *peshi* files or urgent work, convening of Council or Committee meetings were punctiliously carried out by the Maharaja. He worked till about 11.30 a.m, when he retired for his religious observances and midday meal. After a little rest, at 2.30 p.m. work began afresh. Ministers and heads of departments were received and instructed personally. Plans for new buildings were examined, work in progress inspected in person, schemes under consideration discussed in committee with ministers. Audiences to public, forums, delegations, or a petitioners, if any, were granted in the afternoon. The indoor household inspections or special work were done, when necessary. Often the Maharaja kept at his work till late in the evening. At night he either dined with his family inside the palace or joined his guests for an informal meal, casting aside the cares of state.

The Maharaja's daughter, Princess Shiv Kanwar, the Maharani of Kotah State, recalled in *The Lives of the Indian Princes*: 'When my father used to come for dinner, sometimes we were allowed to sit there with him. He would have his pencil and chit-pads and while eating, he would write with his left hand, making notes and we thought it was wonderful, sharpening his pencils and thinking that we were great office bearers.'

Though the Maharaja was well-versed in Hindi and English both, but he invariably talked to every resident of Rajasthan in Marwari. If anyone talked to him in Hindi he would at once retort *Deshi Gadhi Poorvi Chal.*(local donkey with a foreign swagger)

Once at Rajgarh railway station in Bikaner state, Seth Ghanshyam Das Birla, an industrialist, met the Maharaja; the former began to talk in English. The Maharaja retorted: 'Sethji, I know that you have good knowledge of English, but you should not forget that whenever you meet a Rajasthani, you should talk in Marwari, which is the dialect of our forefathers. We should talk to an Englishman in English, and to a non-Rajasthani in Hindi.'

The Maharaja used to address the Bikaner Legislative Assembly in Marwari dialect, though his script happened to be in English. 'As a matter of fact he delivered his speech in Marwari in the form of a free and extempore version of his English speech.'

The Maharaja was invited in May, 1940, by Professor Robert Stanley McCordock of Lincoln Memorial University, Tennessee, USA, to be represented in its Hall of Holography, which contained many autographed photographs and original letters of the great men and women of twentieth century and past generations. The magnitude and uniqueness of this enterprise was quite impressive. In the Hall of Holography, the field of literature, at the time, was represented by autographed photos or letters of Rudyard Kipling, Whitman, Thomas Emerson, James Masefield, Longfellow, Tennyson and others. In the diplomatic realm its collection included men like Gladstone, Disraeli, Austen Chamberlain, Thomas Jefferson, Monroe, Jackson, Abraham Lincoln, Llyod George, and numerous others.

The Lincoln Memorial University earnestly urged the Maharaja to send them his autographed photo, and also, if possible, a letter of tribute to Abraham Lincoln at whose personal request this University was founded. The Maharaja acceded to their request, and along with his autographed photo, had sent the following tribute to the memory of Abraham Lincoln: 'The name of Abraham Lincoln is one that is honoured all over the world as that of the man who secured the emancipation of the Negroes from slavery. In this world torn by national egoisms and conflicting racial claims his name is still an inspiration and a beacon light. The principles for which he stood with such faith, those of the equality of races and of the value of human life, have never been of such importance to the world as they are now, when arrogant claims of racial superiority are put forward as official dogmas by powerful nations.'

The Maharaja's autographed photo is fixed firmly on the walls of the Hall of Holography, amid a galaxy of the brilliant diplomats and statesmen of the world, clearly serving as evidence of his ability and greatness. Wearing a distinctive uniform and a turban, the Maharaja's photo clearly stands out in the hall.

The Last Days of the Maharaja

The Maharaja had developed some trouble with his voice since 1940, as a result of which an operation upon his throat was done in Bombay on June 24, 1942, by Dr. Patzal. The operation was done successfully, the doctors advised the Maharaja to undergo electric treatment for which, they said, special facilities were available in Madras. The Maharaja, therefore, proceeded to Madras direct from Bombay on July 2. In Madras he received a full course of deep therapy treatment under Dr. Rama Rau and returned to Bikaner on August 8. The Maharaja had a great affection for his daughter – Princess Shiv Kanwar, Maharani of Kotah and wrote to her on August 9, 'There was a small nodule on left vocal chord. During operation on the June at Bombay, it was found on examination to have undergone cancerous changes. This I myself suspected all along, but the cancer was of most favourable kind, which yields most satisfactorily to treatment and does not spread to other parts of the body.'

After returning from Madras, the Maharaja began disposing off state work and continued to do so till a short time before proceeding to Bombay on December 2, 1942, when the doctors again advised him to take a little rest. In Bombay, Dr. Souttar, a cancer specialist from London, and other eminent doctors and *hakims* were consulted, but there was neither any improvement in his health nor in voice, and it was later confirmed as a cancer of the throat.

Although the Maharaja, in addition to the acute trouble in throat, later developed breathlessness and a troublesome cough, he showed no sign of any anxiety. He showed exemplary courage and mental equilibrium in calmly bearing the onslaught of the disease. He continued to grant interviews and audiences to the Princes and his subjects. After his malignancy aggravated on December 28, he discontinued going out for a drive.

A gradual deterioration was noticed in the Maharaja's condition and, therefore, Mandhata Singh, prime minister of the state, was called to Bombay in the last week of December. From the second week of January 1943, the Maharaja lived on liquid food and since January 19 he could not take even water. Glucose and saline injections were consequently given to maintain his strength. On January 24, he became a little delirious.

It was at 11.00 p.m. on February 1, however, that his condition suddenly took a turn for the worse. For a moment he regained consciousness, in the early morning, and in a quivering voice, said 'Get me the file of Bhakra Dam'. These were the last words that the Maharaja uttered. He breathed his last at 5.25 a.m., on Tuesday, February 2, 1943. He was 63.

Sir Roger Lumby, the Governor of Bombay, and the Maharajas of Kashmir, Kotah, Gwalior and Palanpur came to Devi Bhawan, Bombay, and paid their homage to the late Maharaja. The *Seths* and *Sahukars*, and many other Bikaneris who were in Bombay at the time, also came to pay their respects to their deceased Maharaja. At 8.20 a.m. the Maharaja's body was taken to the Santa Cruz aerodrome in a closed Buick car. From there the aeroplane (Hudson Bomber), carrying his body, took off for Bikaner at 9.25 a.m.

Cremation at Devi Kund

On hearing of the Maharaja's tragic demise, a paralysing sorrow swept over all of Bikaner. The people of all castes and creeds in grim silence of sorrow had thronged in countless numbers in the Fort and on the road leading to Devi kund. The plane landed at Nal aerodrome at 1.05 p.m. From the aerodrome the *Sowari* was brought direct to the Fort in closed car. The body was given *Sampara* again in the Karan Mahal courtyard. A new, royal *poshak* was worn. The customary rites were completed. The funeral procession or *Mahadol* started from the Fort. The state band played the funeral tune. Sorrow-stricken people rushed from all sides to pay their last homage to their beloved sovereign. On reaching Devi kund the *Mahadol* was taken into the compound and placed there on the ground to the north of the *Deval* of Maharaja Dungar Singh, where the cremation took place. The Brahmins performed the last rites and the corpse of the Maharaja was placed on the *chita* (pyre); *mantras* were recited, *bang*, the last lamentable cry out by the kith and kin given loudly, and the pyre was lit by the Brahmins and the Deodhiwala Rajvis. The flames blazed high as the spirit of the great Maharaja soared heavenwards.

Tributes to the Maharaja

Innumerable telegrams, and messages of condolence poured in, paying rich tributes to the memory of Maharaja Ganga Singh of Bikaner. The cablegrams were received from Queen Empress Mary, the Duke of Gloucester, Queen Empress Elizabeth, and the King Emperor George VI.

A black-bordered *Gazette of India Extraordinary* was issued by the Government of India on the occasion and the Viceroy paying a tribute to the Maharaja, said: 'His career was one of unceasing and varied activity in the course of which His Highness' remarkable talents and forceful personality gained for him an outstanding position of eminence and renown. In his state he inaugurated a new era of progress and prosperity. In the Chamber of

Princes he played a great part which will have its place in Indian history. In the wider sphere of imperial and international affairs he enhanced not only his high reputation but the prestige of the princes and people of his motherland.'

L.S. Amery, the Secretary of State for India, said: 'By the death of His Highness the Maharaja of Bikaner, India has lost her most distinguished public figure and the empire a soldier-statesman of first rank.'

Condolences were sent by Sir Roger Lumby, Governor of Bombay; Sir John Herbert, Governor of Bengal; Sir Maurice Hallet, Governor of United Provinces; Sir Bertrand Glancy, Governor of the Punjab; Sir H.P. Mody, Governor of Madras; Colonel G.V.B. Gillan, Resident for Rajputana, etc. They said that the country had suffered 'a great loss', and that Maharaja Ganga Singh was 'a distinguished Ruler whose friendship we shall always remember'.

Sir Maurice Gwyer, the Chief Justice of India, in his message of condolence, wrote: '... His death leaves a gap which it is impossible to fill among the elder statesmen of this country. He will be remembered both as the ruler of his state and as one of the most eminent men of his time; and he has left for all those who are called to fill exalted positions an example of inspiring and unselfish devotion to duty.'

B.L. Mitter, Advocate General of India, while sending his condolences on February 2, wrote: 'India has lost one of her greatest sons and the princely order one of its soundest pillars. His late Highness was great in thought and deed.'

At a condolence meeting held at the Benares Hindu University, the former President of India, S. Radhakrishnan, then Vice-Chancellor of the University, said: 'His interest in this University was unbounded ... In him we have lost a great patron of this University, a great friend in whose mature judgment and mellowed experience we could always rely.'

At a condolence meeting of the Municipal Corporation, Bombay, held on February 6, the following resolution was passed: '... Maharaja of Bikaner, who was one of the enlightened and illustrious rulers of Indian states, a great statesman and a renowned soldier and by whose death the people of Bikaner have lost a benevolent ruler and the country, one of her great sons.'

The Nawab of Palanpur, a close friend of the Maharaja, wrote: 'This terrible blow has broken my heart and I shall carry this grief to my grave...

Bikaner has lost its father, India its guiding star, the mother country her noblest son, and the Empire one of its pillars ...'

The life of the Maharaja was very aptly summed up by *The Times of India* as 'a fine record of heroic and permanent achievements' which was 'for a major part of his 63 years devoted with exemplary single-mindedness to the service of his people, his country and the British Commonwealth. In so doing he placed Bikaner on the map and himself became a figure of world distinction.'

A marble bust of the Maharaja was unveiled on October 14, 1943, by Lord Wavell, the Viceroy, in the Chamber of Princes Hall. Maharaja Jam Saheb of Nawanagar, the Chancellor on the occasion, said: 'The Maharaja of Bikaner was a towering personality, a treasure of wisdom, a pillar of strength with his characteristic dignity; and the eyes of everyone in the Chamber fell irresistibly on that stalwart leader who typified in his person the highest traditions of Indian kingship...'

Centenary Celebrations

Maharaja Ganga Singh's birth centenary celebrations were held at Bikaner on October 19, 1980. M. Hidayatullah, Vice President of India, who was the chief guest on the occasion, said: 'Maharaja Ganga Singhji's services to the cause of Indian nationalism are such as to entitle him to an honoured place among the ranks of the great Indian patriots'; that 'he was one of the greatest builders of his time'; that 'he was the first Indian to be a full General in the Army'; and that 'he was a great nationalist and was proud of being an Indian'.

As Lord Wavell said of the Maharaja, 'I would only associate myself with all that he has said and again express my gratitude for the opportunity to salute the memory of His late Highness not only as a great and inspiring leader but as one whose personal friendship I am proud to have enjoyed through so many years.'

The inspiration of a great poet enables one sometimes to say in a few pregnant words something that an ordinary mortal could not achieve even in pages of laboured prose. And no one, I think, would grudge to the late Maharaja of Bikaner the application of familiar lines which, though written centuries ago, seem to be incomparably appropriate of this sad occasion: 'He was a Man. Take him for all in all, we shall not look upon his like again.'

Glossary

Chauth	One-fourth share taken or received by.
Cheetah	Panther.
Chita	Pyre, a pile of wood on which a corpse is burnt.
Deval	Cenotaph, monument put up in memory of a person.
Durbar	Court – also Government of an Indian state.
Ekka	An antique wooden carriage driven by a horse.
Farman	A formal order issued by the Sovereign.
Hakim	A practitioner of Hamdard and Unani medicine.
Howdah	A big, comfortable chair, stud with gold or precious stones, put on an elephant, for the ruler or dignitary to sit in a royal procession.
Izzat	Dignity, prestige.
Jagir	Fiefdom.
Jheel	Lake.
Khabar	Information.
Kharita	A formal letter exchanged between Rulers (also with the Viceroy).
Khoma	Pardon Mighty Lord.
Khyat	A hand-written historical manuscript.
Kirti Stambh	Tower of Glory.
Machan	A wooden, leafy structure put temporarily on a big tree for

	the hunter to take position for big game hunt.
Mahadol	Carrying the dead body of the Maharaja on an open, palanquin – like structure, by pall – bearers.
Mahal	Palace.
Maidan	Field, open space.
Mandi	Market Town.
Mansab	Army rank under the Great Mughals.
Murti	Idol.
Nagara	Drum.
Nullah	Streamlet.
Panchayat	A board of five which settles the affairs of the village or of small communities.
Pargana	Part of a country marked out for a special purpose, such as, Tehsil or district.
Peshi	Give a hearing.
Poshak	Royal embroidered dress.
Prole	Big gate.
Pugaree	Turban.
Rath	Carriage.
Ryot	Cultivator.
Sadhu	Ascetic.
Sahukar	A respectable businessman.
Sampara	Washing of the dead body, completely in water.
Sati	A woman who voluntarily embraces a pyre with the corpse of her husband. This practice is forbidden by law.
Seth	A member of the merchant class.
Shikar	Shoot : big game hunt.
Shikari	Hunter.
Sowari	A royal procession.
Tehsil	A unit of revenue administration.
Thakur	A Rajput noble.
Thikana	Estate.
Tilak	A mark (usually red) placed on the forehead.
Tola	Unit of measurement of gold or silver
Tuladan	The weighing ceremony of a ruler against gold or silver.
Vahan	Vehicle
Yuvraj	Maharajkumar, heir-apparent.

Bibliography

Allen, Charles: *Lives of the Indian Princes*, London, 1984.

Bikaner Golden Jubilee Book, 1887-1937.

Goetz, Hermann: *The Art and Architecture of Bikaner State*, Oxford, 1950.

Hooja, Rima: *Prince, Patriot, Parliamentarian: Biography of Dr. Karni Singh - Maharaja of Bikaner*, New Delhi, 1997.

'Indian Princes and the Crown' in *Times of India*, Bombay, 1912.

Morrow, Ann: *Highness: The Maharajahs of India*, London, 1986.

Ojha, G.H.: *The History of the Bikaner State*, Ajmer, 1939.

Original Sources: Files, Documents, Correspondence, Speeches, Notes, Memoranda, Gazettes, Albums, Diaries, etc., pertaining to Maharaja Ganga Singh. (Research Archives, Maharaja Ganga Singhji Trust, Lallgarh Palace, Bikaner).

Patnaik, Naveen: *A Desert Kingdom: The Rajputs of Bikaner*, London, 1990.

Panikkar, K.M.: *His Highness the Maharaja of Bikaner*, London, 1937.

Powlett, P.W.: *Gazetteer of the Bikaner State*, Bikaner, 1932.

'Ruling Princes and Chiefs of India' in *Times of India*, Bombay, 1930.

Reed, Sir Stanley: *The Royal Tour in India: 1905-06*, Bombay, 1906.

Singh, Dr. Karni: *The Relations of the House of Bikaner with the Central Powers*, New Delhi, 1974.

Singh, Rajvi Amar: *Mediaeval History of Rajasthan*, Bikaner, 1992.

Singh, V.P. (ed.): *Son of the Soil: Maharaja Ganga Singhji, Bikaner*, 1981.

The House of Bikaner, Bikaner, 1933.

Tod, James: *Annals and Antiquities of Rajasthan*, Calcutta, 1884.